PRINCE RUPERT

PRINCE RUPERT

Portrait of a Soldier

FRANK KITSON

CONSTABLE · LONDON

First published in Great Britain 1994
by Constable and Company Limited
3 The Lanchesters, 162 Fulham Palace Road
London W6 9ER
Copyright © 1994 Frank Kitson
Paperback edition 1996
The right of Frank Kitson to be identified as the author
of this work has been asserted by him in accordance
with the Copyright, Designs and Patents Act 1988
ISBN 0 09 475500 0
Set in Linotron Sabon 10 on 12pt by
Rowland Photoypesetting Ltd
Bury St Edmunds, Suffolk
Printed in Great Britain by
St Edmundsbury Press Ltd
Bury St Edmunds, Suffolk

A CIP catalogue record for this book
is available from the British Library

TO ELIZABETH

CONTENTS

ACKNOWLEDGEMENTS

I wish to record my grateful thanks to Richard Ollard for his valuable assistance in reading my manuscript and offering advice without which this book could never have been published. I would also like to thank the National Trust at Ashdown House for permission to reproduce the painting of Prince Maurice by Honthorst in this book, the trustees of the Royal Armouries and A. R. Dufty CBE for permission to use the photograph of Egmont's painting of Lord Digby herein and the Trustees of the Leeds Castle Foundation for permission to reproduce the portrait of Thomas Fairfax by Robert Walker here. Finally, I am grateful to David Ryan of Partizan Press for his assistance with certain matters of army organization, weapons and equipment.

FIGURES

ILLUSTRATIONS

PREFACE

THERE HAVE BEEN so many books written about Prince Rupert
that the reader deserves to know why he should have another one
thrust under his nose. The answer is that there is much for the
student of war to learn from his activities that is not apparent from
earlier books, either because they were written to give an overview
of his life as a whole and therefore cover too wide a canvas, or
because they concentrate on the most exciting and spectacular
period of his life and fail to do justice to the breadth of his
capabilities.

There is no criticism implied in this statement. From 1642 until
his death forty years later, Rupert played a prominent part in the
affairs of England as soldier, sailor, artist, scientist, as promoter
of expeditions to explore and colonise and as a prominent member
of the royal family. It would be difficult to do justice to his contribution in all these fields in one book and his biographers have
rightly concerned themselves with painting a portrait of their subject rather than in extracting value from his experiences in any
particular field. Furthermore the immensely colourful and dramatic
circumstances of his life combined with the magnetism and power
of his personality have tended to distract writers from making an
accurate assessment of his ability as a commander and his influence
on the armed forces of this country, especially on the navy.

The purpose of this book is to examine Rupert's performance
as a commander by land. A second book designed to examine his
work as a sailor will, I hope, follow. I have been interested in
writing these books ever since I first read about him in the early
days of my own military service. Throughout my army career I
not only collected material when it came my way, but also compared some of my own experiences with situations that faced him,
particularly with regard to the handling of insurrection. As a result

I hope that I may have gained a better insight into certain aspects of his life than would be available to most of his biographers.

In order to explain how he got his results, I have described the way in which he influenced Royalist policy and the way in which he raised, trained and equipped his armies. I have also tried to indicate the value he set on gaining information about the enemy and the lengths he went to in order to be able to move his men around at great speed. All of this is relevant to an understanding of his success. Naturally his performance on the battlefield is also analysed, including his method of taking and relieving fortified towns.

When it comes to material, there is certainly no shortage and it is interesting to trace how Prince Rupert has been regarded over the years. There is no doubt that he was held in great respect as both general and admiral at the time of his death and that this remained the case for many years afterwards. But gradually the reputation he had built up amongst those who had seen him at work faded and was replaced by that of the gallant, rash, impetuous and arrogant leader of the Cavaliers who burst upon the scene at the start of the Civil War and who rode off into the sunset when the King's cause foundered four years later.

In terms of Rupert's reputation it is a pity that Edward Hyde, later Earl of Clarendon, took such a dislike to him, since his writing has played an important part in shaping the way in which subsequent generations have viewed the events which took place in England during the Civil War and the people who took part in them. A similar situation arose with Pepys after the Restoration. But it must be remembered that neither Clarendon nor Pepys was an impartial historian writing in an academic environment. They were both men of affairs playing a part in the events they were describing. Furthermore both of them crossed swords with Rupert on occasions. In the case of Clarendon, although there was no major confrontation between them in the Civil War, there certainly was during the court's subsequent exile, and Rupert was also involved in the events that led to his dismissal in 1667. Clarendon would therefore have been understandably hostile to Rupert when he revised and completed the great history that he had started twenty-one years earlier.

The business of restoring some depth to Rupert's reputation can be dated to the publication of Warburton's book[1] at the start of the Victorian era and was taken a step forward by Eva Scott[2] in the next reign. These were followed by three further biographies in the 1930s, one of which, written by George Edinger,[3] broke new ground by going into some detail about his naval activities. Morrah's excellent work in the mid-1970s[4] gives a more detailed, reliable and balanced account of his life as a whole. Much information can be obtained from other biographies of Rupert and from references to him in books dealing with the Civil War. But even now, whilst acknowledging the influence that Rupert still exerts on the imagination, most persist in regarding him as no more than a loyal and gallant fighter and have little appreciation of the fact that he brought one of the sharpest intellects of the age to bear upon military problems.

I do not claim to have unearthed any startling new material, nor have I attempted to justify every statement made with a reference. But where I have written something that could be regarded as controversial, I have tried to show where the facts on which I base it came from. My bibliography is merely a list of the books and papers quoted for this purpose and is not designed as a comprehensive reading list.

Finally, in order to achieve its purpose, this book must inevitably concentrate on the warlike aspects of Rupert's varied life. But no study of a commander can be divorced from his character and Rupert's character was the product of many influences that had nothing to do with war. I hope therefore that even those readers who have no particular preoccupation with warfare as a subject will find plenty to interest them in this book about a person who was one of the principal military leaders of this country during a tumultuous period of its history.

1

RUPERT'S WORLD

Prince Rupert was born in 1619 and died in 1682. No man's thoughts or activities can be understood except in the context of the period in which he lived, so this book must start with a brief sketch of the world in which he found himself.

The split within Western Christendom known to us as the Reformation took place about ninety years before Rupert was born. Although it would be wrong to suggest that all the international and internal struggles that took place in Europe over the next 150 years were designed to promote the cause of one religion or another, it would none the less be true to say that religious differences provided the excuse for many of them and exerted some influence on the way in which most of them were conducted, at any rate up to the end of the Thirty Years War in 1648. A rough parallel from our own century would be the effect which the establishment of Communism in Russia had on subsequent events. Although not all of the many wars and insurrections that have occurred since 1917 have been between Communists and non-Communists, this ideological divide has contributed to the outbreak of a number of them and has exerted an influence on the way in which most of them have developed. Those opposing Communism have thought of themselves as standing up for the freedom of the individual and those advocating it have felt themselves to be fighting for a better world, as a result of which both sides have experienced a sense of commitment transcending narrower national interest.

During the years immediately following the Reformation both sides felt a sense of commitment to either the reformed or the old religion. Initially the situation was very fluid so that some countries fluctuated between one religion and the other: an added complication was the fact that the Protestant community itself split into a number of factions. While all this was going on, countries often interfered in each others' internal struggles in order to support the side with whom they sympathised and this greatly added to the level of disturbance in Europe. But as time went by, in most states one religion or the other became firmly established and opportunities for successful outside interference diminished. The more usual causes of conflict between the kingdoms and principalities of Europe gradually reasserted themselves, and these might even involve states of the same religion fighting each other, possibly in alliance with an ally of a different religion. As this trend developed, most individuals found that their allegiance to their prince or country outweighed their attachment to a particular religion when the two were in conflict.

Rupert's life spanned the period when this change-over was most marked. When he was born most wars were, ostensibly at least, wars of religion. When he died they were largely waged across the religious divide for reasons of national or dynastic interest.

It is not necessary to recount in detail the events which took place in each of the European states in the aftermath of the Reformation in order to understand Prince Rupert's position, but a brief description of some of them will avoid distracting diversions at a later stage.

In the sixteenth and seventeenth centuries most of the Germanic states of Europe formed what was known as the Holy Roman Empire. At the time of the Reformation there were two or three hundred such states of greatly differing size. They were ruled by a motley collection of dukes, counts, archbishops, bishops, abbots or even, in the case of very small ones, by knights. In addition there were a number of totally independent cities such as Nuremberg or Augsburg.

There was virtually no cohesion in this empire because the Emperor had few powers in practice, although he did have a court which was capable of making rulings in matters of dispute between the various states and each new ruler had to have his authority confirmed by the Emperor. But the court usually took a long time to resolve a dispute and the Emperor as emperor had no troops or police with which to enforce its rulings. In practice the Emperor's powers derived from his position as ruler of one or more of the states.

When an Emperor died his successor was elected by the heads of seven of the most important states of the Empire. Of these seven, three were archbishops who ruled extensive territories along the northern stretches of the Rhine, one was the King of Bohemia and the remaining three, known as electors, were the rulers of Saxony, Brandenburg and the Palatinate. The Palatinate consisted of two parts. First there was a large area astride the Rhine with its capital at Heidelberg known as the Lower Palatinate. Second was an area known as the Upper Palatinate which lay south of Bayreuth and north of Ratisbon having an eastern boundary with Bohemia.

Well before the Reformation the Habsburgs had become the most influential of the great families of the Empire. When the Habsburg Emperor Charles V abdicated through ill health in the middle of the sixteenth century, he left his many possessions within the Empire to his brother who was already King of Bohemia and of the neighbouring kingdom of Hungary which was not part of the Empire. His brother also became the next Emperor. At the same time he left his possessions in Italy, and the kingdom of Spain which he had inherited from his mother, to his son Philip, and also his possessions in the Netherlands which consisted of seventeen provinces situated in what is now Belgium and Holland.

Prince Rupert's own family, the Wittelsbachs, was also influential within the Empire. Descended from Addelaheren, who succeeded Attila the Hun in the middle of the fifth century,[1] it had over the years provided many famous leaders including an early fifteenth-century Emperor. At the end of the sixteenth century one branch of this family ruled the Palatinate and another Bavaria.

Charles V was the Emperor at the time of the Reformation. Although he was not a religious fanatic like his son Philip, he realised that maintenance of the Roman Catholic faith would be the best way of keeping a hold over his widespread possessions. He therefore consistently supported the established faith, making full use of the Inquisition in Spain and the Netherlands. None the less by the time of his abdication the reformed religion had become established in many parts of the Empire and this evolutionary process continued during the second half of the sixteenth century with the additional complication of the spread of Calvinism.

One of the areas where the reformed religion had taken a firm hold was in parts of the Netherlands, and Charles V put great pressure on the governments of the seventeen provinces there to root it out. When Philip II took over from his father he redoubled this pressure and in addition sent a governor and troops from Spain to help in the task, thereby demonstrating his lack of confidence in the local authorities. In doing this he alienated many of the leading families who might otherwise have supported him, since most of them were as firmly Catholic as he was himself. After ten years of insensitive and cruel Spanish rule several hundred of the nobles of the area banded together, demonstrating and presenting petitions in order to get Philip to suspend many of his edicts: they were soon joined by large numbers of prominent citizens. Philip's reaction was predictable. He despatched the ruthless Alva, together with a first-class army, to suppress and eradicate all traces of opposition: the ensuing blood bath only succeeded in turning a peaceful protest into a full-scale insurrection.

Those opposed to Philip found a leader in William Prince of Orange and Count of Nassau, known to history as William the Silent. In 1568 William started to conduct what would now be known as an insurgency campaign against the Spanish government of the Netherlands. He found his main support in the northern and predominantly Protestant provinces and after a period of guerilla warfare both on land and at sea was eventually able to establish himself in the Brill which became his headquarters. Soon a number of towns in Holland and Zealand had chosen him as their governor. Alva recaptured some of them but his appalling behaviour turned even the more Catholic provinces in the south against him. Eventually Alva was recalled and a more moderate Spanish regime managed to return the southern provinces to their allegiance to Philip. But the seven northern ones refused and set themselves up as the United Provinces, independent of Spain.

Although Philip eventually succeeded in having William the Silent murdered in 1584, the United Provinces were by that time allied to the England of Queen Elizabeth, who sent her long-time favourite the Earl of Leicester with an army of 6,000 men to their assistance.[2] This act, blatantly hostile to Spain, was one of the main reasons for the launching of the Armada in 1588. Had Spain succeeded in conquering England it would have had little difficulty in regaining the United Provinces, but the defeat of the Armada enabled the United Provinces to consolidate their independence. For many years thereafter fighting continued in which the forces of the United Provinces were commanded with great skill by William the Silent's son, Prince Maurice of Nassau. The English contingent played an important part in these battles until James I came to the throne and concluded a treaty with Spain. At this time the English contingent was incorporated into the forces of the

United Provinces, which retained English and also Scottish regiments within its order of battle for many years to come. The threat to the United Provinces' independence gradually receded and virtually ceased altogether when France declared war on Spain in 1609. From then on Spain was too busy defending its remaining Netherlands provinces from France to launch a serious invasion of its lost provinces to the north, but sporadic fighting continued and the English and Scottish regiments remained.[3]

During the second half of the sixteenth century France experienced a series of highly sanguinary civil wars which, although ostensibly fought for religious reasons, were mainly conducted for the political advancement of the various leaders concerned. Furthermore, even when the government was at its busiest slaughtering its own Protestants, it was quite prepared to pursue its rivalry with the Habsburgs by assisting Protestant uprisings against them if any advantage could be gained from doing so: in this way France gained the fortresses of Metz and Verdun in the middle of the century. For France it was the Habsburgs who were the main enemy, because they possessed so much of the territory along her borders that she coveted for reasons both of security and of material gain.

It is unnecessary for an understanding of Prince Rupert's career to recount, even in outline, the twists and turns of events in France during the sixteenth century, although it is worth noticing that Calvin, whose ideas gave rise to the stricter version of the Reformed faith to which the French Protestants known as Huguenots adhered, was a Frenchman. Apart from that, all that needs to be said is that, at about the time Philip of Spain was mourning the loss of his Great Armada, the last of the Catholic Valois kings of France was murdered and his place taken on the throne by the Bourbon Henry of Navarre, a Protestant. This able man immediately became a Catholic in order to conform with the religion of the majority of his subjects. At the same time he confirmed and added to the privileges which the Protestants had won during the civil wars so that they virtually enjoyed equal rights with the Catholics, although there were restrictions placed on the exercise of their religion in certain specified areas. On the other hand they were given a number of fortified towns for themselves including the coastal fortress of La Rochelle. Henry was murdered in 1610.

* * *

Although the ideas of Luther and the other reformers circulated in England, the split from Rome, when it came, resulted from Henry VIII's matrimonial problems and his desire to get his hands on the wealth of the monasteries rather than from a change in his religious convictions. As a result Protestantism in England during the sixteenth century developed along different lines to the way in which it spread across the Continent. By the time Henry's son died, a basically Protestant doctrine had been worked out and was enshrined in Cranmer's incomparable Prayer Book, but a full-scale ecclesiastical hierarchy of priests and bishops was retained: the general idea was that the Church in England should be both catholic and reformed. During the next five years Queen Mary burned and hanged a number of her subjects in order to return the country to the old religion, but her arrangements were reversed at her death by her sister Queen Elizabeth.

By contrast in Scotland, the forceful Calvinist reformer John Knox, together with a number of nobles, had cast out Roman Catholicism and established what became known as the Presbyterian Church at about the time that Elizabeth came to the throne of England. Soon afterwards Elizabeth's cousin Mary Queen of Scots arrived in Edinburgh from France to assume the government. Mary was a Roman Catholic and widow of the King of France but she was unable either to restore the Roman Catholic faith in Scotland, or to retain her position on the throne. Within seven years she abdicated in favour of her infant son, later to become James I of England, and fled into England where Elizabeth held her captive. Although powerless in captivity, she became the focus for a series of plots by those who wished to overthrow Elizabeth, put her on the throne and restore the Roman Catholic faith.

Initially Elizabeth, whilst safeguarding the Protestant Church of England, had pursued a policy of moderation towards her Roman Catholic subjects. But this became increasingly difficult as the plots against her multiplied and were backed by Philip of Spain: the presence of large numbers of Philip's soldiers just across the Channel in the Netherlands added to the danger and directly led to the support which Elizabeth gave to the rebels there and, once they were established, to the United Provinces. Eventually and reluctantly Elizabeth agreed to have her cousin Mary executed. She also did as much damage to Spain as she could, short of declaring open war, by turning a blind eye to the maritime expeditions led by adventurers such as Drake which preyed on Spanish ships and possessions in the New World. As the reign went on and the threat from Spain increased, more and more people became involved in these events and the country closed ranks behind the Queen. Although the defeat of the Armada greatly diminished the threat, Englishmen remained active against Spain at sea and in the United Provinces. By the end of the reign, thousands of Englishmen had witnessed the horrors inflicted by Spaniards in the name of Roman Catholicism, which included the public execution of captured British seamen by the Inquisition. As a result Protestantism, coupled with a hatred of Spain, had become deeply embedded in the minds of the English people.

In the last years of the reign this feeling developed in court and intellectual circles into a sort of mystic ideology in which the Queen was seen as the personification of a holy and romantic Protestantism. Although this movement is of little historical significance in a general sense, it is relevant to the conditions under which Prince Rupert grew up.

Prince Rupert was the third son of the Elector Frederick V of the Palatinate whose mother was the daughter of William the Silent and therefore sister of Maurice of Nassau. Born in 1596, Frederick was a Calvinist, the senior Elector and head of the Evangelical Union which was an association of five of the main Protestant states within the Empire set up in 1608 to resist attacks from their Roman Catholic neighbours. To counter this Union a Catholic League was set up under the leadership of Maximilian of Bavaria the following year. Frederick became Elector at the age of fourteen on the death of his father.

In 1613 Frederick married Princess Elizabeth, the sixteen-year-old daughter of King James I of England and VI of Scotland: James had come to the English throne in 1603 on the death of Queen Elizabeth. James was a learned man with a hatred of war, but he was physically uncouth and a homosexual. He was extravagant and allowed his favourites great influence in the government of the country. Although firmly Protestant himself, he was tolerant of other religions and did not object when his wife, the Lutheran Anne of Denmark, became a Roman Catholic. From the time of his accession he followed a conciliatory policy towards Spain, for sound practical reasons, which was thoroughly unpopular. Neither his appearance, nor his habits, nor his toleration of Roman Catholics, nor his friendship with Spain, endeared him to his English subjects who looked back to the glorious days of Good

Queen Bess and made unflattering comparisons between her and James.

Princess Elizabeth was greatly admired in England because of her vivacious beauty and winning ways. Her marriage to the 'Protestant Champion of Europe' was undoubtedly popular. The people saw it as a commitment by James to the Protestant cause and felt that it would herald an end to the era of friendship with Spain. Splendid festivities marked the wedding, marred only by the recent death from typhoid of the Prince of Wales which left his small, weak and tongue-tied brother Charles as heir to the thrones of England and Scotland.

For a time all went well for Frederick and Elizabeth in the Palatinate and over the next five years two sons and a daughter were born to them, in that order. Frederick was a handsome and popular Prince who, assisted by his mother, ruled his Electorate successfully. The court at Heidelberg was magnificent and adorned with all sorts of unusual mechanical devices.[4] Echoes of the mystical Protestant movement that had built up round Queen Elizabeth of England attached themselves to Frederick and Elizabeth at this time, lending an air of extravagant fantasy to their life which may have adversely affected their judgement with regard to the importance of their position in Europe. Certainly Frederick had neither the material strength nor the ability to challenge the Habsburgs, which is what he did.

When Ferdinand, brother of the Emperor Charles V, died in 1564, his eldest son inherited Austria, Bohemia, and that part of Hungary not occupied by the Turks: he also became the next Emperor. A younger son inherited Styria which lay to the immediate south of Austria. The eldest son's lands together with the title of Emperor went in succession to his two sons. When the second of these died in 1619 the next Habsburg heir was his cousin, the Archduke of Styria, who not only succeeded to all his lands but was also elected Emperor as Ferdinand II.

But whereas Ferdinand's two predecessors had to a large extent tolerated a variety of religious sects within their domains, Ferdinand II, who had been brought up under the influence of the Jesuits, would not. This was particularly resented in Bohemia where Ferdinand immediately started to eradicate the Reformed Church, which was Hussite rather than Lutheran or Calvinist. This sparked off a rebellion and the rebels, maintaining that the crown was elective rather than hereditary, offered it to their neighbour Frederick of the Palatinate in August 1619.

Frederick had a difficult choice to make. As the Protestant leader of Europe he felt that he had a duty to accept the offer in order to curb the power of the Catholic Habsburgs which he would certainly do if he could establish himself firmly in Bohemia. Protestants everywhere were urging him on, including the Archbishop of Canterbury, and the London populace expressed their joy at the news with bonfires and the ringing of church bells. But if he did accept, he would be directly challenging Ferdinand both as the Emperor to whom he owed allegiance as Elector of the Palatinate and as the existing King of Bohemia. There was no likelihood that Ferdinand would meekly accept the situation, so all depended on whether Frederick was strong enough to hold Bohemia if he took the crown. The question of whether he was strong enough would depend partly on what forces he could raise from within the Palatinate and Bohemia and partly on what help he could get from his allies, including his father-in-law James of England, whom he clearly expected to support him despite a non-committal answer to his letter asking for his opinion. James's problem was that he dared not say no in the light of public opinion, but he did not want to say yes because he was still continuing with his pro-Spanish policy even to the extent of trying to marry his heir Charles to the daughter of the King of Spain.

Despite being advised not to accept by nearly all of the leaders of the Evangelical League and despite the urging of his mother not to do so, based on her long experience of the power of the Habsburgs, Frederick accepted. In the last resort it was probably his religious convictions together with his wife's desire to be a queen that tipped the scales although he had reason to hope for some assistance from both England and France. But it was a disastrous decision both for him and for Europe, since his acceptance set off the Thirty Years War, a series of conflicts that devastated the Continent.

In early October Frederick and Elizabeth, together with their eldest son Prince Frederick Henry, set off for Bohemia leaving their second son Charles Louis and their daughter Elizabeth at Heidelberg with Frederick's mother. In early November they were crowned in Prague. On 17 December Prince Rupert was born and later christened with medieval splendour in the cathedral. His chief sponsor on this occasion was the outlandish Transylvanian Prince Bethlen Gabor, more Muslim than Christian, who had recently been elected to the crown of Hungary despite the fact that it too had been left to the Emperor Ferdinand.

For one winter Frederick and Elizabeth were left in peace as King and Queen of Bohemia, but it was their only period of unchallenged rule, as a result of which they became known as the Winter King and Queen. In the spring the Emperor Ferdinand first ordered Frederick to leave Bohemia and then, when he refused, started to mobilise the support of the Catholic League and the Habsburg family. Despite his peril Frederick received little help from his Protestant allies, although King James went so far as to permit a body of 2,000 volunteers, paid for by private subscription, to enlist under Sir Horace Vere and go to his assistance.[5]

The Emperor Ferdinand had more success at drumming up support and as a result a Spanish army from the Netherlands under Spinola entered the Lower Palatinate at the end of August and a second army raised by Maximilian of Bavaria on behalf of the Catholic League crossed into Bohemia in late October. From the start Frederick moved energetically between the fighting in the Lower Palatinate and Bohemia, but he was no great soldier and neither his commanders nor their armies were a match for their opponents. On 8 November Frederick's army in Bohemia under Christian of Anhalt was defeated just outside Prague at the battle of the White Mountain.

Although a contingency plan had been made for the escape of Elizabeth and her retinue,[6] the battle was over so quickly and the rout so complete that they were hard pushed to make their escape. As the coaches were about to rattle out of the palace yard, Frederick's chamberlain found an infant that had been left on the floor of an empty room. He just managed to throw the child into the last coach as it left. It was Prince Rupert.

The details of the family's wanderings during the next few months make strange reading of the sort normally found only in novels. At one stage Elizabeth, heavily pregnant, was forced to leave her carriage, which had become stuck in the snow, and mount pillion behind a young English officer called Ralph Hopton.[7] Little help was afforded by any of the Protestant rulers, who were frightened of offending the Habsburgs and the Catholic League. Frederick's brother-in-law, the Elector of Brandenburg, reluctantly conceding to pressure from the English ambassador,[8] allowed the fugitives to stay in the castle of Kustrin so that Elizabeth could at least have her baby under cover. He was already affording shelter in Berlin to Frederick's mother and the two children originally left at Heidelberg. Heidelberg itself fell to Spinola's army at about this time.

Elizabeth's new baby was born on 6 January and was called Maurice after his great uncle: until his death he would be Rupert's greatest friend and companion. But the Elector of Brandenburg did not want Frederick and his entourage on his territory for any longer than necessary so they left as soon as Elizabeth was capable of setting off on her travels. Eventually they were given sanctuary by Maurice of Nassau and arrived at the Hague on 14 April.

To start with, no doubt, Frederick and Elizabeth thought of themselves as rulers who were temporarily obliged to seek sanctuary in a friendly country. Ever since the battle of the White Mountain, Frederick had been travelling round the courts of Protestant Europe trying to drum up money and material support, and he still had an army of a sort in the field in the Lower Palatinate under the command of the Count von Mansfeld and Duke Christian of Brunswick. But his arrangements seldom produced tangible results and the same can be said for the diplomatic activities of King James who erroneously thought that his friendship with Spain would enable him to get the Palatinate restored to his son-in-law, provided that Frederick renounced his claim to Bohemia. Within a few years all was lost and the Emperor handed the whole of the Palatinate over to Maximilian of Bavaria who also replaced Frederick as one of the seven Electors.

Meanwhile a cult was beginning to form around Elizabeth in her exile in Holland. Partly this was a reaction to her misfortune and partly it was the result of her beauty and personality which exercised such a fascination for so many of the men of the period. But there was also the fact that she remained for many the personification of the Protestant ideal which gave a sort of lustre to her court. To the Jesuits she may have been the 'Winter Queen, melting with the snows' but elsewhere she was still the 'Pearl of Britain', for whose marriage Shakespeare had written *The Tempest*. She was also the 'Queen of Hearts' and 'Helen of Germany'; she was the 'Goddess Diana' and the Rising Moon of Sir Henry Wotton's sonnet which by its presence 'eclipsed the lesser beauties of the night'. So powerful was her magic that a number of otherwise hard-headed men surrendered to the spell and served her without thought of personal gain and regardless of the chances of success. Her rescuer after the battle of the White Mountain, Ralph Hopton, was one such person and her faithful protector throughout her lengthy widowhood, Lord Craven, was another. There were many others who without even knowing her personally, came out from

England as volunteers to fight in the Palatine cause whenever an opportunity for action presented itself.

In concluding this chapter it is only necessary to point out that the disturbances that racked the Empire in the period preceding Prince Rupert's birth caused him to be brought up an exile and were the reason for his long imprisonment as a young man. The struggle between Spain and the Netherlands created the surroundings in which he lived as a child and gave rise to the campaigns in which he was to learn his trade. Events in England culminated in the wars in which he was to exercise command on land and at sea.

2

CHILDHOOD AND EDUCATION

THE UNITED PROVINCES, in which the ex-King and Queen of Bohemia arrived in April 1621 and in which Prince Rupert was to spend his youth, were a republic and not a monarchy. They were governed by the States General which was a body composed of representatives of the seven provinces. The leading political figure was known as the Advocate, later called the Grand Pensionary, but his powers were restricted by the mechanism of government.

Complementary to the powers of the Advocate and the States General was the position of Stadholder, whose somewhat imprecise responsibilities included the maintenance of law and order plus a commission to resolve disputes in the States General.[1] In war the Stadholder was granted the additional position of Captain General of all the forces, an appointment that had originally been given to the Earl of Leicester when England first started to help the emerging United Provinces.

Prince Maurice, who was the Stadholder, was a royal personage by virtue of his position as a prince of the house of Orange Nassau; not because he was the Stadholder of the United Provinces. He was also regarded as the finest soldier in Europe as a result of the immensely successful campaigns he conducted against the Spaniards in the twenty-five years following his father's death in 1584. His court was at the Hague.

Over the years the balance of power between the Advocate (Grand Pensionary) and the Stadholder had varied but they had clashed at the start of the Thirty Years War over the question of whether or not the United Provinces should resume hostilities with Spain when the current truce, which had been entered into in 1609, ended. Prince Maurice took the line that the Habsburgs had to be fought tooth and nail as the re-establishment of Roman Catholicism throughout Germany would threaten the continued existence of the United Provinces. In the event his views prevailed, the

Advocate was executed for treason and his son-in-law sent into exile. Thus, at the time that Frederick and Elizabeth arrived at the Hague, Prince Maurice was in every sense the first citizen of the republic. In the month of their arrival, hostilities with Spain were resumed and Prince Maurice once more became Captain General.

Although the States General were marginally less enthusiastic than Prince Maurice about receiving the royal exiles, the welcome from all levels of society was sincere. Past links between the United Provinces and the Palatinate had been close, not only because of the family relationship with the Stadholder, but also because a friendly Palatinate had made it more difficult for Spain to move its forces between Italy and the Netherlands during the war that had been waged when the United Provinces were establishing their independence. Furthermore Frederick was still the Protestant champion and an uncompromising Calvinist. For political, religious and strategic reasons it was important to help Frederick back to his electorate and look after him meanwhile in a way compatible with his rank as King of Bohemia and husband of the English King's daughter.

Accordingly the United Provinces agreed to pay 10,000 guilders a month towards the upkeep of the exiles, to which was added a further 26,000 provided by England. Frederick raised extra money by selling the principality of Lixheim in Lorraine for 130,000 rix dollars.[2] In addition to the money, the Dutch put two large and adjoining houses in the Hague, which had formerly belonged to the late Advocate and his son-in-law, at the disposal of Frederick and Elizabeth. Despite their hope that they would soon return to the Palatinate, they were to make this their main residence up to the time of Frederick's death and thereafter Elizabeth lived there until the year before she herself died in 1661. Accompanying Frederick and Elizabeth in April 1621 were two of their children, Frederick Henry and Rupert.

Altogether Frederick had brought around 2,000 followers from Bohemia with him when he first arrived.[3] All of these people, to say nothing of Frederick and Elizabeth, were profoundly shocked when news was received that the twenty-seven principal nobles and court officials left behind in Bohemia had been tortured, mutilated and then killed in the Market Place in Prague by the Emperor's orders, as an example to anyone else who might be thinking of opposing his rule.[4]

In 1622 Frederick rejoined his troops in the Lower Palatinate in an attempt to prevent the quarrelling that had been going on between the commanders of the various parts of his army, notably Mansfeld, Sir Horace Vere and Elizabeth's passionate admirer, Duke Christian of Brunswick. Frederick had some minor successes and was able to spend a short time at Heidelberg, but partly as a result of pressure from King James, who still thought that he could gain more by negotiating with Spain than could be achieved by fighting, Frederick retreated from the Palatinate and Heidelberg finally fell in September.

As Frederick could not pay his army once it had left the Palatinate, the various parts of it, including Sir Horace Vere and his English contingent, were taken into the service of the United Provinces. Mansfeld and Duke Christian arrived back in the United Provinces just in time to prevent Spinola from capturing the important frontier town of Bergen-op-Zoom. Meanwhile Elizabeth, who had remained at the Hague, had, in April, produced her sixth child, the Princess Louise Hollandine.

In May of 1623 one of the more important events of Rupert's young life occurred when Frederick, on his return with the Stadholder from a visit to the latter's castle at Breda, obtained a house in Leiden some ten miles away from the Hague, where his children could be brought up. This had become necessary as there was insufficient room at the Hague and in any case Elizabeth did not welcome the presence of children around her. It is said that she preferred her dogs and her monkeys and in any case she spent as much of her time as possible out hunting and had no desire to become involved in the supervision of a nursery.

Leiden was a good choice both because it was a convenient distance from the Hague and also because the house was immediately opposite the university, which had been established there when the United Provinces broke away from Spain and which already enjoyed a considerable reputation. The close proximity of the university would enable the children to make use of its facilities when they were old enough: the boys were enrolled in due course, Rupert starting there in 1630 at the age of ten.

The house at Leiden had originally been a convent but it had been converted into an official residence for the Prince of Orange and was known as the Prinzenhof. Not needing it for himself, Prince Maurice was happy to pass it on to Frederick for the use of his children. An elderly nobleman from the Palatinate and his wife, Frau von Plessen, who had been Frederick's governess at the turn of the century, were put in charge. As time went by Frau von Plessen was helped by an increasing number of tutors and sub-governesses.

The first group of Palatine children to occupy the Prinzenhof in the summer of 1623 consisted of Frederick Henry, Rupert and Louise, who had up to that time been with their mother at the Hague. In the following year they were joined by Charles Louis who had been staying in Brandenburg and some time later, possibly as much as four years later, by Elizabeth and Maurice. It is difficult to work out exactly when the family were reunited, but in any case new children were born nearly every year, i.e. in 1623 Louis; in 1625 Edward; in 1626 Henrietta Maria; in 1627 Philip; in 1628 Charlotte; in 1630 Sophie; and finally in 1632 Gustavus Adolphus. Although Louis and Charlotte died as infants, the rest joined the company at the Prinzenhof as soon as they were old enough to withstand the journey.

The regime at the Prinzenhof was designed to be one of spartan formality based on the procedures of the Heidelberg court underpinned by firm adherence to the Calvinist religion. Although Elizabeth's entitlement to worship in accordance with the rites of the Church of England was guaranteed by her marriage settlement,[5] she and Frederick were both Calvinists.[6] Frederick was in fact a strict and somewhat intolerant Calvinist who managed on at least two occasions to alienate those whose help he most needed by the rigidity of his beliefs. Fortunately religious teaching at the Prinzenhof was based on the old Heidelberg Confession which had been designed by Frederick's father in such a way as to make it possible for his Lutheran subjects to co-exist with his Calvinist ones as far as possible. It was therefore less uncompromising than the Calvinism practised by Frederick himself.

French was the only language that Frederick and Elizabeth had in common[7] and it became the language that their children used when speaking to each other, although they spoke English to their mother. In the Prinzenhof much of the instruction was carried out in German, especially that to do with religion. As the children grew older and moved around outside the Prinzenhof, they would have been among people who spoke Dutch, known at that time as High German. They grew up to be fluent in all these languages.

To the modern mind the children of Frederick and Elizabeth were Germans because their father was a German, but in common with royalty as a whole, their blood was very mixed. Their four grandparents were German, Dutch, Scottish and Danish and these grandparents were themselves of mixed race. In practice nationality is mainly a matter of what a person feels and in these terms it is fair to think of Rupert as being primarily a Prince of the Empire for the first half of his life and a member of the English royal family for the second.

Frederick's fortunes had sunk to a low level in 1622 when he was forced to evacuate the Palatinate, but by 1624 they had recovered to some extent. This came about because James and his powerful favourite the Duke of Buckingham had at last decided that it was no longer worth pursuing a policy of close friendship with Spain, following the breakdown of their efforts to marry James's son and heir to the Spanish Infanta. In March the English Parliament voted money to help Frederick and it was decided that an Anglo-French force of 13,000 men would invade the Palatinate itself.

In the event this did not happen, mainly because of decisive Spanish action against the Dutch. In August 1624 they invested the important frontier fortress of Breda and Prince Maurice, who was by now a sick man, was unable to relieve it. In April 1625 Maurice died and in May Breda fell. Soon afterwards King James also died and Elizabeth's brother came to the throne as King Charles I.

Prince Maurice was succeeded as Stadholder and Captain General by his half-brother Frederick Henry (not to be confused with Rupert's brother of that name). Frederick Henry was nearly twenty years younger than Maurice and consequently far closer in age to Frederick and Elizabeth, whose close friend he had been ever since they had passed through the United Provinces on their way to Heidelberg at the time of their marriage twelve years earlier. Furthermore he had recently married one of Elizabeth's Maids-of-Honour who was the daughter of Frederick's Chief Steward.

Untried in war or diplomacy, Frederick Henry succeeded to his high offices at a time when Dutch morale was at a low ebb. By contrast the fortunes of Frederick and Elizabeth appeared to be rising in a spectacular manner, Elizabeth having become heir apparent to the English throne. Ever since the Winter King and Queen had arrived at the Hague they had been treated with courtesy and friendship by Prince Maurice; now they really were of importance and their blue and yellow livery commanded the greatest respect. Many pictures painted at this time bear witness to their pre-eminence[8] which persisted for a year or two and which must have been apparent even to Rupert and his brothers despite their youth.

1625 was taken up by negotiations designed to get the Danes, backed by English money, to put an army into the field and an Anglo-Dutch army under Mansfeld was also raised. During the course of these events the magnificent Duke of Buckingham, who had retained his influence on the conduct of affairs in England despite the death of King James, came to the Hague to confer with Frederick and the Stadholder. One of the matters raised was the possibility of Buckingham's daughter Mary marrying Frederick's eldest son and Buckingham rode over to the Prinzenhof to meet Frederick Henry and his brothers.[9] In the end nothing came of this, as Buckingham was murdered before the matter was concluded. But although Mary never set eyes on Frederick Henry, she became the great love of Rupert's early years.

Despite the efforts of Buckingham and the Stadholder, the strategy of the war was flawed. In 1626 Mansfeld's army was totally destroyed by the Emperor's great general, Wallenstein, and the Danes also suffered defeat. By the end of the year both Mansfeld and Duke Christian of Brunswick were dead and in the following year the Danes were defeated again. Despite further English subsidies they withdrew from the war and Frederick's chances of recovering the Palatinate, which had recently seemed so good, had once more disappeared. Indeed Protestants throughout the Empire were now in greater danger than they had been at any time since the days of Charles V. After ten years of war it must have seemed as if the Emperor and the Catholic League had triumphed. But the Thirty Years War still had twenty years to run.

Meanwhile Prince Rupert was growing up at the Prinzenhof. There is a picture painted of him by Ravensteyn when he was six or seven, which makes it clear that he was a mischievous little devil despite the rich formality of his clothes. Indeed he was known amongst his brothers and sisters as Rupert the Devil. Another picture of him painted by Van Dyck when he was twelve shows him in black with a plain white collar, unsmiling and with a disdainful look on his face. From an early age it was clear that he would have to make a living for himself as a soldier and it is equally clear that he set about preparing himself for the task with unusual singleness of purpose. It is said that by the time he was eight years old he had learnt the pikeman's eighteen postures and the musketeer's thirty-four and knew how to handle a rider's sword both for cutting and thrusting;[10] also that he handled his arms with the readiness and address of an experienced soldier.

As he grew older he was given the assistance of the best masters to help in his study of the complicated art of fortification and military architecture[11] which was always one of his particular interests. An English officer called Sir Jacob Astley who had long experience in the Dutch wars was one of his military tutors:[12] Astley was a great favourite with Rupert's mother who used to call him her monkey. Rupert had a natural gift for drawing and sketching which helped him greatly in his study of fortification. Art was a subject that appealed to several of the Palatine children, particularly Louise. Gerard Honthorst, who was then at the height of his powers, was employed to help them develop their skills. Over the years Honthorst painted a number of portraits of Rupert and the other members of the family.

Rupert's education was not restricted to military subjects but included the all-pervasive religious studies, mathematics and languages. Rupert set his mind resolutely against the classics as being of no practical value to a soldier, but he was outstanding at modern languages, which he would need for talking to his men, and by the time he was thirteen he had added Spanish, Italian and some Czech to the four that he had learnt to speak as a child.

Notwithstanding his aptitude for study, Rupert was happiest out of doors and rapidly became a first-class horseman, swordsman and shot. Like his mother he was passionately fond of hunting and remained so throughout his life. He was a natural athlete with an iron constitution which also came from his mother. When full grown he was immensely strong and tall, standing around six foot four in his socks. As a boy his uncontrollable temper and blunt speaking made him a difficult companion at times, but his energy, charm and sheer devilry more than compensated so far as the younger members of the family at the Prinzenhof were concerned: Maurice was completely devoted to him. Not unnaturally Rupert's elder brother Charles Louis, who had been separated from his parents and brothers in his earliest years, did not react so favourably. He was in many respects the opposite of Rupert, being well controlled, devious and sarcastic. Within the family he went by the name of Timon. He was none the less his mother's favourite son, a fact which she fully acknowledged.[13]

In 1629 the Palatine family suffered a severe loss when the eldest son Frederick Henry was drowned on a visit to Amsterdam with his father. To save money they were travelling on a public ferry which sank after hitting a barge. Frederick survived, but he was greatly shaken and it is said that his spirits never properly recovered. Rupert's feelings are not recorded, but he must have felt the loss since Frederick Henry was the one member of the family who had been with him from the day he was born and was widely accepted as being an exceptionally clever, pleasant and affectionate young man.

The following year, 1630, was notable in two ways from a domestic point of view. In the first place the country house that Frederick had been building for some years at Rhenen in the Province of Utrecht was now completed. It stood close to the Rhine about fifty miles upstream of Leiden and was a splendid place for the family to visit for hunting and other outdoor activities. A story later recorded by the captain of one of Prince Rupert's ships tells of an incident that befell the Prince one day when hunting near Rhenen. Apparently a dog that he particularly liked went to ground in pursuit of a fox. When it did not reappear Rupert squeezed down the hole after it and eventually got hold of its hind legs, but was unable to extract either himself or the dog. By this time the gentleman who was accompanying him was getting worried, so he too got himself far enough down the hole to reach Rupert's legs, but could not get him out. Eventually this man's legs were discovered and after much effort he was pulled out, followed by the Prince still hanging on to the dog which was firmly gripping the fox.[14]

The second event of 1630 was Rupert's entry into the university. This may not have been particularly significant, as it would have involved no change in his lodgings which were as close as they could be to the university in any case, and he had already been making use of university facilities for some time. None the less it would have entailed some change in his methods of study and it would have brought him in touch with a number of new teachers. His first university tutor, Dr Alting, was considered a man of great learning who soon left to become a professor at Groyning, after which Rupert was taken in charge by a man called Hausemann.[15] In the outside world 1630 was significant as the year in which King Gustavus Adolphus of Sweden set out on the remarkable series of warlike operations that shook the Empire and rekindled the hopes of Protestants throughout Europe.

At this time Rupert was developing fast. It would have been impossible to think of a better place for an exiled prince to grow up, especially one who would have to make his own way in the world. Quite apart from the university, the town was full of interest and Rupert and his brothers were allowed to move around it in their high-spirited way, talking to whomever they met, which they also did when staying at their mother's court at the Hague.[16] The Dutch were said to have treated them with kindly tolerance.

Rupert is known to have talked freely to the common folk, particularly the sailors of the ships that were tied up nearby. This was a time of great maritime expansion for the Dutch and the men and boys he met could easily have been newly returned from distant expeditions to Java, Ceylon, Celebes or Brazil. Rupert had a great interest in what was then known as cosmography, that is to say the study of lands, people, animals and vegetation that would now be included under the heading of geography. He was also fascinated by ships of all sorts and at an early age knew the rig of the various craft that were to be found around the coast and canals of the United Provinces. At the same time he learnt about their signal flags, ensigns and other distinguishing marks.[17]

In later life Prince Rupert was often considered aloof by the great men and courtiers with whom he came into contact, probably because their main occupation was the pursuit of power or the pursuit of pleasure, neither of which interested him greatly. But he always got on well with practical and skilled people, however humble, whether they were the soldiers in his regiments or the sailors in his ships or the huntsmen with his hounds or the men that broke and made the horses that he rode or even the farriers with their forges, beating their red-hot metal into tools, horseshoes or weapons. Rupert eventually became adept at all these activities himself and enjoyed talking to people who shared his skills. Throughout his life he was intrigued to discover how things worked and he liked nothing better than to design, and then make, articles that had some practical purpose. It must have been during his boyhood at Leiden that he developed this characteristic, so unusual in a prince.

Gustavus Adolphus, King of Sweden, landed at the mouth of the River Oder to take up the leadership of Protestant Germany at the end of June 1630. The military operations that ensued over the next two and a half years constitute one of the great campaigns of history. They temporarily changed the face of Europe and totally revolutionised the way in which warfare would be conducted for years to come. Rupert was closely affected by these events in both the short term, in that they governed the Palatines' chances of recovering their homeland, and in the long term, because they exerted a strong influence on his military thinking and methods. It is therefore neccessary to run over them in outline.

In the course of defeating the Anglo-Danish-Dutch assault of 1626, the Imperial army led by Wallenstein and the army of the Catholic League led by Tilly had marched through and devastated most of the Protestant states of Europe right up to the Baltic. In early 1629, confident in the supremacy that he had now achieved, the Emperor issued the 'Edict of Restitution', designed to reverse the rights that the Protestant states had enjoyed ever since the Peace of Augsburg in the previous century. At the same time he set about rooting out all Protestant institutions within his own domains and expelling any individuals who would not embrace the Roman Catholic faith. At last he and his ally the Duke of Bavaria seemed to be on the threshold of achieving the aims that had been instilled into them by their Jesuit mentors many years earlier. So confident was the Emperor that he even got rid of Wallenstein, ostensibly because the Electors were complaining of the barbarous behaviour of his troops, but more probably because of intrigue by those who were jealous of his power. It is even suggested that Richelieu, wishing to smooth the path of Gustavus Adolphus, indirectly involved himself in undermining Wallenstein's position.[18]

Although a large part of Wallenstein's army melted away when its leader was removed, there seemed to be good cause for the Emperor's confidence. The force which landed with Gustavus in Pomerania was numerically weak and in addition there was great reluctance on the part of the rulers of the northern states to defy the Emperor and afford support to the Swedish King. This was particularly serious in the case of the two main Protestant Electorates of Saxony and Brandenburg, since Gustavus's operations depended on being able to cross the bridges over the main rivers, most of which were firmly held by these rulers. But their reluctance came as no surprise: they had been equally reluctant to help Frederick when, as the former leader of the Protestant cause, he had been chased out of Bohemia nine years earlier. And the Elector of Brandenburg was not only married to Frederick's sister, he was also the brother of Gustavus's wife.

But the Swedish army was unlike any other army and in

Gustavus Adolphus it had a leader who was more than a match for any other commander living. He had been at war for much of the time since he came to the throne at the age of seventeen in 1611, first consolidating his position against the Danes and then fighting in Poland. He had completely rebuilt his army in the light of his experience, tempered by what he had learnt from the large number of English and Scottish officers who had joined his forces at the time of the truce with Spain, after serving with Prince Maurice in the United Provinces.[19]

His reforms were based on a number of clearly thought out requirements. First he improved the speed at which his men could deploy and fight by reducing the size and weight of weapons, particularly with regard to much of the artillery. Second he improved the capability of his engineers to fortify positions and to cross water obstacles. Third he developed a logistic system which enabled his forces to exist and move in a way that was largely independent of the country within which they were travelling, especially if his line of communication to Sweden remained intact. He thereby avoided the need to alienate the population by devastating their homeland. He achieved this by establishing magazines, collecting large numbers of wagons in which to move stores, and by levying money with which to buy stores from allies in return for the security he brought, or from enemies in return for not laying waste their countries in the usual manner. Fourth he improved the clothing of his army so that they could continue to operate in the winter when other armies had moved into winter quarters.

In addition to this, he greatly altered the tactical grouping of his soldiers on the battlefield and the way in which they engaged the enemy: for example he altered the proportion of pikemen to musketeers in the line of battle and used the horse to scatter the enemy by shock action rather than by fire-power. Last and by no means least he was always well to the fore in every action at which he was present, moving unerringly to the point of greatest danger. He did this partly because he thought that it encouraged his men to excel themselves in bravery and partly because he could not help himself. He was totally addicted to danger and would not keep away from it, despite the entreaties of his officers and councillors and the numerous wounds he had suffered over the years. In the end it was his undoing.

At thirty-six Gustavus Adolphus was physically strong and immensely energetic. With a record of military success behind him he was supremely confident in his own ability,[20] although given to displays of temper which he clearly regretted afterwards. After one such outburst he gave the following explanation to his generals: 'I am thought by many of you to speak hastily and angrily in certain conjunctures, but consider, my fellow soldiers, what a weight I have upon my mind! I am to perform all and be present everywhere, and when the human thoughts are on the stretch, obstacles to, and interruptions of the main pursuit make men irritable. You must bear with my infirmities, in the same manner that I submit to yours. One general has a tendency to avarice, another has a passion for wine, a third wishes to wage war with Croatian barbarity, yet without going further than admonishing and advising you, I have discarded no man, but, on the contrary, have kept you all about my person, and more or less esteemed you all.'[21] This passage says a lot about Gustavus as a man and also, incidentally, helps to explain why Prince Rupert's control of his temper was so imperfect during much of his active life.

No description of Gustavus Adolphus or his army would be complete without some reference to the religious background against which both he and his soldiers went about their work. Sweden had adopted the Lutheran religion which, though fully reformed, retained, like the Church of England, an ecclesiastical hierarchy of priests and bishops. Gustavus himself was a firm follower of this religion, drew great strength from it and attended divine service frequently, sometimes as often as three times a day. But he was tolerant in religious terms, so that Calvinists from the United Provinces and Scotland or Anglicans from England could all exist comfortably in his army. He was also completely at ease with the Roman Catholics in the countries that he conquered, reserving his hostility for Jesuits and others who had been deliberately persecuting Protestants.

Many of Gustavus's soldiers shared his fervour; each regiment had its establishment of chaplains to lead the men in worship and a special soldiers' prayer book was introduced by the King himself. It is said that the common sight of generals and soldiers kneeling together in prayer left an indelible impression on the people of Germany. Also that the Swedish army mixed prayer and powder into an explosive compound that would shatter all resistance.[22] Even more important was the fact that the articles of war governing the army's discipline, which were written out in full in Gustavus's own hand,[23] were firmly based on religious principles which meant among other things that the soldiers dared not rape and plunder the population in the countries in which they found themselves, which was clean contrary to the practices of most of the armies of the time, particularly those of Tilly and Wallenstein.

Having once landed at the mouth of the Oder, Gustavus spent the next nine months consolidating his position in Mecklenburg and Pomerania, building up his forces and establishing a base at Stettin. During this period he exploited to the full his ability to stay in the field during the winter months, much to the detriment of the enemy's detachments. He then set off at the end of March 1631, taking Frankfurt-on-Oder in April and forcing his way through Brandenburg despite token resistance from his brother-in-law who was still unwilling to commit himself. One of the penalties of this delay was that Tilly was able to take the city of Magdeburg in early May before Gustavus could come to its relief. Unlike Brandenburg, this small state had declared for Gustavus too soon and had been subjected to a lengthy siege. On capturing the city, Tilly's soldiers burnt it to the ground and massacred the entire population. The death toll of 42,000 sent a wave of revulsion throughout the people of Europe, hardened though they were by the terrible events of recent years. By August Gustavus, although still greatly inferior to Tilly in terms of numbers, was firmly established in a fortified position on the Elbe.

The Emperor now decided to call on the Elector of Saxony to come down firmly on his side and join forces with Tilly in order to destroy Gustavus. Realising that he could no longer sit on the fence and not wishing to fight against his co-religionist, he refused the Emperor's summons and sent an urgent message to Gustavus to come to his assistance. Together they would be strong enough to face Tilly, whom they decisively defeated outside Leipzig on 7 September. Tilly, with the remnants of his force, retreated towards the Weser and Gustavus, having despatched the Saxons to recover Bohemia and a detachment of his own troops to mask Tilly, set off to capture Wurzburg and then move down the Maine to the Rhine. He captured Frankfurt in mid-November, took Mainz on 12 December and settled down there for the winter in order to rest his soldiers after the exertions of the past eighteen months.

Gustavus was joined by his Queen at Mainz where he set up his court. To it came representatives of all the Protestant states of Germany together with the ambassadors of England and France. His great victory at Leipzig had firmly established his position as the Protestant leader of Europe. Amongst those that came to his court was Frederick, who felt that his return to the Palatinate, much of which was already occupied by Swedish troops, must at last be imminent. Before leaving the Hague he had paid a visit to his sons at Leiden where he attended a public examination of the university students in which Charles Louis and Rupert, who were both thought to be highly intelligent, gained much distinction. This was the last they were to see of their father.

On arrival at Mainz, Frederick was well received by Gustavus, whom he already knew, as Gustavus had visited him at Heidelberg in 1618. But although Gustavus had stated his intention of restoring Frederick, he was not yet prepared do so. Many reasons have been put forward for this, such as the fact that Gustavus took offence at the intolerance of Frederick's Calvinism or that he was only prepared to restore him as a vassal of Sweden, which Frederick would not accept. But a more likely reason was that English support, which was the price being paid to him for Frederick's return, had proved inadequate. Admittedly a contingent of 9,000 men under the command of the Earl of Hamilton had been sent as a contribution to the Swedish forces, but they were poorly trained and equipped, insufficiently backed financially and had arrived in the wrong place. Furthermore Gustavus did not get on well with the English ambassador, Sir Henry Vane. An even more important reason may have been that Gustavus, with French backing, was trying to drive a wedge between Maximilian of Bavaria and the Catholic League on the one hand and the Emperor on the other. Clearly the restoration of Frederick would be at the expense of Maximilian who was in possession of the Palatinate. Until a general settlement could be reached under which Maximilian could be compensated in some other way, Frederick would have to wait.[24] Meanwhile Gustavus extended to him all the courtesy due to a reigning sovereign.

But the negotiations achieved nothing and by the spring Gustavus had no option but to continue his advance into the heartland of the Empire having delivered a list of conditions that the Emperor would have to accept if he wished to avoid further bloodshed. These included the restitution of Frederick to Bohemia as well as to the Palatinate. In early March Gustavus set off in search of Tilly, who had replaced the losses of the preceding year and was ready to avenge his defeat at Leipzig.

During the next month Gustavus advanced to the Danube. On 6 April he again defeated Tilly in a battle fought at the junction of the Danube and the Lech about twenty miles upstream of Ingolstadt, Tilly receiving a mortal wound in the process. As a result of this victory Gustavus, who was accompanied by Frederick, was able to occupy first Augsburg and then Munich itself. It must have seemed as if nothing could now prevent Gustavus from gaining complete control of the Empire.

But during the winter the Emperor had, at a colossal and humiliating price, persuaded Wallenstein to re-enter his service and while Gustavus was defeating the army of the Catholic League and occupying Bavaria, Wallenstein was busy turning the Saxons out of Bohemia. Having been joined by Maximilian, he next moved into the Upper Palatinate which caused Gustavus to move north to cover Nuremberg, where the two sides watched each other through most of the summer and then fought a bloody and indecisive battle at the end of August. In September, when it was too late for Wallenstein to initiate a major siege of Nuremberg, Gustavus moved north to join up with the Saxons. In early November, Gustavus won his last great victory at Lutzen near Leipzig, a few miles away from the scene of his victory the previous year. Wallenstein's army was smashed but Gustavus was killed. Frederick had meanwhile returned to Mainz, where he became a victim of a minor outbreak of plague. He too died in that fatal November.

It is difficult to know exactly how the events of these stirring times would have presented themselves to Prince Rupert at Leiden. Being interested in military operations he would undoubtedly have listened eagerly to the stories that reached the university about Gustavus's battles and sieges. Tilly's destruction of Magdeburg would also have been a topic of horrified discussion. After Frederick left the Hague to join Gustavus at Mainz, Rupert would have taken a more direct and personal interest in events. For one thing all the children were very fond of their father, who had been more directly concerned in their doings than had their mother: the older ones might even have been worried about his safety during the operations of 1632. Above all, they were all expecting a quick return to Heidelberg, if not to Prague. Right up to November, the year 1632 must have been one of intense excitement.

And then from the heights of triumph they were plunged into the depths of despair by the sudden deaths of their brilliant ally Gustavus and their much-loved father. The shock must have been terrific and even Rupert was reported as being in floods of tears;[25] one of the few occasions during his life on which he is recorded as having expressed any emotion other than anger. The young Philip, then aged five, was so surprised by this outburst that he

[41]

asked whether the whole battle was lost because the king was dead.

Although the effect on the children was great, it was as nothing compared with the grief experienced by Elizabeth. In many ways Frederick must have been a disappointment to her as all his military combinations and diplomatic efforts since the Bohemia gamble had ended in disaster. Furthermore, in recent years his health had not been good and he had added irritability to his ineffectiveness. But from the start Elizabeth and Frederick had really loved each other, which was unusual amongst royalty in the seventeenth century when marriages were made for dynastic purposes. The Stadholder, Prince Maurice, summed up their relationship best when he said, 'Elizabeth is called by some the Queen of Hearts. But she is far more than that. She is a true and faithful wife and that of a husband in every respect her inferior.'

When Elizabeth heard of Frederick's death she broke down and went into deep mourning: after all her misfortunes her spirit seemed broken at last. But she was too robust a personality to repine for ever and she eventually recovered enough of her optimism and vitality to run her court and make it attractive to outsiders. None the less her last chance of being restored to anything better than a dower house had gone: she had ceased to be heir to the English throne two years earlier when her brother Charles's first child was born. At thirty-six years of age all she could look forward to was a prolonged struggle to keep herself and her nine remaining children in a way that befitted their position, in the face of an ever-increasing mountain of debt. It would inevitably be difficult to marry off the girls properly without adequate dowries and the boys would have to make their own way as soon as they could. Meanwhile her eldest surviving son Charles Louis became the Elector Palatine, in exile.

3

EARLY CAMPAIGNS

The Stadholder, Frederick Henry, had taken over from his brother when the situation was fraught with danger. For a time he continued with Maurice's defensive policy while he reorganised his forces in the face of combined attacks by Spanish and Imperial troops. As he gained experience he emerged as one of the great masters of siege warfare. In 1629, after a number of minor successes, he won his first great victory by capturing Hertogenbosch, although Imperial troops penetrated for a short time as far as Amersfoort, a mere twenty-five miles from Amsterdam. In 1632 he advanced into what was then Spanish territory and took three key fortresses along the Meuse (Dutch: Maas): Venloo, Roermund and Maestricht. In 1633, with his reputation soaring, he set out across the Maas north of Venloo almost as far as the Rhine, to besiege Rheinberg. At this time Rupert was nearly thirteen and a half which the Stadholder, who liked him greatly, considered to be about the right age to start a military career. He therefore took Rupert and his brother Charles Louis along to the siege.

It cannot be denied that Rupert's first campaign started badly. He had set out from the Hague fully equipped for war, which was then, as it remained throughout his life, his great and absorbing interest. After years of study he was desperately keen to take part as a soldier. But within a few weeks Elizabeth recalled him to the Hague because some of her courtiers had persuaded her that army life might corrupt his morals: danger to his person was not the issue. Rupert had no alternative but to comply with her commands despite the appalling humiliation involved. He would be the laughing stock of Leiden University and the Prinzenhof. No record exists of what he said to his mother when they met, but the incident must have scarred him for life.

Fortunately Rupert's discomfiture was not to last for long, because Frederick Henry was able to prevail upon Elizabeth to think again. Rupert was soon back at Rheinberg and was able to take part in the operations that led to the fall of the town in October.

Rupert's biographers have skated over the events of this campaign, partly because there are no detailed records of his part in it and partly perhaps because they thought it to have been of little importance anyway. But nobody's first campaign can really be regarded in this way. Rupert was probably kept in the Stadholder's immediate party to act as an assistant aide-de-camp, taking the less important messages around, or going to find out where someone or some body of troops had got to. He would for the first time have been engaged in operations, putting his armour on and off, seeing that his weapons were kept clean of mud or dust, looking after important officers as they waited to see the Captain General, and so on. He would also have seen people killed and wounded and become familiar with the process of dealing with such casualties, and he would have learned the procedures for handling prisoners of war.

No doubt his duties were of minor importance, but he would have been talking to men who were experienced soldiers; he would have had the opportunity to question them about what was going on, and also about what this great man or that was really like, and what exactly they had said or done, and what it was like to have been present at some of the great engagements of the past twenty or thirty years. If anyone there had served with Gustavus Adolphus, Rupert would have been particularly interested to hear about him.

Best of all for Rupert, in those precious five months, was the opportunity it gave him to watch Frederick Henry conduct a siege, which was a complicated activity. The mechanics of the business involved setting up a chain of fortifications to prevent interference from the besieged garrison (line of contravallation) and another line to prevent interference from the outside world (line of circumvallation). The next thing was to set up batteries of cannon to batter a breach in the wall and at the same time to tunnel under the wall in order to cause it to fall down. The besiegers would also dig trenches towards the place where the breach was to be made, so as to give their infantry a covered approach when the moment came to make the assault.

While this was going on it was necessary to ensure that the besiegers were kept well supplied with rations despite possible attacks on the supply lines by an enemy trying to delay the siege.

At the same time the besiegers would be trying to prevent any supplies getting into the fortress, which was particularly difficult if the fortress could be reached by boat from the sea or along a river. Finally there was the problem of dealing with any force sent to relieve the garrison, which might involve the use of as large a force as was being used for the siege itself. Frederick Henry's capture of Maestricht the previous year was particularly admired as he had done it in the face of two separate relieving forces, repulsing first one and then the other without at any time letting go of his stranglehold on the town. In later life Rupert was at his best when capturing or relieving fortified towns; it was one of his specialities. It is not too far-fetched to suppose that it was his early campaigning with Frederick Henry that laid the basis of his skill in this respect.

By the end of the year the Stadholder and the two Princes were back at the Hague. Frederick Henry marked the successful termination of the campaign with a medieval-style tournament. On this occasion Rupert not only excelled with his weapons but did so with so much grace that he won the admiration of most of the ladies present. Descriptions of this occasion give the first indication of the fascination that Rupert was to exert over so many people during his youth, despite the fact that he went out of his way to keep his distance and was sometimes abrupt to the point of rudeness. The following extracts from an account of Rupert being given his prize serve as an indication of the enthusiasm felt at the time. 'The ladies contended among themselves which should crown him with the greatest and most welcome glories ... There was one, more eminent than all the rest, both in quality and beauty ... whose loveliness transcended that of the rest of her sex, as much as his worth had the noblest of his, and it was not possible that the greatest bravery could be showed without the admiration of the greatest beauty ...'[1] And Rupert had only reached his fourteenth birthday a few days earlier. So ended Rupert's first campaign.

Unfortunately there were no operations in 1634 suitable for the young Princes as Frederick Henry was busy negotiating with the French. These negotiations resulted in a sizeable French army being put under his command for the campaign of 1635. Meanwhile Rupert had to spend another year at Leiden University, although his thoughts were so focused on war that he had little interest in anything else.

The 1635 campaign was on a far bigger scale than the Rheinberg siege. This time the forces of France and the United Provinces combined to fight the Spaniards in Brabant. Their common purpose

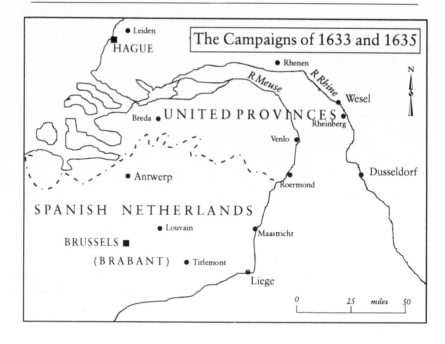

The Campaigns of 1633 and 1635

was to weaken the power of Spain but beyond that the aims of the two countries did not coincide precisely. Richelieu was already looking forward to a time when France would secure her frontiers by occupying a series of fortresses along the Rhine, which was hardly a prospect that would appeal to the Stadholder. None the less the campaign started well with the defeat of the Spaniards by a large French army, after which the two forces joined together to besiege Tirlemont (Dutch: Tienen).

Rupert had decided that in this campaign he would learn the job of soldiering from the bottom and had become a volunteer in Prince Frederick Henry's life guard. This amounted to being an ordinary trooper in a regiment of horse which had the primary job of looking after the safety of the Stadholder: the regiment would automatically be in the thick of any fighting. The commanding officer, Mr Beringham, was regarded as being an exceptionally brave man; he later became the chief equerry to King Louis XIV of France.

In this campaign Prince Rupert, who was now fifteen, was thrown in at the deep end from the start, as the siege of Tirlemont was an intense and bloody affair. Indeed, when the defenders were finally overcome, the French sacked the city in such a revolting way as to disgust and estrange their allies.[2] From Tirlemont the combined force moved to besiege Louvain.

The siege of Louvain was badly co-ordinated and failed. In view of Frederick Henry's skill in the conduct of such operations some people thought that the failure was deliberate. Having witnessed the fate of Tirlemont at the hands of the French, the Dutch had no desire to see the same thing happen to the inhabitants of Louvain, although they would naturally have been happy to bring about the destruction of the Spanish garrison. But whether the failure of the siege was deliberate or not, there was plenty of fighting and Rupert was frequently engaged in it.

There is a story to the effect that whenever Rupert was not required for duty with his troop, he would slip away to find the young Turenne who was fighting with the French army and 'together they would ride out under the cannon that defended the breastworks, each anxious to show the other that he was unmoved by the whistling of balls and each secretly admiring the other for his unconcern.'[3] In reality it is unlikely that they would have wasted time impressing each other in this way, but it is almost certain that they would have met. Turenne was eight years older than Prince Rupert, and a first cousin of Rupert's father. He was also a nephew of Prince Frederick Henry and would doubtless have been with him on occasions. It was more than likely that Turenne would have talked to Rupert from time to time and it is even possible that, as the story goes, they gave vent to their impatience at the way in which the siege was being conducted.

The anonymous writer of the *History of Prince Rupert*, which was prepared in the Prince's lifetime, remarks on the fact that Rupert openly expressed disagreement with the way in which the campaign was being directed, but goes on to say that although Rupert did not understand the political aspect of the business, he did at least realise that, for a soldier, obedience was more important than success.[4] This sentiment is in full accordance with Prince Rupert's subsequent career. As a commander on land and at sea he frequently expressed his disagreement with the policy of those above him, sometimes in the most forceful manner, but having done so he invariably carried out his instructions to the best of his ability, regardless of danger or of the likely consequences.

After a time the siege of Louvain was abandoned and the French, who had suffered heavily, withdrew to France. The Dutch also withdrew to their border and laid siege to the fortress of Schenk which they eventually captured. But in December, before the fortress had fallen, Rupert was recalled to the Hague in order to join his brother Charles Louis who was visiting England as the guest of his uncle, King Charles I.

Despite the fact that so little is recorded of this campaign, there can be no doubt that Rupert learnt a lot from it. By the time he left for England he must have had a detailed knowledge of what life was like for a soldier in the ranks. In particular he would have realised that the first priority in their lives was to get enough sleep and food and to remain warm and, if possible, dry. He would also have noticed that the best officers were the ones that managed to carry out their operational tasks successfully, whilst at the same time taking account of their soldiers' needs.

It is worth pointing out that the campaign did not consist only of reducing fortresses. There was a certain amount of open warfare between one siege and the next and Rupert is known to have distinguished himself at a battle which developed when the army was forcing a crossing over the River Florival. In fact Rupert's bravery was said to have astonished the older soldiers; he must have been rather a nuisance for those who felt themselves responsible for his safety and who were obliged to take more care of him than he took of himself.[5]

There could be no greater contrast with the life Rupert was leading as a trooper in Brabant than the existence that awaited him when he arrived at his uncle's court in February 1636. His mother as usual was worried about him. To start with she was frightened that his manners would be too rough and that he would create a bad impression, but he quickly endeared himself to both King Charles and Henrietta Maria, his Queen. Furthermore his straightforward way of speaking, which contrasted so markedly with the artificial manners of the court, combined with his great height and graceful bearing, made him immensely attractive, especially to the ladies. The only trouble was that up to the time of his arrival, his sophisticated and personable brother had been the centre of attraction. Once Rupert arrived this was no longer the case.

It would seem that Rupert and Charles Louis did not see much of each other during the fifteen months in which they were both in England, except when they attended public functions together. King Charles was at first reluctant to recognise Charles Louis as the Elector Palatine for fear of offending Spain but he did eventually do so. For his part Charles Louis spent much of his energy, time and considerable diplomatic skill in mobilising support for his cause. In doing this he did not fail to ingratiate himself with the growing number of influential politicians, many of them Puritans, who were out of sympathy with the King. Charles Louis was quite capable of sensing the political turmoil that seethed below the surface in England and he had no wish to be left high and dry should a different set of people become influential later on.

Rupert took little interest in the political scene: what struck him was the beauty, peace and prosperity of his mother's native land. He was also impressed by his uncle's court where the aesthetic beauty of the surroundings and the sparkling vivacity of the inmates contrasted so markedly with the Stadholder's modest establishment at the Hague, or with the battered and impoverished remnant of past glories over which his mother presided. The court at Whitehall enchanted Rupert.

Rupert also developed a great respect and affection for his uncle which he retained throughout the frustrations of the Civil War and the stormy confrontation that arose between them in the final months. When Rupert first came to England, King Charles was a few months past his thirty-fifth birthday. He had started life with legs too weak to support him and a serious impediment in his speech. Although small, about five foot four inches, he had out-grown his early defects and become an elegant and dignified man of great charm, albeit with a slight hesitancy when speaking which made him seem shy and withdrawn. He was a superb horseman and, like Elizabeth his sister, was passionately fond of hunting. He was certainly the greatest connoisseur of pictures ever to have sat upon the English throne and he was an accomplished musician as well. His love of hunting and pictures were two characteristics that he shared with his nephew. They also shared a strong sense of personal honour, although in Charles's case this did not extend to his public life. Unlike Rupert, Charles was basically a weak man who could also be stubborn. He was fatally indecisive and incapable of sticking to a course of action even when he decided on one. But on his first visit to England, Rupert only saw Charles's good points. The rest would become apparent as the years went by.

Charles's Queen, the daughter of King Henry IV of France, was twenty-six years old when Rupert arrived at his uncle's court. In the early days of their marriage Charles had taken little notice of her, beyond finding her Catholicism and her French attendants an embarrassment. At that time he was firmly under the influence of the Duke of Buckingham. But when Buckingham was murdered, he discovered that the girl he had married three years earlier had developed into a fascinating woman and he fell in love with her. She was a strong character and gained an ascendancy over him which she did not scruple to use in public as well as in private affairs. In some ways she was good for him, in that she gave him confidence and drew him out of himself to some extent. But her political judgement was unsound and, above all, she showed no restraint in the way in which she exercised her religion, taking any opportunity to convert those with whom she came in contact and fuelling the suspicion that Charles himself was sympathetic to the old faith, which was completely untrue.

Rupert was no more conscious of Henrietta Maria's bad points during his visit to England than he was of the King's. On the contrary he fell under her spell and became as devoted to her as he was to his uncle, although in this case his devotion would later turn to fierce hostility. But for the moment Henrietta Maria adopted Rupert with enthusiasm and absorbed him into the brilliant circle of her friends and attendants: not, incidentally, the French ladies who had accompanied her from France and who had been packed off home some years earlier, but the flower of the aristocracy, beautiful and seductive, by whom she was now surrounded.

For a while it appears that Rupert uncharacteristically thrust his preoccupation with warfare into the background, in order to savour the delights of this magical court to the full. But the King, not wanting to be burdened with Rupert's upkeep for ever and desirous of helping his unfortunate sister's children, looked round for ways of getting him well started in the world. During the next sixteen months a number of ideas were examined.

In the event none of them bore fruit. One was instantly rejected by Rupert, namely that he should become a bishop of the Church of England. A second, that he should marry the very rich daughter of the French Huguenot Duke de Rohan, took many years to negotiate. Although Rupert never encouraged the idea, he did not finally turn it down until agreement was almost reached some seven years later. Two more opportunities that he might well have been happy to accept failed to materialise, namely that he should command a Dutch force designed to invade Brabant and that he should command a contingent of 6,000 Englishmen to serve with the French army in an attack on the Empire. By contrast an offer was made by Emperor Ferdinand II shortly before he died in February 1637, to provide for Rupert if he would but convert to the Roman Catholic faith. Ferdinand had clearly heard that Rupert was showing great military promise.

The last proposal was that Rupert should command a sizeable English expedition to capture Madagascar and thereafter that he should rule it as Viceroy. This idea, fantastic as it may sound, was taken seriously at the time. An order in council was passed authorising the fitting out of twelve warships and twenty-four merchantmen and Rupert threw himself heart and soul into the project with his usual abundant energy. He had always been interested in the sea and he now turned eagerly to the subject of ship-building.[6] On one occasion he visited Woolwich in company with the King where he met Phineas Pett, the great master-shipwright, and saw a new ship of 105 guns being built called the *Sovereign of the Seas*.

At the Hague, Rupert's mother was by now thoroughly alarmed. In the first place she was totally opposed to her son sailing off into the Indian Ocean on an enterprise which she regarded as being absurd as well as perilous. More alarming still were the stories she was hearing about Rupert's close relationship with the Queen and her Roman Catholic entourage, who Elizabeth correctly assumed would be working for a conversion. For both these reasons Elizabeth tried hard to get Rupert back, saying that he would be far better employed fighting the Spanish with Frederick Henry. Rupert on the other hand was enjoying himself and was determined to spin out his stay for as long as possible. It is interesting to record that when he did return to the Hague, he admitted that had he remained in England for another fortnight, he would have succumbed to the pressure from his aunt to become a Roman Catholic![7]

In the end events in Europe led to the termination of Rupert's visit to England. The death of the Emperor Ferdinand II, combined with Richelieu's desire to extend France's interests at the expense of the Empire, appeared to provide a possible opportunity for the recovery of the Palatinate. Since the death of Gustavus Adolphus five years earlier, the Swedes and their Protestant allies had retained their hold over a considerable part of the Empire, although the Emperor and the Catholic League had improved their position to some extent. In 1637 two large Swedish armies financed by France were in the field, one under the command of Duke Bernard of Saxe Weimar about 100 miles to the south of the Palatinate in the region of Basle and the other under Marshal Banier in Saxony about 200 miles to the north-east. Each of these armies had tactical aims that were unconnected with the Palatinate, but if their operations developed well and drew off enough of the Imperial forces, it was hoped that Charles Louis with quite a small force of his own might be able to pass between the two main battle zones and recover his Electorate.

To take advantage of his opportunity, Charles Louis needed an army and it was now that his painstaking work over the past year bore fruit. As usual King Charles was reluctant to involve himself in Continental adventures, but on this occasion the natural affection that he bore his nephews, reinforced by pressure from the Puritan elements that Charles Louis had been canvassing, persuaded him to support the enterprise and to encourage volunteers to join the Elector. The King may also have hoped that his support would persuade Richelieu to stop meddling in Scottish affairs, which he was doing at the time, as the Palatine expedition would at the very least draw off Imperial troops from the Swedish operations that France was backing.[8]

But King Charles was not intending to go so far as to put an army into the field on his nephew's behalf. What he did was to open a subscription list to raise money for the expedition to which he contributed £10,000, and he promised £12,000 a year for the support of the force. He also called for volunteers to join the Elector's army. The Palatine cause was very popular in England and many contributed, the faithful Lord Craven matching the King pound for pound.

The prospect of invading the Palatinate immediately drove all other ideas such as the conquest of Madagascar out of Rupert's mind and he enthusiastically threw in his lot with his brother. Together they returned to the Hague in June 1637 to raise an army. But despite the excitement, Rupert was sad to be leaving and wrote to his uncle after their last day's hunting, saying that he wished he had broken his neck so that he could leave his bones in England. In the event he had many more days' hunting in England before finally leaving his bones there.

Although Rupert learnt little about warfare during his visit to England, he had established his position as a member of the English royal family and a person on whom the King could rely while his own sons were still children. In addition he had met many of the leading members of the nobility and their wives and daughters at court and would have gained some idea of who was influential in what part of the country and how the great families were connected with each other. He had also seen what the countryside was like, particularly in the south and west where he travelled, and as a soldier he would have noticed the state of the roads and rivers and the extent to which the land could support armed detachments. He would certainly have noticed how the defences of most of the towns and cities had decayed during the long period of peace that had pertained since the end of the Wars of the Roses. Finally his time at court should have given him an understanding of the code of manners used in English society and the relationship between what people said and what they meant. Unfortunately he was not good at picking up such nuances, which he probably dismissed as being unimportant, and which he did not attempt to follow, either then or later.

Inevitably, on their return to the Hague, much needed to be done by Charles Louis before Rupert could be given any men to command. In order to fill in the time profitably, Rupert joined his brother Maurice who was with the Stadholder Frederick Henry, besieging the fortress of Breda. At this time there was still a sizeable English contingent in the army of the United Provinces, consisting of four infantry regiments and some troops of horse. Several of the noblemen known to Prince Rupert in England were present, including Lords Grandison and Northampton who had travelled with him from London; his one-time tutor, Sir Jacob Astley, was also there.

It would seem that during his visit to the siege, Rupert stayed in Frederick Henry's immediate circle, but it is clear that after so long an absence from the field of battle he could hardly contain himself and took every opportunity to become involved in the fighting, usually with his brother. One early account states that they 'let not one day pass in that siege, without doing some action at which the whole army was surprised'.[9]

On one occasion at least, Rupert and Maurice did the Stadholder an important service when, as night fell, the brothers entered a trench that had been pushed forward towards the outer sloping wall of the fortress known as the glasis. Whilst there they heard faint sounds from within which made them suspicious. Under cover of mist and darkness they left the trench and quietly climbed the glasis until they could hear some of the defenders talking among themselves. From what they heard they realised that a sortie was intended that very night and they were even able to discover from which gate the sortie was to be made and what its objective would be. They quickly made their way back to the Stadholder's quarters and passed on the information. As a result a strong body of troops was ready to meet the enemy as they emerged. By their daring action the two young Princes had encompassed the doom of many of their enemies.

Rupert's next recorded exploit happened when a detachment of English volunteers were told to storm a small fort on the outward face of the defences called a hornwork. Frederick Henry, realising that it was a highly dangerous undertaking, told Rupert that he was not to join in. As compensation he let Rupert go to Captain Monk, the officer in Goring's regiment who was to lead the assault, with the order to attack. Needless to say, as soon as the message was delivered, Rupert took advantage of the activity preceding the assault to mingle with the front rank of the attackers and was next observed in the thick of the fighting, which turned out to be prolonged and intense. The English prevailed, but not before many were killed and wounded. One of the wounded was Goring, who walked with a limp for the rest of his life as a result: Lord Wilmot was another casualty. Both Goring and Wilmot would later hold senior positions under Rupert in the Civil War. Rupert himself emerged unscathed.

Much to Rupert's disappointment Breda surrendered soon after this incident on 10 October. Maurice, like Rupert after Rheinberg, was sent back to school, going with two of his younger brothers to Paris. Elizabeth was concerned about the outcome of Charles Louis's expedition and wanted to keep Maurice safe at least.

Rupert returned to Charles Louis who had by this time made some progress in raising an army with which to invade the Palatinate. The Elector had also bought the small German town of Meppen on the River Ems about fifty miles south of Emden and ten miles east of the Dutch frontier, with money supplied by Lord Craven. This was to be the assembly point for the men he was recruiting from Hamburg and North Germany. Unfortunately the town was surprised and overrun by Imperial troops, so Charles Louis got permission from Frederick Henry to assemble his force at Wesel on the Rhine instead.

There were three regiments of horse in the army which Charles Louis was raising and Rupert was made colonel of one of them.

His first task therefore was to prepare his regiment for war, which occupied him throughout the coming months. While he was doing this, two other regiments of horse were being formed under the command of officers called Ferentz and Loe, and Lord Craven was building up a regiment of guards and two troops of horse. There was also a small artillery train.

Charles Louis had also arranged to be joined by a detachment of Swedes under the command of Count Konigsmark which would bring the total of his army to around 4,000, comprising roughly two-thirds horse, including dragoons, and one-third foot. The Swedish contingent would be accompanied by James King, a forty-nine-year-old Scot who had spent many years in the Swedish army and who had been made a major general by Gustavus Adolphus in 1632. As the most experienced officer present he would act as the Elector's military adviser.

The direct route from Wesel to the Palatinate lay straight up the valley of the Rhine, but there were strong Imperial garrisons in the way which the Elector's little army could not expect to overcome. It was therefore necessary to take a circuitous route through countryside where the rulers were well disposed to the Protestant cause, or where hostile centres of population were weakly held. It was also desirable for the force to stay within a reasonable distance of Swedish garrisons, into which it could retreat if a superior Imperial army were to appear and from which it might expect information and help.

Historians with the benefit of hindsight invariably describe the venture as hazardous to the point of folly, but at the time it must have seemed that there was at least a chance of success. Had this not been the case, neither Frederick Henry nor King Charles would have encouraged it as they did. During 1638 both Marshal Banier in Saxony and Duke Bernard along the upper reaches of the Rhine had won victories, so that a favourable climate for a descent on the Palatinate existed. By securing one area after another, by building up alliances with Protestant rulers along the way and by co-ordinating each step with the local Swedish garrisons, it might have proved possible to appear on the borders of the Palatinate with a strong enough force to oust Maximilian of Bavaria. This, after all, was the method adopted by Gustavus Adolphus when he built up the limited force with which he invaded the Baltic coast of Germany into the armies which so greatly damaged the interests of the Emperor and the Catholic League.

Unfortunately Charles Louis had neither the military ability nor

The Campaign of 1638

the negotiating skills of Gustavus. Although the raising of his little army was an achievement of a sort, there seems to have been no agreement reached with any of the Protestant rulers nor any firm arrangements made with the Swedish garrisons along the way.[10] Perhaps Charles Louis thought that he would be in a better position to negotiate after his expedition had at least made some headway into Imperial territory. At any rate it was decided to move off through Westphalia and Lippe and then to follow the Weser valley into Hesse Cassel,[11] from where a descent on the Palatinate could be made.

The rendezvous with the Swedish contingent was well to the north of Wesel at Bentheim. From there the combined force set off into Germany in early October. Its first objective was the town of Lemgo, weakly held by the Imperialists, which would, if captured, provide a foothold in Germany and useful additional supplies for the army. Lemgo was on the route to the Weser valley and the Elector's army could expect some cover from the Swedish garrison in Minden, twenty miles to the north. Under the circumstances they should have been able to capture the town before an Imperial army could come to its assistance.

On the way to Lemgo the Elector's army passed within a short distance of the town of Rheine which was held by a small Imperialist garrison, and it was decided that a detachment should turn aside to reconnoitre the place. The practical reason for doing this was to collect information, but the medieval custom of delivering 'an affront' to a hostile town was still occasionally observed and in this case could conveniently be combined with the reconnaissance. The normal procedure was for the 'affront' to be 'resented' by the garrison of the town who would draw up some horsemen outside the walls. The two sides would then attack each other, the horsemen trotting briskly forward, firing their pistols and then engaging in sword-play. After a time the two sides would disengage and the defenders would retire behind their walls.[12]

On this occasion Charles Louis, accompanied by Lord Craven and Richard Crane, later to become commander of Rupert's life guard in the Civil War, went with Rupert's regiment to look at Rheine. On arrival they found a number of the enemy drawn up under the walls and Rupert with three troops of horse was told to engage them in the approved manner. But what happened next had nothing to do with medieval customs, or traditional methods of handling cavalry. Although Rupert's regiment was untried, it included Germans who had served in many past campaigns and a large number of volunteers raised from the English gentry the previous year. Furthermore they had been trained together by Rupert at his most forceful, over a period of many months. When ordered to charge, the three troops of heavily armoured men rode straight at the enemy without halting to discharge their pistols. There was just one colossal crash as the two sides met, followed by the complete disintegration of the enemy's line. Rupert and his men found it difficult to get control of their excited animals and some, Rupert included, were nearly carted through the gates of the town, together with the retreating enemy. Eventually he got his men together and they rode off to rejoin the rest of the party.

Thus ended the first of a number of irresistible and virtually uncontrollable charges made by Prince Rupert. No one was ever able to devise a way of withstanding them, although eventually Fairfax and Cromwell discovered ways of exploiting the ensuing chaos. During the charge an Imperial soldier came right up to Rupert and pointed a gun at him which miraculously misfired.

Shortly afterwards the army reached Lemgo and prepared to lay siege to it. But within twenty-four hours a reconnaissance patrol reported the presence of a large hostile army commanded by Count Hatzfeldt approaching from the rear. It is not clear where this army had sprung from but judging by the direction in which prisoners were taken after the ensuing battle, it probably came from the south-west, having been put together from Imperial troops stationed in principalities along the lower Rhine valley.

The unexpected presence of so large an army called for a change of plan. Return to the United Provinces was ruled out by the position of the hostile force. Withdrawal to the shelter of the Swedish garrison at Minden seemed the best alternative. There were two possible ways of getting there. First to march north to Vlotho and then along the west bank of the River Weser to Minden. Second, to march north-east to cross the Weser at Rinteln and thence to Minden. The first choice was the most direct and avoided crossing the river, but it meant that the line of march would take them close to Hatzfeldt's army. The second depended on getting the whole army across the Weser before the enemy could catch up and interfere with the crossing. General King also said that this course would expose the army to the risk of encountering hostile troops from Luneburg which might appear from the north and oppose the crossing, or interfere with the subsequent move to Minden. On balance he favoured the first course and Charles Louis accepted his advice.

This decision was made on 16 October and that night some of the artillery train and the baggage set off for Minden followed early next morning by the rest of the force.[13] But Hatzfeldt had anticipated the move and had managed to reach Vlotho ahead of the Elector's army so that as they approached the Weser, they discovered the enemy drawn up in front of them. Hatzfeldt had with him eight regiments of horse, one regiment of Irish dragoons and 1,800 infantry which was greatly in excess of the Elector's strength.

On realising that a battle was inevitable, General King wanted to take up a position on a small hill known as the Eiberg[14] and advised the Elector to deploy the regiments of horse there while he went back to bring up the foot soldiers and the remaining guns. But while he was away Konigsmark persuaded Charles Louis that the cavalry would be better placed if they descended from the hill and took up a position in a narrow valley closer to the enemy. This would restrict the enemy to attacking on a confined front, one regiment at a time, which would even out the disparity in numbers. Charles Louis agreed, so Konigsmark as the senior commander present took his own regiment, together with the three Palatine regiments of horse, into this position, deploying them one behind the other in the valley.

Although it was Konigsmark's turn to occupy the most honourable position, that is to say to command the leading regiment, he 'courteously' conceded the honour to the Elector's regiments which deployed with Loe's in front followed by Ferentz followed by Rupert. Konigsmark took up the rear promising to do the part of a trusty second.

No sooner were these regiments in position than they were vigorously attacked by the enemy. Such was the momentum of their attack that they broke through the two leading Palatine regiments. But Rupert did not wait for them to reach him, charging them full tilt with his whole regiment as he had attacked the Imperialists outside Rheine with his three troops. The result was the same and the Imperialist horse wavered and then turned. Rupert pursued them down the valley sending a messenger to Konigsmark to back him up.

But Konigsmark did not stir and when Rupert reached the end of the valley he was attacked by a fresh enemy regiment. At this time Lord Craven with his two troops of horse had pushed his way through the mêlée to join Rupert and together they again forced the enemy out of the valley into the open with great slaughter. But at this point a fresh enemy regiment commanded by Colonel Lippe attacked Rupert's exposed flank which was no longer protected by the sides of the valley. Also some more enemy worked their way down the sides of the valley and got behind the remains of the three Palatine regiments which gradually broke up into a number of small groups each assailed by superior enemy detachments.

After a time Rupert found himself isolated, but unmolested because the white cockade that he was wearing to identify him to his men turned out, by chance, to be the same as those worn by the Imperial troops that day. He could easily have slipped away in the confusion but at that moment he saw a young officer from one of the other regiments being assailed by Imperial troops and he charged to his rescue thereby identifying himself as a member of the Palatine forces. By this time Ferentz, Crane and Lord Craven were all prisoners, Craven being severely wounded into the bargain. In a last effort to break free, Rupert put his horse at a stone wall, but the tired animal was unequal to the challenge and Rupert was borne to the ground by sheer weight of numbers. At that moment Colonel Lippe appeared, impressed by Rupert's ferocious resistance, and pushing up the visor of his helmet, asked who he was. Rupert replied that he was a colonel to which Lippe replied that he was a very young one. Soon afterwards Rupert was recognised and thereafter his captors took great care that he should not escape.

Meanwhile General King, observing the battle from the Eiberg, realised that all was lost and left the field with Charles Louis in a coach. But in the confusion the coach got stuck in flood water by the River Weser and Charles Louis only escaped drowning by clinging on to the branch of an overhanging tree. Konigsmark, anticipating the defeat to which he had so generously contributed, abandoned his allies and managed to extract the Swedish contingent more or less intact. The Elector's army was totally destroyed.

For the rest of his life, Rupert attributed the disaster to General King, first for choosing the Vlotho route rather than the one via Rinteln and then for his conduct of the battle itself in not backing him up when his dynamic counter-attack put the leading Imperial regiments to flight. That was the one moment in the battle when the Palatine army had a chance of victory. In common with many others Rupert suspected that King had betrayed the expedition to the Imperial forces for profit, inventing the threat from Luneburg to add weight to his choice of the Vlotho route.[15] In support of this contention people have pointed to the fact that King got his own personal belongings away to safety at a very early stage.

But even without the threat from Luneburg, the Rinteln route would have been risky. King was perfectly capable of working out how long it would take to get the army across the Weser using the bridge and whatever boats and ferries were capable of breasting the flood. He would also have known how difficult it would be for the small number of foot soldiers in the Elector's army to defend the approaches to the bridge from Hatzfeldt's leading troops for long enough to get the rest of the army across.

So far as the battle itself was concerned, it was hardly King's fault that the horse moved forward from the position on the Eiberg that he had selected for them. On the other hand there is no guarantee that a battle fought on the Eiberg would have been successful. The real trouble was that there was no clear concept for the battle which everyone understood and followed. It would have been possible to fight a battle on the Eiberg as King advised, or one in the defile in front of it as Konigsmark suggested. Either might have worked if implemented with determination. What was sure to fail was a battle in which part of the force was doing one thing and part another.

King, incidentally, attributed the disaster to Rupert for advancing beyond the end of the valley and thereby exposing the Palatine horse to the enemy's superior strength.

4

THREE YEARS A PRISONER

AFTER THE BATTLE Prince Rupert spent one night in the open nearby and the next at Bad Salzufflen where a sympathetic woman helped him in a vain attempt to escape. From there he was taken to Warrendorf near Munster where he and the other prisoners stayed for some days in order to give Lord Craven a chance to recover from his wounds. At this time Crane was released to take the news of Rupert's capture to King Charles: originally it was thought that Rupert had been killed in the battle.

The party then went through Nassau and Wurtzburg to Bamberg where Ferentz and Craven were ransomed, despite the fact that Craven offered to pay a sum equal to his own ransom to be allowed to stay with Rupert during his captivity. He subsequently offered an immense amount for Rupert's freedom but this too was refused: the Emperor, like his father before him, wanted to convert Rupert to the Roman Catholic faith and take him into his service.

From Bamberg, Rupert was taken to Regensburg and then to the castle at Linz on the Danube, about 100 miles to the west of Vienna, which was to be his prison for the next three years. He was nineteen years old, he had devoted himself to the study and practice of arms since his childhood, he was bursting with energy and he had taken part in four campaigns. He was by the standards of the day qualified for the command of an army and would doubtless have been thinking that Maurice and Gustavus Adolphus, the two great commanders of the age, had first commanded armies at seventeen. And he was stuck in an impregnable castle in the very heart of the Empire. Nothing could have been worse.

At this point it is worth assessing Rupert's military qualifications. So far as his characteristics were concerned, he had time and again demonstrated that he was possessed of unusual physical courage; he was always prepared to take his own line regardless of opposition or support, which indicates moral courage. That he was immensely energetic, both physically and mentally, is apparent from numerous contemporary references to his 'restlessness' (a word which had to be taken literally at that time) and from the number of different skills that he had mastered. He could not, at the age of nineteen, have excelled at fencing, shooting, horsemanship, languages, drawing and his military studies, without possessing a vast amount of physical and mental energy. His actions at Breda and in the battle at Vlotho show that he was decisive and determined in the face of danger, and the enthusiasm with which his soldiers followed him indicates that he was fully capable of inspiring confidence.

But although certain basic characteristics are essential in a commander, it is his knowledge of the job combined with his military experience that enables him to exploit them. From an early age Rupert had a thorough knowledge of the skills needed by pikemen, musketeers and horsemen, and by the time he was captured he would have known what was involved in organising, training and equipping regiments of horse and foot. As Stadholder, Prince Maurice had introduced the study of fortification at Leiden University[1] as a result of which Rupert was well grounded in the subject, and he would have gained some practical knowledge of it from taking part in the sieges of Tirlemont, Louvain and Breda. He would also have had some knowledge of artillery, which later became one of his particular interests, and of military engineering.

Although Rupert would have studied the business of commanding a force of different arms, e.g. foot, horse, artillery and engineers, he had not had the opportunity of practising it himself. Broadly speaking it involved working out, or being told, exactly what the force was required to do, making a plan for doing it and then putting that plan into effect. An essential prerequisite for this was the collection of adequate information about the enemy and the terrain, both difficult in a period when maps were either non-existent or unreliable and communications slow.

As always, much depended on a commander's ability to move his force quickly, thereby enabling him to concentrate superiority at a critical point and to surprise his opponent. Speed of movement depended partly on the state of the roads and of the bridges and fords across rivers, and partly on how the force could be supplied.

An army on the move could be supplied either by taking the required food and ammunition along in carts, or by prepositioning replenishment in magazines along the way, or by dispersing the force each evening into areas where small groups could get their own food by purchase or pillage. Prepositioning was the system that enabled the force to move the fastest, because it reduced the number of baggage wagons in a column. It also avoided wasting the time taken to disperse the force each evening over an area large enough to support it and to reassemble it next morning. But this system was not easy to manage when advancing into enemy-held territory unless there were friendly fortified centres of resistance which the enemy had not overcome and which had a surplus of supplies, or unless enemy magazines existed that could be overrun and appropriated. Living off the land would only be quicker than taking along the necessary supplies in carts if the land was able to support the force moving through it without too much dispersal. If it had recently been laid waste and the productive population reduced by years of strife, as was the case over much of central Europe, this would not be the case. Another problem of fighting over depopulated country was that there were fewer people from whom to get information.

Rupert would have been very conscious of these considerations as his condition as a prisoner was the direct result of Hatzfeldt's ability to move a superior force into the path of the Elector's army without the latter knowing what was going on until it was too late. In the English Civil War Rupert proved himself a master of the rapid movement of forces. Time and again he succeeded in concentrating superior forces at places that his opponents thought he could not reach in the available time. This proved particularly useful for taking or relieving fortified places on which so much depended.

His ability in this respect could only have come from long hours of study which enabled him to know exactly how much time was needed to move the component parts of an army under lots of different circumstances over a given distance under differing conditions. With his sharp intellect he would then have been able to apply this basic knowledge to planning and executing particular operations. Possession of this knowledge, together with the ability to apply it rapidly, was one of the things that distinguished the professional commander from the amateur.

There is a splendid passage in Clarendon's *History of the Great Rebellion* which depicts the very essence of Rupert's mastery in this respect, although Clarendon may not have meant it in this way. Speaking of the relief of Newark he says: 'His highness resolved to try what he could do for Newark, and undertook it before he was ready for it, and thereby performed it. For the enemy, who had always excellent intelligence, was so confident that the prince had not a strength to attempt that work, that he was within six miles of them before they believed he thought of them.'[2]

Because of the risk of fighting a set-piece battle in the seventeenth century, most commanders tried to avoid it altogether, preferring to achieve their aims by taking from their opponents fortified towns which controlled the surrounding countryside. Wars tended to take the form of a series of sieges and relief operations, in which one side or the other negotiated a settlement when it was clear where the advantage lay. If a besieged town refused to yield when it could not defend itself and when there was no reasonable expectation of relief from outside, the attackers were entitled to slaughter the garrison: the assault often led to the sacking of the town as well. If a state refused to attack, or negotiate with an enemy occupying part of its country, the enemy would probably lay the country waste in order to force matters to a conclusion. Even if the country was not deliberately laid waste, the presence of the enemy army would have much the same effect, as it took what it needed to support itself. During the Thirty Years War, operations of this sort shattered the states of Germany, causing an estimated loss of two-thirds of their combined populations. In some states, such as the Palatinate where a population of 500,000 was reduced to 48,000, the loss was far higher.[3]

When set-piece battles did occur they usually took the form of two bodies of foot soldiers armed with pikes and muskets pushing against each other until one side broke. Once soldiers turned, they became vulnerable to their opponents, particularly any enemy horsemen that might be nearby, and there was often great slaughter. The horse was usually posted on the flanks of the line of foot to protect them. If one side's horse could be put to flight by the other, its foot would be exposed and, if attacked, would probably collapse. The initial clash between the horse of the two sides could therefore have a major effect on the outcome of the battle.

If one side had a great numerical superiority in terms of foot soldiers, the other side had to man their line more thinly in order to avoid being outflanked, unless they could fight in a position where their flanks could be covered by some natural obstacle such as a river, cliff or swamp. In this context manning more thinly meant having fewer rows of men from front to rear, which naturally made the line easier to break. But weakness of this sort would be more than offset if the enemy's horse was chased off the field, as this would provide the opportunity for attacking his foot from an unprotected flank. And there were other considerations, such as the ability of the artillery to weaken the enemy before the two sides closed with each other, the state of training, the physical condition and morale of the two sides, and so on, all of which could affect the result. For all of these reasons it was difficult to predict the outcome of a battle regardless of the numerical superiority of one side over the other.

As with all battles, commanders tried to keep a reserve to commit at the critical moment, in order to avert defeat or exploit success. Once they had committed their reserve they would try to form another one in case of need. But in an age when the only communication was by messenger and when the battlefield was so obscured by smoke that commanders could seldom see what was going on, it was difficult to know when or where to commit a reserve and virtually impossible to form a new one, once the first was committed. An added hazard of a battle was the personal risk that the commander had to run if he was to be successful. Gustavus Adolphus was one of the few commanders of his time to favour the set-piece battle in spite of the risk and his death at Lutzen turned a great victory into a disaster for the Protestant cause.

Rupert had shown at Vlotho that he had the ability in a full-scale battle to provide an opportunity for success, although on that occasion there was no one capable of exploiting it: he probably felt that had he been in King's shoes, he would have won a victory. Judging by his future conduct, Rupert must have concluded that battles sometimes offered opportunities that outweighed the risks involved, because in years to come he was sometimes prepared to offer battle when circumstances required it.

A further point regarding Rupert's qualification for high command was that he was becoming known throughout Europe. In some way difficult to explain, he captured people's attention. Partly, no doubt, this was due to his striking appearance and to the dramatic circumstances of his family's misfortunes, not to mention his own close confinement as the Emperor's prisoner. Partly it was due to his legendary courage and his skill at arms.

His apparent immunity on the battlefield was also a subject of comment. Stories of this had started to circulate at the sieges of Tirlemont, Louvain and particularly at Breda, when he came out of the murderous assault on the hornwork without a scratch. They had been reinforced at Rheine when his opponent's carbine misfired at point blank range and again at Vlotho when two bullets passed through his cloak without touching his body. Altogether

Rupert was beginning to build up a formidable reputation which, if not strictly a qualification for command, was undoubtedly a great asset, since it inspired confidence in his leadership and added authority to his opinions.

The circumstances of Rupert's confinement varied from time to time throughout the three years of his imprisonment, as the Emperor tried first one thing and then another to achieve his aim of converting him and taking him into his service. Even before it became known that he had been captured, Rupert's mother had written to Sir Thomas Roe saying that she wished him dead rather than a prisoner. She had a horror of any of her children becoming Roman Catholics and had on one occasion said that she would rather strangle them with her own hands than let that happen. Knowing how his mother felt, Rupert told Richard Crane, when they parted company at Bamberg, to reassure her that he would change neither his religion nor his party to achieve his release.

From the Emperor's point of view it was important to isolate Rupert entirely from anyone who might encourage him to stand firm, as a result of which efforts made by his mother and brother to send him a gentleman companion were turned down: he was eventually allowed a page and two servants who could be English or Dutch, but not German. Furthermore he was at first strictly confined to his apartments except for exercise periods in the castle garden and occasional invitations to dine with the governor.

The governor of the castle was Count von Kuffstein, an experienced soldier who had started life as a Lutheran. Although sympathetic towards Rupert, he pursued the Emperor's interests with the enthusiasm of the convert. He immediately set about the business of converting Rupert, but made no headway whatsoever. Rupert refused to talk about religion, nor would he go and discuss it with the Jesuits, let alone allow them to visit him. The misery of his captivity accentuated a natural bloody-mindedness that was never far below the surface of his personality.

It is impossible to know exactly how Rupert occupied his time in the early days of his imprisonment, but all accounts mention that he spent much of it drawing and painting. It was at this time that he perfected an instrument for drawing in perspective that Albert Durer had devised but had been unable to render practical. Many years later he presented it to the Royal Society, of which he was by then a member.[4]

Count von Kuffstein had a daughter, Susanne Marie, who was two or three years younger than Rupert and later accounted one of the great beauties of her day. She took pity on Rupert and was clearly attracted to him. Von Kuffstein, possibly hoping that the feminine touch might succeed where his own best efforts had achieved so little, put no obstacles in the way of their meeting and they spent much time in each other's company. Thanks to her influence Rupert was allowed more freedom within the castle and was able to practise shooting, ride in the school and play tennis. He also spent more time at the governor's residence where he was treated almost as one of the family, von Kuffstein helping him with his military studies in the intervals of trying to convert him.

The exact nature of Rupert's relationship with Susanne is diffi-cult to determine. It would seem that she was in love with him and that he became extremely fond of her. It is unlikely that she became his mistress: one of his biographers suggests that in his younger days he tended to idealise women, treating them in the same sort of way as his mother's admirers treated her.[5] Certainly he was grateful to Susanne and always spoke of her with great respect and affection. In years to come Susanne married three times and, although Rupert made several visits to Austria, there is no indication that he ever renewed the acquaintanceship.

After about two years the Emperor made a firm offer to release Rupert if he would become a Roman Catholic. His uncompromis-ing reply was that he had not learnt to sacrifice his religion to his interest, and he would rather breathe his last in prison than go out through the gates of apostasy. The Emperor then gave up the idea of conversion and said that all he need do was to ask pardon for the crime of rebelling against the Holy Roman Empire. Rupert could not do this without denying Charles Louis's right to his Electorate, so he replied briefly that he disdained to ask pardon for doing his duty. Finally the Emperor agreed to waive the apology if Rupert would take a command in his forces against the French. But this would inevitably result in Rupert having to fight against the Swedes and probably some of the Protestant princes as well. Rupert's answer was that he took the proposal as an affront rather than as a favour, and that he would never take arms against the champions of his father's cause.[6]

Throughout these exchanges Rupert had defied the Emperor with courage but with a lack of tact that played into the hands of his most uncompromising enemy, the old, and by this time repul-sive, Maximilian of Bavaria. Despite his great age this man, who had been the close ally of Ferdinand II in the early days of the century, was now married to the new Emperor's sister. Through her he urged that there should be no further truck with Rupert, who should be taught a lesson that he would never forget. As a result all Rupert's privileges were removed and he was closely confined in his quarters, watched day and night by a guard of twelve musketeers. And so he continued for some time in great unhappiness.

At this time Rupert was thrown back on the company of a pet hare and of a dog that had been given to him by the English ambassador in Vienna. Rupert, who had inherited his mother's interest in animals, managed to train the hare to do a number of tricks, but after a time he released it because he was afraid that it was finding captivity as irksome as he found it himself. The dog, named Boy, remained a close companion and became famous during the Civil War.

Luckily for Rupert, Linz was at this time visited by the Emperor's brother, the Archduke Leopold, who was in the area directing operations against a detachment of Banier's forces. Leopold, nick-named the Angel because of his sweet temper and piety, was several years younger than his brother and only four years older than Rupert, formerly nicknamed the Devil. For some reason Angel and Devil took to each other and became friends. On his return to Vienna, Leopold persuaded his brother to restore Rupert's privi-leges and extend them to the extent of permitting him to leave the castle on parole for up to three days at a time. Rupert made full use of this concession and paid a number of visits to the local landowners, with whom he got on well. Indeed, it was reported in England that he was greatly admired by these people, who treated him with as much respect as if they were his subjects.

When Rupert's release finally came it was as a result of pressure exerted jointly by Cardinal Richelieu and King Charles, who was getting into difficulties with his subjects and wanted to be sure of Rupert's services should he find himself involved in a civil war.

The causes of the English Civil War are too complex to be covered adequately in this book, but an attempt must be made to outline them because they form the background to the operations in which Prince Rupert played so prominent a part and influenced the way in which they were conducted.

Rumblings of discontent were audible in the reign of King James I, who became unpopular because his pro-Spanish policy offended the deeply held feelings of many of his subjects, despite the benefits it brought them. Another cause for offence was the extent to which the King handed power and wealth to his young favourite Buckingham who, for all his natural attributes, was plainly incapable of exercising adequately the various functions allotted to him. So great was Buckingham's unpopularity that, when in the closing stages of the reign he persuaded the King to abandon the Spanish alliance, Parliament refused to vote money to carry on any policy while Buckingham remained in power. To save him from impeachment James dissolved Parliament.

When King Charles succeeded his father in 1625, he remained as attached to Buckingham as his father had been. By the time that Buckingham was murdered three years later, a strong anti-court party had become established in Parliament led by Sir John Eliot, which was determined to curtail the royal power so that, as they would put it, evil counsellors would find it more difficult to come between the King and his subjects' loyal representatives. Finding that he could not work with a Parliament dominated by these people, Charles dissolved it in 1629 and ruled without one for the next eleven years. During this period he raised the money that he needed to govern the country in a number of ways, the legality of which often gave rise to disputes amongst his subjects.

One of the results of this policy was that the King could not go to war, even in defence of the rights of his sister and her children, because he could not afford to do so. From the point of view of the common people this was a blessing, and gave rise to the impression of peaceful prosperity that Rupert had found so attractive when he visited England in 1636. However, discontent was seething amongst those sections of the nobility and gentry who were excluded from the conduct of affairs but none the less being taxed in ways over which they had no control.

Further discontent arose from developments within the Church of England. In the reign of Queen Elizabeth, when the country had been so severely threatened by the Roman Catholicism of Spain, the Church of England embraced men of widely differing Protestant views. At this time the heirs of Cranmer found little difficulty in making common cause with the more severe and disciplined followers of Calvin who were content to pursue their faith within an episcopalian Church.

When King James came to the throne this partnership continued to prosper. As King of Scotland, James had ruled a country dominated by a Presbyterian Church whose doctrine he shared, but whose excesses he had only been able to control by the reintroduction of bishops appointed by himself.[7] On becoming King of England and therefore Supreme Governor of the Church of England, he accepted the organisation of the Church as he found it whilst retaining his Calvinist faith. This put him in the same category as a small but influential number of his English subjects.

During the course of his reign the ideas of a German theologian called Arminius gained some adherents within the Church of England. These people considered themselves to be the heirs of the pre-Reformation liberalism of Erasmus.[8] Whilst accepting the Reformation and refuting the authority of the Pope, they were more tolerant in terms of doctrine than the rest of the Church of England and were therefore thought to be less firm in their opposition to Roman Catholicism. So long as James was King, preferment to high office in the Church of England usually passed these people by.

By contrast, Charles I favoured them and within seven years of his accession one of their number, William Laud, had become Archbishop of Canterbury. Although the doctrine that Laud professed may have been liberal in the sense that it was less clear cut and dogmatic than that of the Calvinists, there was nothing liberal about the way in which he imposed it on the Church in an attempt to achieve uniformity throughout the country. Laud has been described as an unattractive man of humble birth; red-faced, short, harsh of speech, bad-tempered, fussy, humourless and little liked by his contemporaries, whatever their religious opinions.[9] Not surprisingly his attempt to impose a liberal doctrine in an authoritarian way had the reverse effect of that intended. Far from unifying the Church, Laud split it down the middle by offending all those who leant towards Calvinism, and many others who, wrongly as it happened, regarded his reforms as paving the way to a reconciliation with Rome.

Within the Church of England, ever since the days of Queen Elizabeth, there had been a number of Calvinists who, like King James, happily accepted that the Church should be run by bishops. There had been others who would have preferred the full Presbyterian system that had prevailed in Scotland for a time, under which each congregation elected its own minister and in which bishops had no place. In England these people were known as Puritans. Thus all Puritans were Calvinists, but not all Calvinists were Puritans.[10] Whatever else Laud succeeded in doing, he

certainly brought about a dramatic increase in the number that
wished to be done with bishops, once and for all.

Laud was not only the Archbishop of Canterbury, he was also
one of the inner ring of Privy Councillors that helped the King to
govern the country during the years when no Parliament was
called. In addition to the unattractive qualities mentioned earlier,
he was courageous, determined and above all thorough. Another
man who shared these characteristics was Thomas Wentworth,
Earl of Strafford. Originally a member of the anti-court party, he
became one of Charles's most effective supporters and was
employed by the King as Lord President of the North. In 1633 he
also became Lord Deputy of Ireland and in the course of the next
six years, by ruthlessly rooting out the corruption and inefficiency
that traditionally characterised the way in which the country had
been governed by the English, gave it an unusual but short period
of stability and peace. Because of the direct bearing that events in
Ireland had on the course of the English Civil War, it is necessary
to take a more careful look at the situation that existed there at
the time.

In the centuries following the original incursion into the country
by the Norman Kings of England, a small area along the east coast,
known as the Pale, was secured, settled and ruled directly from
Dublin. But many Norman lords settled well beyond the Pale and
virtually identified with the native Irish: these people were frequently at loggerheads with the authorities in Dublin, particularly
after the Reformation. In Elizabeth's reign Protestant adventurers
from Devon set up a number of settlements in the extreme south
of Ireland beyond the control of the authorities in Dublin, slaughtering many native Irish in the process. In the north-east of Ulster,
from where in prehistoric times Celtic tribesmen had invaded the
western Highlands of Scotland, there had been return settlement
so that from as early as the beginning of the fifteenth century the
Catholic Macdonnells of Antrim were a branch of the Scottish
Macdonnells of the Isles and a nuisance to both the Kings of Scotland and the English authorities in Dublin.[11] Finally during the
reign of James I there had been further intensive settlement in
Ulster by Lowland and Protestant Scots which involved displacing
many families of native Irish.

Strafford's reforms covered the administration of the law, the
legislative system and the Church. In addition he greatly enlarged
and reorganised the army so that by the time he left the country it
consisted of around 8,000 well-found Irish troops[12] led by properly

trained officers drawn from the mainly Protestant Anglo-Norman gentry.[13] Although his reforms were greatly admired by the majority of people of all races, he made a number of deadly enemies amongst those of the nobility whose notorious but profitable activities he had curbed, especially as his own activities did not leave him out of pocket, and they wasted no time in undermining him and his reforms as soon as his back was turned.

Strafford's departure from Ireland came about as a result of events in Scotland. When James I came to England on the death of Elizabeth, he had been ruling Scotland for many years and had little trouble in continuing to rule it through his Scottish council, which consisted of a mixture of the most powerful Highland clan chiefs and Lowland landowning nobility. Charles I was an infant when he came to London and he grew up with little understanding of the position in Scotland. Furthermore, although some of the principal Scottish nobles remained in the south, they, like the King himself, seldom went to Scotland: indeed the two most important, the Duke of Lennox, soon to become Duke of Richmond, and the Marquis of Hamilton, were members of the English Privy Council. They were both cousins of the King and his close friends. The King, like his father, ruled Scotland through his Scottish council, only the secretary of which stayed with the King in England.[14] This was hardly a satisfactory system in the light of the King's scant understanding of the country, and it became worse as he eroded the council's strength by appointing to it men of little influence, including a number of bishops.

When Charles paid his first visit to Scotland in 1633 he was misled into supposing that the people were reconciled to the concept of episcopacy which his father had cautiously and in a limited manner imposed on them. Charles, throwing caution to the winds, decided to have a new prayer book prepared for Scotland that would bring his two kingdoms closer together from a religious point of view. It took a few years for the Scottish bishops to produce one, but by the time Rupert was leaving England, in the summer of 1637, it was ready. Charles told his Scottish council to impose it, but when they did, it was vigorously rejected with riots both inside and outside church. The unrest culminated in March of the following year when a group of prominent men, led by the Earl of Rothes and supported by the Earl of Montrose set about getting signatures to a National Covenant supporting the Presbyterian version of the Protestant religion traditional in Scotland. Over the coming months copies of the Covenant were circulated throughout the country, attracting thousands of signatures.

The King's reaction was to order an army to assemble at York in the spring of 1639 to subdue the Scots. The Scots also set about raising an army with which to oppose the King, recalling many professionals from the European countries where they were serving. A veteran from the wars of Gustavus Adolphus called Alexander Leslie became the Covenanters' commander-in-chief with the Earl of Montrose as one of his principal subordinates. The King's army was composed of levies grudgingly raised by Lords Lieutenant, but there was little enthusiasm. The English Puritans supported the Covenanters, and many others, already fed up with the King's methods of raising money, had no desire to finance war against a neighbouring country with which they largely sympathised. When the two main armies confronted each other at Berwick it became apparent that the King's army was no match for the Scots and a truce was called in the middle of June before any fighting took place. At the end of July the King decided to send to Ireland for the Earl of Strafford.

During the autumn of 1639 the Church Assembly continued to defy the King who, despite some conciliatory gestures, remained determined to crush all opposition. But he would only be able to do this if he could raise an effective army, the financing of which would necessitate the recall of Parliament. Whilst he waited for this to assemble, elaborate plans were made for the production of muskets, cannon, powder, shot and swords, much of which was stored in a great arsenal at Hull. Efforts were also made to collect efficient English and Scots officers serving with foreign armies, many of whom were Roman Catholics, as soldiering abroad was one of the few occupations available to the younger sons of Catholic landowners. At the same time the efficient army that Strafford had built up in Ireland was enlarged in case it too should be needed by the King.

From the King's point of view the Parliament which assembled in April 1640 was a disappointment, because instead of voting money for the war it concentrated on the grievances of the past eleven years. The Short Parliament, as it was called, sat for only three weeks before the King dissolved it. Thereafter Strafford was obliged to resort to ways of raising money that further undermined the King's position, particularly in the city of London. Throughout the country there was an increase of Puritan influence and in some urban areas whole congregations deserted their clergy to become Presbyterians.

In the end the army raised to confront the Scots was little better than its predecessor. There had been some dissension within the Scottish ranks, mainly between the Earl of Montrose who wished to avoid confrontation with the King providing that he would allow a Presbyterian Church in Scotland and the Earl of Argyll who, in effect, wished to prevent the King from interfering in the government altogether. But the King was making no concessions and when the Scots crossed into England in August, Montrose led the advance.

The war did not last long. The Scots occupied Newcastle and the royal garrison at Edinburgh, commanded by Patrick Ruthven, surrendered in mid-September. At the end of that month the King summoned a 'Great Council of Peers' to York to help him rally the country in the face of the Scottish invasion. But many peers were opposed to the war and within a month the King was obliged to agree an armistice with the Scots and call a new Parliament for November.

By the time that this Parliament, known to history as the Long Parliament, assembled, support for the King was at a low ebb. But despite his hesitancy and indecision over methods, the King was utterly determined to defend his sovereign rights. Charles believed that, having been appointed by God, he alone had the right to decide government policy and that any attempt to restrict his authority was ultimately an offence against God. He considered that Parliament was entitled to express the views of those it represented, but that it had a duty to raise the money and other support that he needed in order to govern the country.

John Pym, who on the death of Sir John Eliot had taken over the leadership of those in Parliament opposed to the King's policies, was equally determined not only to revert to a more traditional balance between Crown and Parliament but also to curtail the King's power so that it would be impossible for him or his successors ever again to rule without Parliament for a protracted period. Pym and his followers therefore decided to get rid of Strafford and Laud, to exclude the bishops from the House of Lords, to declare some of the methods for raising money used by the King during the period of his personal rule illegal, to abolish the prerogative courts by which he had raised money, e.g. the detested Court of Star Chamber, and to pass an act obliging the King to call a new Parliament every three years. All this, with the exception of excluding the bishops, was accomplished within a year with the unwilling support of the King, who was even forced to authorise the execution of Strafford and the imprisonment of Laud.

But the majority of the people in the country were as unhappy with the radical measures introduced by Parliament as they were with the King's interpretation of his rights. Furthermore, although the King never wavered from his underlying position, he often disguised it and appeared to compromise in order to attract support, a game that the equally intractable Pym could also play.

By November 1641, a few well-respected men such as Lord Falkland and Edward Hyde, who had previously been critical of the King's policies, had rallied to his support in Parliament and nearly succeeded in preventing Pym and his friends from passing a gratuitously offensive bill known as the Grand Remonstrance which gave form to the resentment felt towards the King and his advisers. By this time the King had also recruited a few of the Parliamentary moderates to his Privy Council and under their guidance could reasonably have expected a gradual improvement in his fortunes. But a major uprising in Ireland, which had taken place the previous month, was about to provoke a new constitutional crisis and push events beyond the point of no return. This was the situation that existed when Prince Rupert was finally released from his captivity.

The circumstances of Rupert's release were as colourful as those of his captivity. The Emperor's sister pleaded on bended knee for Rupert's continued imprisonment, but was countered by the Archduke Leopold and the Empress who, many years earlier as the Spanish Infanta, had been courted by King Charles, then Prince of Wales. Siding with his brother and wife, the Emperor sent word to Rupert that he would release him providing that he would give an undertaking not to bear arms against him in the future. Initially Rupert was reluctant to give even this assurance, but on writing to King Charles for advice received the order to do so forthwith.

Rupert was then told that he would have to sign a document guaranteeing his undertaking, to which he replied that if it was to be a lawyer's business they had better look well to the wording. The Emperor wisely decided that Rupert's assurance would provide the best security: all that was now needed was that he should seal the bargain by kissing the Emperor's hand. Soon afterwards Rupert was hunting near Linz and managed to kill a boar with his spear on foot, an action that was much admired in Austria at the time.

Whilst he was being congratulated by the assembled company the Emperor rode up and extended his hand to Rupert, who kissed it and so became a free man.

A short time later Rupert travelled to Vienna where he was immensely popular. The Emperor himself became attached to the young man who had defied him for so long and redoubled his efforts to get Rupert to enter his service. Although Rupert took a liking to the Emperor and remained friendly to him ever afterwards, he wanted to get home and was determined to leave as soon as he decently could. The Emperor warned him to keep well away from the territory of Maximilian of Bavaria, so he returned to the Hague via Prague, Dresden and Hamburg. At Dresden he was lavishly entertained by the Elector who soon discovered that Rupert would not drink in a way compatible with Saxon hospitality and greatly preferred hunting to banquets.

Such was the energy with which Rupert pursued his journey that he arrived at his mother's court on 20 December, the same day as the letter from Vienna telling of his departure and well before anyone dreamt that he could himself appear. He was three days past his twenty-second birthday.

5

THE UNFOLDING WAR

Rupert was not the only member of the Palatine family to have
spent time as a prisoner. While he was incarcerated at Linz, Charles
Louis, Maurice, Edward and Philip had all been detained for short
periods in France for one reason or another. At the time of Rupert's
homecoming Charles Louis was again in England, but the three
others were at the Hague together with the younger members of
the family: money was still short and employment for the men a
pressing problem. The Prinzenhof had been closed down earlier in
the year on the death of the youngest child, Carl Gustav.

Prince Frederick Henry, though pleased to see Rupert, could no
longer employ him because of his undertaking to the Emperor. In
any case Rupert's first obligation was to King Charles, who had
taken so much trouble to secure his release. Elizabeth of Bohemia
seemed unaware of the changes that had taken place in her son
during the last three years. Despite his record in captivity, she
remained jealous of Henrietta Maria's influence and worried that
she might yet convert him, thereby jeopardising Charles Louis's
prospects. She was accordingly reluctant to let Rupert go to
England. But Rupert was determined to visit his uncle and thank
him for his release.

King Charles's difficulties had multiplied in the few weeks that
followed Rupert's departure from Linz. The uprising in Ireland
had taken place when the King was visiting Scotland and he had
immediately ordered a brigade of Scottish troops under General
Munro to be sent to Ulster. Both King and Parliament realised that
English troops would also have to be sent to stem the blood bath,
because most of the efficient Irish army raised by Strafford had
been disbanded at Pym's insistence in case the King tried to use it
to coerce Parliament in England. But Pym's supporters were not
prepared to leave control of such a force in the King's hands. They
wanted Parliament to appoint the commanders and direct their

activities, which meant depriving the King of one of his most fundamental functions.

Throughout December Pym and his friends had been pressing
for the passage of a militia bill which would give Parliament control
not only of the force sent to Ireland, but also of the part-time
county levies and city trained bands in England as well. They had
also been pursuing the issue of debarring the bishops from the
House of Lords which the Puritans wished to extend to abolishing
bishops altogether. In order to force these measures through Parliament, Pym organised mobs of apprentices from the city to intimidate the King's supporters and engineer an atmosphere of crisis.
Over the Christmas period it seemed probable that Parliament
even intended to impeach the Queen, who was being blamed for
encouraging the revolt of the Irish Catholics. Charles, banking on
support from those who thought that the militants had gone too
far, decided to act.

On 4 January 1642 the King, with a detachment of his guards,
walked from Whitehall to Westminster, intending to arrest and
charge with high treason five members of the House of Commons,
namely Pym, Hampden, Haselrigg, Holles and Strode, together
with Pym's principal supporter in the Lords, Viscount Mandeville,
soon to become Earl of Manchester. On arrival he went into the
chamber of the Commons accompanied only by Rupert's brother,
Charles Louis. But in the King's words, the birds had flown: they
had in fact taken refuge in the city. This fiasco undid all the good
work that the King's supporters had been doing to discredit Pym.
Uproar followed. Six days later the King left London.

The King went first to Hampton Court and then to Windsor.
In February he escorted the Queen to Dover on her way to the
Netherlands. Ostensibly she was taking the young Princess Mary,
who had recently married Prince Frederick Henry's fifteen-year-old
son, to join her husband. In fact her purpose was to sell some of
the Crown Jewels and to buy arms and equipment which the King
would need if it proved necessary to use force against his rebellious
subjects. Charles planned to establish himself in York once the
Queen had gone. He thought that it would be a good place from
which to secure Hull with its arsenal left over from the Scottish
wars; through Hull also he could receive such assistance as the
Queen was able to raise abroad. He also felt that it would be easier
for him to raise an army in the north than in the south, should it
prove necessary for him to do so.

It was at Dover Castle on 17 February that Prince Rupert met up with his uncle and aunt. Although he received a warm welcome, he found them anxious and greatly changed. King Charles was trying hard to conciliate Parliament, and felt that the presence at court of such a formidable soldier as Prince Rupert might be misconstrued by the moderates. Rupert therefore returned with the Queen and her daughter when they sailed for the Netherlands a few days later.

They were met on arrival by a great gathering led by the Stadholder Frederick Henry, his son Prince William of Orange and by the Queen of Bohemia who thus for the first time came face to face with the sister-in-law she so greatly distrusted. Although the two Queens were destined to spend the next year together at the Hague, it does not seem that they developed any great liking for each other. Whilst Elizabeth accepted that Henrietta Maria was a loving wife and a stalwart supporter of her brother from a personal point of view, she thought that in other respects she was 'a disastrous mate for him'. She is on record as saying that she had 'too warring a mind for her sex' and she deplored the fact that Henrietta Maria and her entourage were consistently hostile to Parliament, not wishing for matters to be patched up and wanting everything done by force.[1] Elizabeth's assessment is confirmed by a letter that Henrietta Maria wrote to King Charles at this time, threatening to retire to a convent unless he stood up more firmly for his rights and those of his children. Amongst the Queen's Ladies-in-Waiting was the young Duchess of Richmond, formerly Mary Villiers, daughter of the murdered Duke of Buckingham.

Rupert spent the next five months helping his aunt to raise money and buy arms, a task made difficult by the fact that the Dutch, though anxious for profit, sympathised more with the Puritan elements within Parliament than with the King. But the Queen tackled the task with her customary energy and achieved much success. Rupert meanwhile was collecting together a group of officers to accompany him to England when the time arrived.

Once established in York, the King set about securing Hull, although it is likely that much of the contents of the arsenal had been moved to London by sea in accordance with Parliamentary instructions issued at the end of March.[2] At any rate on 23 April he sent his eight-year-old son, the Duke of York, together with Charles Louis and a number of courtiers, to visit the Governor, Sir John Hotham. Whilst they were at dinner, Charles himself appeared outside the walls and asked to be let in. But Hotham, whose main concern was to safeguard his estates, had no wish to alienate Parliament and refused to open the gates. The party accompanying the Duke of York were unable to force the issue and Charles was obliged to return to York empty-handed. Charles Louis, who had by this time calculated that the King was unlikely to prevail in the long term, left York. Having sent a message to Parliament saying that he had been an unwilling tool in the attempt on Hull, he returned to the Hague. Meanwhile the Duke of York and Rupert, *in absentia*, had both been made Knights of the Garter.

By this time Parliament had passed the Militia Ordinance which governed the way in which it would raise its forces using Lords Lieutenants and their deputies to appoint officers, raise the men and collect the necessary funds for their support. It also removed those Lords Lieutenants and Deputy Lieutenants who did not support Parliament and replaced them with men who did. With Parliament in control of the normal process for raising troops, the King fell back on the old system of issuing Commissions of Array to selected people throughout the kingdom, including the recently deposed Lords Lieutenants and Deputy Lieutenants, together with Justices of the Peace and other leading members of the gentry. Three of these Commissioners acting together were entitled to issue commissions to individual officers, to raise and command regiments or troops of horse or companies of foot soldiers. In this way both sides raised their armies.

The King had in fact been raising troops before the Commissioners were appointed. He said that he intended to lead them to Ireland to fight the rebels, but in Puritan circles it was thought that he wanted to win the rebels over and use them in England against Parliament. In practice there were several separate sources of trained manpower in Ireland which the King might be able to tap if he could negotiate an end to the uprising. First there were the English regiments, officered by professionals such as Richard Grenville and George Monk, which had been sent there in recent months to handle the uprising. Second there was the remains of Strafford's Irish army, well-trained troops, officered for the most part by Protestants and commanded by the Earl of Ormonde, head of the influential Anglo-Irish Butlers. These two categories, together with Monro's Scottish brigade which had arrived in April, amounted to about 12,000 men. Opposed to them were large numbers of rebel Irish troops, commanded mainly by Anglo-Irish gentry, although in Ulster the military commander was the redoubtable native Irishman, Owen Roe O'Neill. These groups nominally owed allegiance to Lord Mountgarret as President of the General Assembly of the Confederate Catholics.

Throughout the Civil War the possibility of tapping this varied source of military manpower affected the strategy of both sides. Right up to the end when all seemed lost, the King thought that troops from Ireland were going to swing the war in his favour and much effort was expended on holding a port in the north-west through which such reinforcement could pass. Furthermore the King endlessly engaged in secret negotiations designed to reach a settlement that would make this possible. In modern parlance it was as if he was trying to incorporate into the Royalist forces units of the British Army in Northern Ireland, the part-time members of the Royal Irish Regiment (formerly the Ulster Defence Regiment) and the Irish Republican Army. Furthermore he was trying to do it at a time when the whole of England was horrified by tales of the massacres perpetrated by the Irish rebels on the English and Scottish settlers. From the start Parliament was conscious of the military danger. It was also conscious of the propaganda opportunities provided by the King's negotiations which it exploited to the full.

But whatever the King's chances may or may not have been of acquiring a war-winning capability from Ireland, there is no doubt that the position in England greatly favoured Parliament. As men's commitment to one side or the other took shape it could be seen that Parliament would have control of London, the Home Counties, Bristol and most of the prime sources of wealth, including all the main ports with the exception of Newcastle. Parliament was therefore in a better position than the King to pay and equip its forces.[3] A further advantage, on which so many of the other advantages depended, was Parliament's control of the fleet. Charles had built a number of excellent ships during the 1630s but had alienated the navy by his failure to have them properly maintained and supplied. Worse still was his tactless treatment of the Lord Admiral, the Earl of Northumberland. As a result of this, in the summer of 1642 Northumberland appointed the Earl of Warwick to command the fleet as his deputy. Warwick was not only an experienced and competent soldier with additional experience of war at sea gained as a privateer, but he was also at the very heart of the Puritan movement and deeply committed to the Parliamentary cause. He retained command of the fleet throughout the Civil War and directed its activities superbly.[4]

By comparison, the King's strength lay in the traditional loyalty felt for his position by those of the nobility and gentry not specifically committed to Parliament as a result of their experiences of government, their personal prospects, their family connections, or their attachment to the Puritan religion. Geographically his hold was strongest in the north and west of the country, but he had some supporters in other places, even in the city of London itself. That the King had managed to rally as much support as he had was in part due to the way in which Edward Hyde had presented his case in Parliament during the first half of 1642. As a result of his advocacy many members of both Houses discreetly left Westminster in the early summer, either to join the King or to muster support for him in their home areas.

By mid-July King Charles had with him at York the Secretary of State Lord Falkland, the Chancellor of the Exchequer Sir John Culpepper, the Lord Keeper of the Great Seal, who was the senior law officer in the kingdom, and Hyde himself. Hyde, Falkland and Culpepper had all opposed the King during the time that he was ruling without Parliament and they remained dedicated to the search for a solution to existing problems that would safeguard the position of both King and Parliament. Whilst opposing Pym's revolutionary demands, they certainly did not look for a military solution that would destroy Parliament's legitimate rights and influence. Hyde and Falkland had for some years been at the centre of a circle of influential and cultured people who used to meet at Falkland's house near Oxford. They were close personal friends, civilised and rational, who shared a dislike of violence in all its forms: the very idea of civil war was an affront to their convictions and their sensibilities.

From a material point of view everything was in Parliament's favour and opinion abroad was that the King would speedily be forced to submit. In July, accepting at last that war was inevitable, the King appointed his chief commanders. In accordance with ancient custom, he commanded his army in person as Captain General. Under him and with direct access to him were the Lord General and the General of the Horse. The Earl of Lindsey, who was sixty years old and the owner of extensive estates in Lincolnshire, was appointed Lord General. He had served as a soldier on a number of occasions since his youth, but with long gaps in between: his military thinking was based largely on his experiences in the Netherlands. Prince Rupert, with ideas derived mainly from Gustavus Adolphus of Sweden, was appointed General of the Horse. Although the Lord General was to have authority throughout the army, Prince Rupert was not obliged to take orders from anyone but the King himself; a sure recipe for friction and confusion. Sir Jacob Astley was appointed to command the foot and Henry Wilmot was second-in-command and commissary general of the horse. As soon as these appointments were made the King sent word to Rupert to join him.

At last Rupert had the major command for which he had waited so long. At twenty-two he was at the peak of his immense physical strength and this, together with the frustrations of the past and his addiction to war, unleashed a torrent of energy within him that remained undiminished for the next three years. But although he possessed the military qualities required of a commander to a high degree, he did not understand the political background to the struggle in the way that his brother or mother did. To his mind the issue was simple. Those who were about to take up arms against the King were rebels who were not susceptible to reason. If they had been susceptible to reason, they would have settled for the generous concessions that the King had already offered. The only sensible course was to overcome them as soon as possible. Once this was done and the King restored to his rights and to his capital, it would be time for such negotiation to take place as the King thought fit. Until then, there should be no compromise. This at least was the gist of the advice he had offered his uncle in February[5] and there is no reason to suppose that he saw things differently in August.

This approach would inevitably bring Rupert into conflict with the King's civilian advisers such as Hyde and Culpepper in the same way as the muddled chain of command would bring him into conflict with some of the officers in the army. Rupert's short temper and the direct way in which he expressed his views, contrary to the normal manners of the court, would ensure that these conflicts were bitter and tempestuous. In retrospect some historians have wondered whether Rupert's contribution outweighed the disruption that he caused from time to time. The answer must be that without his aggression, drive and skill the Royalist cause might well have foundered in the first few months, whereas in the event he established a military ascendancy over Parliament that was to last for nearly two years.

Rupert wasted no time on receiving the King's summons and embarked in the *Lion*, which was the ship that had brought him and the Queen to the Netherlands in February. But Elizabeth of Bohemia and Charles Louis had no wish to see Rupert fighting against Parliament and sent word to the captain to avoid taking him to England. Soon after sailing a storm provided the excuse to put Rupert ashore and when the weather improved the ship slipped away without him. Rupert then borrowed a ship from the Stadholder and set sail a second time with his brother Maurice, an engineer called de Gomme, an ammunition expert called La Roche, Dan O'Neale who was to be lieutenant colonel of his regiment, Richard Crane who was to command his life guard, Somerset Fox, the dog Boy and a pet monkey. After a rough crossing they were intercepted off Flamborough Head by a Parliamentary ship, which they evaded, and finally landed in the evening at Tynemouth. Notwithstanding the perils and fatigue of the voyage, Rupert insisted that they set off at once on the 130-odd miles to Nottingham where he expected to find the King. Riding through the night Rupert's horse slipped and fell on top of him, putting his shoulder out of joint. Luckily a bonesetter was found and after a delay of three hours, despite the pain, he resumed his journey. On arrival he discovered that the King had left a few days earlier to secure Coventry.

Even Rupert could go no further without a rest, but this was soon interrupted by the Governor of Nottingham, Lord Digby, who wanted him to identify a particular weapon in the armoury that the King urgently required. George Digby was a courtier and friend of King Charles who must have been well known to Rupert, as he had spent part of the previous six months in the Netherlands with the Queen. As a soldier he was typical of many of the Royalist officers that Rupert would have to train: willing, gallant, but totally ignorant of war. Digby was also a politician, whose advice to the King was usually disastrous: he had for example played a leading part in the King's bungled attempt to arrest the five members of Parliament in the previous January. He was thirty years old, amusing, intelligent, articulate and good-looking in a golden, blue-eyed way. He was also quick-witted, a born intriguer, a dissimulator and a man of no fixed principles. If a policy was being followed that someone else had suggested, he would usually try to change it for one that would put him at the centre of events without much regard for the merits of the case.

Rupert found the King outside Leicester. At that time the Royalist horse consisted of 800 untrained men under officers, some of whom had previous military experience. Rupert immediately took over command from Lord Wilmot, eight years his senior, whom he had known at the siege of Breda. On the previous day Wilmot had failed in an attempt to attack a weak detachment of enemy troops outside Coventry, as a result of which spirits were low. The whole party then returned to Nottingham where next day, 22 August, the King raised his standard, thus formally signalling the start of the war. During the following night the standard blew down, which was considered an ill omen.

For the next three weeks the King stayed at Nottingham in order to collect together those units being raised by his supporters in Yorkshire and the East Midlands. At this time the horse were billeted outside the town and Rupert energetically set about the task of turning them into soldiers. He also sent a characteristically direct demand to the Mayor of Leicester for £2,000 as his contri-bution to the cause, adding that 'if any disaffected persons with you shall ... persuade you to neglect the command, I shall tomorrow appear before your town in such a posture with horse foot and cannon as shall make you know that it is more safe to obey than resist His Majesty's command.' As Leicester was still wondering whether to support the Royalist cause, the King quickly repudiated his nephew's demand, but he kept the first instalment of £500 sent by the Mayor to keep Rupert pacified.

Whilst still at Nottingham Rupert had the first of many disputes with George Digby, who was in the process of raising a regiment of horse. Apparently Digby had been making unpleasant comments to the effect that Rupert was mixing with people below his station. As always Rupert preferred talking to those with whom he had business, such as his regimental officers or even armourers and saddlers, rather than drinking and gambling with courtiers. But he did so for practical reasons and was angry with Digby who was obliged to make an abject apology to the detriment of their future relationship.

At the same time as Rupert was recruiting and training the horse, he was also ranging widely across the Midlands seizing Parliamen-tary assets and interfering with their recruiting. His first engage-ment with the enemy took place on 11 September when he assaulted and captured a house in Warwickshire belonging to a Parliamentary supporter. The house was defended with vigour and when it was overcome Rupert was amazed to find that the defence had been conducted by the owner's wife and son-in-law assisted by no more than three servants and a few women. He so admired the fortitude of the lady of the house that he permitted nothing to be touched and offered a command in his own regiment to the son-in-law who politely declined it. To Rupert the rules of war were as sacred as the laws of God and he was always meticulously correct in his dealings with those that surrendered. On the other hand it was unusual for him not to wring the maximum advantage out of any situation and he would have been within his rights to have removed everything of military value.

During this period Rupert was constantly on the move, appearing in one place after another, demanding in the King's name the weapons, armour and horses that he needed to build up his command. So often was his appearance reported that he gave the impression of being in several different places at once and the notion got around that he possessed supernatural powers. Furthermore, as most of his business involved stripping the countryside of military resources, he gained a reputation for ruthlessness and fierce hostility that terrified his enemies and left even his friends in awe of him. That this was the case is confirmed by numerous contemporary sources.[6] Indeed, so great was the clamour from Parliamentary propagandists that within a few months Rupert felt himself obliged to answer allegations of savage conduct in two pamphlets prepared by the Oxford University printer. Needless to say, fear of Rupert generated by his enemies rebounded on their own heads, because it fostered the idea that he was invincible.

Meanwhile a Parliamentary army was being built up at Northampton, strategically placed between London and the King. On 9 September the Earl of Essex arrived to take command, by which time his force had reached a strength of about 15,000, far in excess of the King's army. Essex was the son of Queen Elizabeth's executed favourite. In his youth he had been forced into a bad marriage by James I which had left him feeling hurt and foolish. But at fifty-one he was an experienced soldier of the Dutch school, having served as a company commander in Sir Horace Vere's force in the Palatinate and later as a colonel in the Netherlands. He had for a time been King Charles's lieutenant general in the first Scots war: latterly he had been Lord Chamberlain until dismissed on refusing to join the King at York. As a commander he was deliberate rather than inspired, but he was honest and reliable which made him popular with soldiers, who trusted him. He was a firm supporter of the Parliamentary cause, a moderate Puritan and a first cousin of the Earl of Warwick.

On 13 September the King's army, consisting of five regiments of foot, a detachment of horse and an artillery train of twelve guns, left Nottingham and headed west. Rupert with the remainder of the horse moved on a parallel course between the King and Essex. Although numerically the Royalists compared unfavourably with the Parliamentary army their morale and discipline were far better.[7] Furthermore recruiting was going well and around sixty experienced commanders who had been serving with Prince Frederick Henry in the Netherlands were returning to join the King. From Nottingham the King marched via Derby to Stafford, collecting additional units as he went.

Rupert met up with the King on 18 September at Stafford where a remarkable demonstration of his skill at arms took place, recorded in a document that still survives.[8] Whilst standing sixty yards away from the church of St Mary, Rupert fired his pistol at the weathercock, the bullet piercing a hole in its tail which was plainly visible to those below. When the King said that it was a fluke, Rupert fired another shot which also went through the weathercock's tail. It would be difficult to repeat this feat with the current service automatic.

From Stafford the Royalist army moved to Shrewsbury, arriving there on 20 September. Soon afterwards the King took a detachment to secure Chester. Meanwhile Essex, who had left Northampton on 19 September, also marched his army westwards through Coventry, Warwick and Stratford towards Worcester which was garrisoned for the King by Sir John Byron.[9] In an attempt to prevent Essex taking Worcester, the King sent Rupert with eight troops of horse and ten companies of dragoons to reinforce Byron. Rupert arrived on 23 September and immediately realised that Worcester could not be held against Essex's army as its defences were virtually non-existent. He also discovered that the road into Worcester from the east was blocked and rightly guessed that Essex's forces would approach from the south which would take them across the River Teme at Powick Bridge some one and a half miles south of the town. Ordering Byron to withdraw towards Shrewsbury, Rupert moved his detachment, less some of the dragoons who stayed in Worcester, into a large field called Brickfield Meadow between Worcester and Powick Bridge to cover the withdrawal.

Essex had already sent a similar-sized detachment of horse and dragoons ahead of his main army to secure the bridge. They had arrived on the previous day and encamped to the south of the river. But it would seem that they failed to notice the coming of Rupert's force,[10] probably because he had kept his horse well back from the river and merely pushed the dragoons forward to a position from which they could bring fire to bear on the bridge. Having sent Wilmot with a detachment to reconnoitre forward, he ordered the horse to dismount and rest.

Although Rupert had with him no more than 500 horse and some dragoons, a large number of senior officers were present including Prince Maurice, Wilmot, Digby and Rupert himself, each colonel of a regiment, and Sir Charles Lucas, the lieutenant colonel of another regiment. It can safely be assumed that his eight troops were drawn from a number of different regiments so that any practical experience gained would quickly spread throughout the Royalist horse.

Despite the fact that Wilmot's reconnaissance sent back no warning of any enemy in the area, a column of heavily armoured Parliamentary horse under the command of Colonel Sandys started to cross the bridge at 4 p.m. Although fired on by Rupert's dragoons, they rode up a narrow lane and started to deploy into Brickfield Meadow.

Having divested themselves of their helmets and their back and breast plates, the Royalists were at a considerable disadvantage and would be in grave danger if the superior enemy detachment was given enough time to emerge from the lane and deploy in the meadow. Realising that there was no time to put on armour and form his troops into a regular line of battle, Rupert jumped on the nearest horse and rode straight for the enemy, calling on his men to follow. The result was unlike anything that the Parliamentarians had been taught to expect and most turned tail as soon as the Royalists' avalanche hit them, those in front running into those still emerging from the lane. In the ensuing mêlée a number of the enemy were killed and others drowned in the river. So great was the panic that some of the enemy did not draw rein until they reached Essex's main army at Pershore. By contrast a small part of the Parliamentary force, commanded by Captain Fiennes, managed to mount a counter-attack against a troop of Prince Rupert's regiment commanded by Sir Lewis Dyve, which received them standing still and which was in consequence routed with some loss. But Fiennes was soon obliged to withdraw as a result of the situation elsewhere on the battlefield.

In terms of the numbers involved, the battle of Powick Bridge was insignificant and Royalist losses light, although many of the Royalist commanders, including Maurice, Wilmot, Lucas and Dyve, received minor wounds. A larger number of the enemy were killed, possibly as many as 150, in addition to which fifty were taken prisoner including the mortally wounded Colonel Sandys. But the main advantage gained by the Royalists was the tremendous boost that it gave to their morale and the even greater boost that it gave to Prince Rupert's reputation. From now on he was not only a terror to the enemy, but a commander who inspired devotion in the hearts of thousands of Royalists.

After the battle Rupert sent a report of the engagement to the King at Chester where his messenger, Richard Crane, the commander of his life guard, was knighted. Rupert himself withdrew his detachment first to Ludlow and then to Shrewsbury where he joined the main Royalist army on 26 September. Meanwhile Essex occupied Worcester.

During the withdrawal, according to a Parliamentary publication of the following year,[11] Rupert was moving around in disguise sizing up Essex's army. On one occasion, dressed as a country gentleman, he is alleged to have entered the house of an old widow within a mile of Worcester asking for something to eat. Whilst preparing his food the woman inveighed against the Royalists, describing them as rude knaves and expressing the hope that a plague would choke Prince Rupert who should have kept himself where he was born. In the story Rupert is said to have agreed heartily and rewarded her with some money. He then got his own back by giving her a letter to the Mayor of Worcester which said that she had been entertaining Prince Rupert in her house. Another story from the same source tells of Rupert coming on a farmer who was about to sell a load of apples to the Parliamentary army. In this story Rupert paid the farmer for the load, changed clothes with him and drove through the enemy's lines selling the apples. Having done this he returned the cart and told the farmer to go amongst the army asking the men how they liked the apples that Prince Rupert had sold them in person. Most authorities take the view that these incidents could not have happened, as Prince Rupert would have been far too busy. But Rupert always set great store by the collection of information and would have heard stories of Gustavus Adolphus passing among his enemies in disguise, even talking to their sentries on occasions. Given his extreme daring, it is by no means unlikely that Rupert would have tried to emulate him, especially in the early stages of the war. Furthermore it would have appealed to the sardonic sense of humour for which he was noted in his younger years.

It was at this time also that Rupert wrote to the Earl of Essex

offering to settle the war either by what he described as an encounter in a pitched field between the two armies on Dunsmore Heath
on 10 October or, if assembling his army was too much trouble,
by straightforward single combat between the two of them. Such
challenges, seemingly more suitable to the medieval period, were
still made from time to time, mainly for propaganda purposes. In
declining the offer Essex made the point that he was not waging
war against the King but merely trying to obtain a peace between
the King and his Parliament in opposition to those who were trying
to prevent it.[12] Parliament's claim that it was only trying to free
the King from his evil counsellors remained unchanged throughout
the war and was endorsed by their war-cry, 'For King and Parliament.' By contrast, the Royalist war-cry was 'For God and King':
the Puritans, convinced that God was on their side, doubtless
considered this to be inappropriate.

It is not necessary to go into great detail regarding the weapons,
organisation and procedures adopted by the Royalist and Parliamentary armies in order to assess Rupert's ability as a commander.
On the other hand it is difficult to follow events without some idea
of the way in which the two armies were organised.

Each army was divided into foot, horse, dragoons, and the artillery train: there was virtually no staff system to help commanders
direct operations which they had to do for themselves with the
assistance of aides-de-camp and a secretary. The most senior
officers such as the King or Prince Rupert or the Earl of Essex had
life guards consisting of various-sized detachments of foot and
horse, whose job was to escort and guard the commander
concerned in battle, on the move and in camp.

A regiment of foot or horse was raised by its colonel; he could
be a senior officer in the army or a local magnate who might or
might not have had previous military experience. Sometimes a
group of gentry from a given area would club together to raise a
regiment, selecting one of their number to be the colonel. Regiments bore their colonel's name, e.g. Lord Lindsey's regiment of
foot or Lord Digby's regiment of horse. A few people might raise
a regiment of foot and a regiment or part of a regiment of horse.
Initially Rupert had a regiment of horse, but later in the war he
took over a regiment of foot as well when its colonel was killed.

A regiment of foot was supposed to be 1,200 strong divided into
ten companies, each consisting of one-third pikemen and

two-thirds musketeers. One of the companies was commanded by the colonel of the regiment, one by the lieutenant colonel, one by the major (technically sergeant major) and the other seven by captains. If the colonel was involved elsewhere as a senior commander or as one of the officers of state, the regiment was commanded by the lieutenant colonel. When deployed for battle, the resources of all the companies were combined, so that the regiment could deploy with the pikemen in the middle and the musketeers on the flanks, or in two equal blocks divided in the same way, known as grand divisions, or in any other way desired by the overall commander. The pikeman's role was to protect the musketeers from cavalry. The widespread use of armour for pikemen was abandoned early on in the war. Musketeers never wore armour and were armed with the matchlock musket which was heavy, clumsy and took up to a minute to reload. Firing by volley was preferred to individual marksmanship and the matchlock round was dangerous up to 100 yards. When the enemy closed matchlocks were often used as clubs. Each company had its own distinctive ensign or colour to which men could rally if separated in combat. Instructions were given by beat of drum. Each regiment had its own baggage train.

A regiment of horse was supposed to consist of six troops, three of which were commanded by the colonel, the lieutenant colonel, and the major respectively, and the other three by captains: in the Parliamentary army there were no lieutenant colonels in regiments of horse. The troops commanded by captains were supposed to have seventy all ranks each and those commanded by field officers rather more, so that the total in the regiment would amount to around 500 if up to strength, which was seldom the case. The officers, who, in the Royalist army at least, were usually country gentry, were mounted on quality horses of around 15 hands. Troopers would normally have to be content with heavier animals and at the start of the war there was little uniformity within troops or regiments. A very few regiments, mostly in the Parliamentary army, were equipped with three-quarter length armour i.e. armour covering the front, back, arms and thighs, with a helmet that gave protection to the head and neck. Regiments so equipped were known as cuirassiers. Most regiments had to be content with back and breast plates and a simple pot helmet. Troopers carried a sword and two pistols. Each troop had its standard on which to rally and instructions were given by trumpet.

Dragoons were musketeers mounted on cheap, small horses or ponies. They were expected to fight on foot and to use their nags for getting between one place and another. They were theoretically organised in regiments of ten companies in the same way as the foot and had colours and drums rather than standards and trumpets. Apart from the horses, the main difference between foot and dragoons was that dragoons had no pikemen and their muskets were the shorter and more modern firelocks rather than matchlocks.

There were ten different sizes of cannon that could be included in the artillery train, each with its own special name, the biggest of which, the cannon royal, had a bore of 8 inches, weighed 8,000 pounds, fired a shot that weighed 63 pounds and needed sixteen horses to pull it. By contrast the smallest, known as a robinet, had a bore of only 1¼ inches, weighed 120 pounds and fired a shot weighing a mere 12 ounces. Cannon could be used in battles or in sieges, but clearly the problems involved in moving the larger ones around meant that they were not suitable for mobile operations. The mainstay of the field artillery was the saker, with a 3½-inch bore and weighing 2,500 pounds, which could be pulled by five horses. The artillery train also included pioneers and miners.

When possible, soldiers in the field were issued with two pounds of bread or biscuit and one pound of meat or cheese per day. It would be normal for the men to carry about seven days' supply in their knapsacks and they would be replenished from time to time from the regimental wagons. As the war developed each army collected a wagon train which could transport food from base areas to detachments in the field. When troops were not in the field they were often quartered on the civil population who were obliged to house and feed them in return for tokens which would, in theory at least, be redeemed for cash later. In terms of supply the Royalist armies were consistently better organised than those of Parliament, although the King had more difficulty in raising money than did Parliament.[13]

When Prince Rupert rejoined the Royalist army at Shrewsbury, it was growing daily in size and efficiency, although none of the regiments of horse or foot could be regarded as being fully trained. None the less by early October there was a general feeling that the time had come to take the offensive. Two courses of action were considered. First to move directly on Essex's army around Worcester in order to destroy it in battle. Second to move toward London and to bring Essex to battle under favourable circumstances when he tried to interpose himself between the King and his capital. The second course was chosen because the country round Worcester would not enable the Royalists to exploit the superiority of their mounted troops. The Royalist army left Shrewsbury on 12 October.

At this time the Royalist army consisted of thirteen regiments of foot, ten regiments of horse and three regiments of dragoons, many of the regiments being considerably under strength. There was also an artillery train of twenty assorted guns. By contrast Essex had twenty regiments of foot, sixty-one troops of horse, not all of which had by this time become incorporated into regiments, two regiments of dragoons and forty-six guns of various sorts. But unlike the Royalists, Essex had already committed himself to detaching sizeable garrisons to towns such as Hereford, Worcester, Banbury, Coventry and Northampton, so he would take longer than the King to assemble his army at any point of confrontation. Furthermore it would seem that his scouts and his intelligence service were not yet working effectively, because it was not until 19 October that he started in pursuit of the King and even then he was uncertain as to the exact direction in which the Royalist army was moving.

The Royalist army, travelling at about ten miles a day in a south-easterly direction, moved from Shrewsbury to Bridgnorth and then to Kenilworth which was half-way between the Parliamentary garrisons at Coventry and Warwick. From there it moved towards Banbury, billeting the soldiers in a number of villages spread across an area that was roughly eight miles from east to west and four miles north to south for the night of 22 October. The King with the headquarters of the army was at Edgecote in the south-east quarter of the billeting area which at its nearest point was four miles north of Banbury. The King's intention was that on the next day a detachment of 4,000 men under Sir Nicholas Byron should move forward and capture Banbury whilst the remainder of the army rested.

Meanwhile Essex, who had been marching due east from Worcester at a slower pace than the Royalists, arrived a few miles away in the area of Kineton that same evening and started dispersing his troops around the nearby villages without realising that the King's army was so close at hand. Despite a reconnaissance by Digby's regiment earlier in the day, the Royalists knew no more of Essex than he knew of them until a party of Essex's soldiers looking for billets ran into some of Rupert's men at Wormleighton, which is where Rupert himself intended to spend the night. In the ensuing scuffle the Parliamentarians were captured and soon afterwards Rupert sent a patrol to Kineton which confirmed the presence of Essex's main army there.

It would seem that Rupert's first reaction was to launch a night attack on Kineton, which would certainly have thrown Essex into confusion, but would not have achieved the sort of victory needed to permit the King to advance unmolested on London. He therefore sent a message to the King suggesting that the army should concentrate next morning on top of a steep ridge called Edgehill three miles distant from, and overlooking, Kineton. As this was on the extreme western edge of the area over which the Royalist army was spread, some of the regiments would have to march as much as eight miles to get there, but against this the position itself was an immensely strong one and lay between Essex and Banbury. The King received Rupert's message at about midnight, agreed with his suggestion and sent out the necessary orders. At 4 a.m. he wrote a brief note to Rupert saying that he had given orders as he desired and had no doubt that all the foot and cannon would be at Edgehill in good time next morning where Rupert would also find his loving uncle and faithful friend etc. The attack on Banbury was of course cancelled.

Although Essex had reached Kineton, his army was more spread out than the King's, partly because of the garrisons already mentioned and partly because Essex had been obliged to leave a force of two regiments of foot and some horse to guard his artillery train which was moving very slowly. Furthermore, although some of his outposts must have realised that there were Royalist forces nearby, it was not until about 8 a.m. on the morning of Sunday, 23 October, as he was going into church at Kineton, that Essex became aware that the whole Royalist army was present and concentrating at Edgehill. He immediately gave orders for his own army to draw up in the Vale of the Red Horse between Kineton and Edgehill itself. Allowing time for the orders to be passed, and for the troops to be assembled and marched to the rendezvous, it is likely that his first regiments started to deploy about three-quarters of a mile from the bottom of the escarpment at around midday.

Rupert arrived at Edgehill as it was getting light at about 6.45 a.m. He had ordered the horse to be there by 8 a.m. to cover the army's deployment but it was nearly 11 a.m. before the last regiments arrived. The foot started to arrive soon afterwards but it was not until 1 p.m. that the regiments with the furthest to march and the artillery arrived. Considering the distances involved, the Royalist deployment indicates a fair standard of staff work and battle procedure. Furthermore the King had managed to concentrate all thirteen of the foot regiments that had been with him at Shrewsbury, together with an extra two that had joined him on the march, plus all but one of the ten regiments of horse, the three regiments of dragoons and most if not all of his twenty guns.

By contrast only twelve of Essex's twenty regiments of foot arrived in time for the battle together with forty-two of his sixty-one troops of horse (equivalent in Royalist terms to about seven regiments), his two regiments of dragoons and an indeterminate number of guns generally estimated as between thirty and thirty-seven. But depite Essex's absentees he probably had a slight advantage of numbers in the battle, with 14,900 troops against the Royalists' 14,300. He certainly had more guns and a preponderance of foot, to the tune of 12,000 as opposed to the King's 10,500, but he was inferior with regard to the horse, the King having 2,800 to Essex's 2,150.

Whilst the Royalist forces were assembling, the King held a council of war which led to a dispute over the way in which the battle should be fought. Although the concept generally accepted at the time, of the horse fighting off the enemy's horse and then attacking the flanks of the enemy's foot whilst it was being assaulted from the front, was agreed, a difference of opinion arose regarding the way in which the foot should deploy for battle. On both sides regiments of foot were grouped into brigades or tertias as they were sometimes called. The Lord General thought that within each brigade the regiments should form up in line abreast as was customary in the Dutch service, but the Field Marshal, whose job it was to draw up the army for battle along the lines desired by the Lord General, wanted to do so in a way in which the regiments took up a diamond formation as practised by the Swedish army. The advantage of the first system was that it was simpler. The advantage of the second was that it was more flexible and gave foot regiments a better chance of defending themselves against attack from the enemy's horse.

Patrick Ruthven, Earl of Forth, was the Field Marshal. He was a Scot who had held Edinburgh Castle for the King in the second Scots war. He was seventy years old and had spent many years in the Swedish army, rising to the rank of major general under Gustavus Adolphus who highly esteemed his company. He had joined the King's army when it was at Shrewsbury and had spent most of the time since assisting Prince Rupert with the horse. Rupert backed him in this dispute and the King came down on their side, whereupon the Earl of Lindsey said that if he could not be trusted to draw up the army as Lord General, he would return to his regiment and fight as a colonel – which he did, being mortally wounded in the ensuing battle.

The five brigades of foot eventually deployed with three in the front line and two behind. The horse deployed on either flank. Prince Rupert led the right wing which consisted of his own regiment and life guard, the Prince of Wales's regiment and Prince Maurice's regiment, a total of nineteen troops. Behind them was Sir John Byron's regiment of six troops. Wilmot led the left wing which consisted of his own regiment, Lord Grandison's regiment and the Earl of Carnarvon's regiment, a total of fifteen troops. Behind them were the regiments of Sir Thomas Aston and Lord Digby with six troops between them. Each regiment deployed in three ranks which was the custom in the Royalist army. The regiments in the second line would have stood some way behind the leading regiments, ready to attack the enemy's foot if all went well, or to support the forward regiments of horse if they failed to break the enemy's horse.

This should have left the mounted element of the King's life guard two troops strong, plus the one troop of Gentlemen Pensioners, in the rear of the army to act as protection for the King and as a general reserve, but the mounted troops of the life guard had been so teased about their smart appearance that they begged the King to let them join in the initial attack, which he foolishly allowed them to do. Rupert therefore gave them the place of honour on the right of his front line. One regiment of dragoons covered the Royalists' right flank, the other two regiments being on the left.[14]

Essex deployed his foot with two brigades forward and a third one behind his left forward brigade. The vacant position behind the right forward brigade was occupied at the start of the battle by a reserve of two undeployed regiments of horse, one being Essex's own regiment commanded in the battle by Sir Philip Stapleton and the other being commanded by the lieutenant general of horse, Sir William Balfour. The remainder of the horse were on the flanks, the vast majority, consisting of two regiments and seventeen independent troops under the commissary general of horse, Sir James Ramsey, being on the left opposite Prince Rupert where the terrain was open. Only one regiment of six troops, under Lord Feilding, was on the right opposite Wilmot. The two regiments of

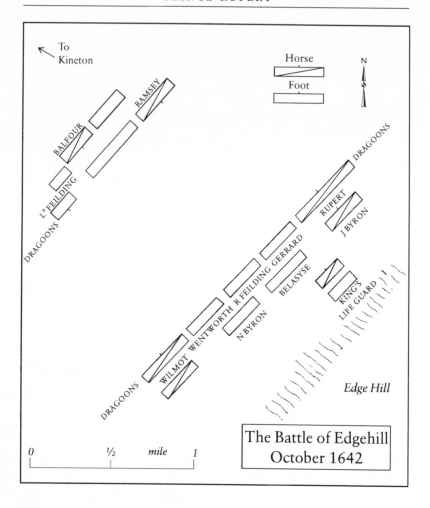

The Battle of Edgehill
October 1642

dragoons were both deployed covering Lord Feilding's regiment on the right while some musketeers did the same for Ramsey on the left.

By around 1.30 p.m. both sides were deployed, the slight numerical inferiority of the Royalists being more than offset by the strength of their position on the ridge. But Essex showed no indication of being prepared to launch an attack on such a strong position, especially as he had much to gain by waiting for the regiments with his artillery train and the garrisons at Warwick and Coventry to join him. It was equally important to the Royalists that the battle should be fought before these reinforcements joined

Essex. In addition the Royalists were very short of rations and could not get more until after the battle. They therefore decided to abandon their impregnable position in order to encourage Essex to attack and advanced their whole line from the top of the ridge to the plain below, a difficult manoeuvre, especially for the guns, because of the steepness of the hill. It must have been well after 2 p.m. before they were drawn up about half a mile short of the Parliamentary line.

Once they were drawn up the King, with the Prince of Wales and Duke of York, aged twelve and nine respectively, rode round each of the brigades to encourage the soldiers. Rupert meanwhile spoke to the regiments of horse on each wing giving clear instructions that when ordered to charge they were not to halt short of the enemy so that the front rank could fire their pistols, as was the Swedish custom, let alone go through the complicated Dutch procedure of firing and wheeling, but to go straight in with the sword, using their pistols only when the enemy was on the run. Rupert had no illusions about his men's ability to manoeuvre and was equally sure that the enemy horse would turn tail if ridden into by hundreds of his own men at a good pace. Even if the riders wanted to stay to do battle, most would be unable to prevent their horses swinging round and going with the Royalist horse. Anyone who has been hunting knows what it feels like when the field comes thundering past and most hunts muster no more than the equivalent of one troop of horse, except perhaps on Saturday.

The sight of the King's party progressing through the Royalist ranks was too much for Essex's gunners who started the battle by bombarding the Royalist line. Soon afterwards the Royalist dragoons moved forward to clear the enemy dragoons and musketeers from their positions on the flanks of the Royalist advance, which they did quickly and efficiently. While this was going on, a few minutes before 3 p.m., a lone horseman from the Parliamentary ranks rode up to Rupert to tell him that as soon as the Royalists charged, a whole troop of Sir William Waller's regiment would move forward, fire their pistols into the ground and join his forces. Shortly afterwards Rupert gave the order to advance. The three ranks of the leading regiments moved forward, initially at a walk and then at a trot, being joined by the Parliamentary troop as promised. During their advance they were shot at by enemy cannon and by musketeers of a foot regiment, posted in gaps between the troops of Ramsey's horse, but they came on without hesitation. At some point, perhaps 200 yards short of the enemy, they broke into a canter and continued to gain speed so that they crashed into Ramsey's line at full gallop.

The result of this unorthodox behaviour was more dramatic than even Rupert could have expected. The whole of Ramsey's horse turned tail and fled pursued by the Royalists who cut down the musketeers as they passed and overran many of the enemy's cannon. Furthermore the left forward brigade of Parliamentary foot was so dismayed at witnessing the rout of their horse that they too took to their heels as soon as the Royalist foot advanced. On the Royalist left Wilmot's horse easily routed the single Parliamentary regiment, at the same time putting to flight one regiment of foot on the right of Essex's line. The only Parliamentary forces now in the field were the eight regiments of foot in the two remaining brigades and the two undeployed regiments of horse.

At this point a serious mistake was made by the second line of the Royalist horse, which should have supported the advance of the foot by attacking their opponents' flanks. Instead, on both wings of the army, they joined in the pursuit, leaving the battlefield at the mercy of the two remaining Parliamentary regiments of horse. It is difficult to know why this happened since it is clear from reports and accounts written by participants[15] that the regiments concerned knew what was required of them and had orders to that effect.

By this time the horse of both sides on the King's right, totalling well over 2,000, would have been mixed up together, hurtling along through the smoke of battle and the cloud of stones, dust and bits of turf thrown up by the horses' feet, some flying for their lives, others trying to cut them down with their swords or shoot them with their pistols. Most of the officers and nearly all of the men were new to war and far from expert at handling a frenzied horse with one hand and a selection of unfamiliar weapons with the other. In less than ten minutes after passing the enemy's guns, sweating and panting from their efforts to control their horses, they would have reached Kineton and the enemy baggage wagons.

It is impossible to know when Rupert discovered that Sir John Byron's regiment had followed his charge instead of staying on the battlefield, but it is clear that he was trying to turn his own men well before they reached Kineton. But because of the difficulty that he would have had in making himself understood in the midst of such confusion and the problems that his men would have had in controlling their horses, it was some time before he could muster even a few troops and lead them back. On the other wing Wilmot was content to pursue the enemy to Kineton, but the lieutenant colonel of Lord Carnarvon's regiment, Sir Charles Lucas, ably assisted by Lord Grandison, Captain Smith and one of Wilmot's troop leaders, succeeded in rounding up around 200 troopers drawn from several different regiments and leading them back to the battle.

Meanwhile the Royalist foot had closed with Essex's two remaining brigades which, despite being outnumbered, had managed to hold the attack for a while, probably because of their superior weapons and equipment and the basic strength of the straight and deep Dutch formation that Essex employed. Certainly there was no lack of courage on either side and many casualties occurred at this stage of the battle. But just as things were looking bad for Essex's foot, Sir William Balfour decided to launch the two regiments of horse that he was holding in reserve. By this time the two rear Royalist brigades had moved up into the gaps between the three forward brigades so all five were in a straight line. Stapleton attacked the left centre Royalist brigade commanded by Sir Nicholas Byron while Balfour himself attacked Richard Feilding's brigade in the centre. Although Stapleton's attack was repulsed, Balfour broke right through and made for the guns behind, which he put out of action by cutting the traces. Meanwhile Essex's foot exploited the confusion in the area where Balfour had broken through.

The King, who had been watching the battle from a high point behind the foot with his two young sons and a few courtiers, feared that the Royalist centre might break up altogether. He therefore sent the princes to the rear with Edward Hyde, and moved forward into the battle, placing himself with a company of his life guard (foot). At this time Balfour, who had caused so much damage with his regiment, rejoined Stapleton behind Essex's foot.

Having broken through the King's centre, Essex now launched a further attack on Byron's brigade which had already repulsed Stapleton's first attack. This time Essex, using both the regiments of horse to help his foot, succeeded in pushing the Royalists back. In desperate fighting the royal standard was captured and the standard bearer, Sir Edmund Verney, killed. It was at this time too that the Earl of Lindsey was killed at the head of his regiment, the lieutenant colonel of the life guard captured and the brigade commander, Sir Nicholas Byron, wounded. But at this moment Sir Charles Lucas with the 200 men he had rallied from Wilmot's regiments charged into the rear of Essex's position, doing great execution amongst two regiments of foot that were already in retreat and incidentally recovering the royal standard, which it is estimated was only in enemy hands for a total of six minutes.

Although for a time the situation had looked bad for the two brigades in the centre of the Royalist line, the brigade on the extreme left and the two on the right were never in danger of breaking and they, together with groups of horse that were by now returning from the original charge, swiftly secured the position. On the left wing the Secretary of State, Lord Falkland, who had attached himself for the day to Wilmot's regiment, begged Wilmot to make one more charge in order to put the enemy to flight, but Wilmot refused on the grounds that the day was already theirs so why not live to enjoy it. On the right, where the horse had been involved in much harder fighting and where the regiments were more fragmented, it was considered impossible to launch a further attack in the fading light. In any case the horses themselves had been short of forage for days, had been on the move since the early hours of the morning and could do no more without rest and water. Those foot that were still in contact with the enemy pulled back a few yards and continued firing muskets at each other until it became dark. The battle fizzled out with the participants too shocked and exhausted to continue any longer.

After dark the Royalist line withdrew a few hundred yards to the side of the hill where they could light fires and collect together the men of companies and troops that had become separated in the fighting. The night was bitterly cold and next morning the two armies stood to arms and watched each other. Despite the fact that Essex had now been joined by the extra regiments that might have won him the battle on the previous day, he could not make up for the disintegration of one of his brigades and most of his horse, some of whom, including Ramsey himself, had by now reached London with tales of a terrible defeat. Not only was Essex unable to renew the fight, but the loss of most of his baggage train at the hands of Rupert's horse on the previous day meant that he would not even be capable of moving his army any distance until he had replaced it.

In the afternoon Essex started to pull back towards Warwick and the Royalist army returned to the billets it had been occupying before the battle. Next morning Rupert was out with the horse harrying Essex's withdrawal and he managed to capture another twenty-five enemy wagons, containing among other things ammunition and medicines, to add to the seven cannon, the many weapons and the seventy-odd standards and colours that the Royalists had captured during the battle itself. It is estimated that in the battle Essex lost at least 1,000 men killed and many more who had deserted: the Royalists are thought to have had around 500 killed, although losses amongst the Royalist horse are reported as being fewer than fifty. On 27 October Banbury surrendered to the King without a fight, most of the garrison changing sides in the process, which was another direct consequence of the victory at Edgehill.

But the greatest consequence of the victory was that the road to London was open and Essex was in no position to interfere with the King's movements. Nor would he be until he could collect together his scattered horse and reassemble some sort of baggage train. Immediately after Banbury surrendered, Rupert proposed that he should take a flying column of 3,000 horse and foot to march on Westminster and secure Parliament. With no heavy guns to move he would easily be able to cover the seventy-odd miles in three or four days and would arrive before the end of the month while the capital was still stunned by the news of Essex's defeat. It seemed as if nothing could prevent Rupert from bringing the war to a successful conclusion. Rupert's proposal was strongly supported by Lord Forth who had by now been appointed Lord General in place of Lord Lindsey.

It was only two months and a few days since the King had set up his standard at Nottingham. At that time everything had seemed to favour Parliament, which not only controlled the fleet, the ports and the armouries, but had also raised a larger army than the King. So weak were the Royalists that Sir Jacob Astley could not even guarantee the safety of the King in Nottingham Castle. Royalist morale was low, many being half-hearted about fighting the rebels who were often their friends and relations. Now the scene had changed dramatically. Although Parliament's long-term strength in terms of fleet, ports and access to wealth remained, there seemed little reason to think that the war would last long enough for it to matter. The King's army had become well trained, confident and even well disciplined compared to Essex's men. It had out-manoeuvred and defeated its enemies, scattering their horse, destroying their transport and exposing London in the process. Parliament stared defeat in the face.

It would be an exaggeration to claim that Rupert was solely

responsible for this remarkable change, since it could not have happened without the generosity and effort of those that raised additional forces for the King, nor should the training skills of such professionals as Astley be discounted. But, according to Sir Philip Warwick, it was Rupert who on arrival at Nottingham 'put that spirit into the King's army that all men seemed resolved' and it was Rupert who, having developed an original system of attack in his earlier campaigns, trained his regiments in such a way that he became the terror of the Parliamentary forces. It was Rupert who inflicted the first defeat on the enemy at Powick Bridge, thus fostering the belief that the King's soldiers were more than a match for those of Parliament and it was the ferocity of Rupert's charge at Edgehill that caused most of the enemy horse and some of his foot to leave the field of battle with scarcely any resistance.

It is less easy to know how much influence Rupert exercised on Royalist strategy and tactics during this period. In theory all major decisions were discussed by a council of war, consisting of senior officers of the army, the two Secretaries of State and the Chancellor of the Exchequer, to say nothing of other influential persons whose advice the King valued, such as the Duke of Richmond and the Earl of Bristol. Sometimes as many as twenty-five people attended these councils, including brigade commanders and the commanders of some of the regiments. Decisions taken by the King, based on the council's advice, would then be implemented by whoever was responsible, such as one of the Secretaries of State, or the Lord General, or the General of Horse, all of whom would already have had the opportunity of giving their views when the matter was being discussed in the council of war.

In practice the King paid most attention to those closest to him. Initially the Lord General's views on military matters had prevailed, but according to Hyde, once Rupert arrived, the King took his advice on all things relating to the army[16] even when it differed from that given by Lindsey. It may therefore be assumed that Rupert either initiated or approved the idea of moving from Nottingham to Shrewsbury in order to build up the army in safety. It is clear that he advocated the move from Shrewsbury towards London and opposed the idea of attacking Essex at Worcester. It is equally clear that it was Rupert who persuaded the King to fight when Essex caught up with the Royalists at Kineton; who selected the position at Edgehill; and who physically took possession of the high ground with his horse before Essex could do so. In short Rupert not only built up the Royalist horse and raised Royalist morale in the two months following his arrival, but he was also largely responsible for the strategic and tactical decisions that had turned out so well.

But there had been a price to pay for this success. In order to make his influence paramount, Rupert had to persuade the King to support his ideas on how to achieve the Royalist aim of destroying Essex's army and re-entering the capital.[17] Rupert was clear in his own mind about how this should be done and as a result of his past experience, the breadth of his study and the strength of his intellect could argue his case convincingly when necessary.

But some of his ideas cut across those held by other influential Royalists, many of whom found difficulty in arguing with him, either because they had less knowledge of military affairs, or because they were less good at marshalling their arguments, or because they were reluctant to contradict the King's nephew directly. Some of the civilians even had reservations about the Royalist aim, hoping for a compromise agreement rather than military victory and a triumphal return to the capital. Had Rupert been a tactful man he might have treated the arguments of these groups with more consideration. In polite society, the response to a proposition with which one does not agree is 'Yes, but . . .' followed by gentle demolition of the other person's argument. Rupert, with no time for such niceties, merely said the equivalent of 'rubbish' or 'balls', thereby causing offence to some who might otherwise have been his friends. He also made no effort to get to know the non-military members of the council of war, which gave them little chance of explaining their views to him privately.[18]

Many historians maintain that Rupert's unpopularity at this time was due to the fact that he was arrogant and impetuous. In practice the reason must have varied between one man and the next; for example Digby, who had been the King's closest confidant, was jealous of being displaced by Rupert, whereas Falkland was offended by the extent to which Rupert asserted his independence of all authority other than that of the King himself. Wilmot, who was genial and reasonably competent but also devious, ambitious and a compulsive womaniser, felt that Rupert's brilliance was putting him in the shade. For most, the problem was that Rupert literally had no time for them. He had saddled himself with so much work that he grudged every moment spent in what he would have seen as unnecessary discussion. He did not keep courtiers at arm's length because he thought them to be his social or intellectual inferiors, but because he thought they were militarily irrelevant.

Sometimes he was wrong, but it was an error of judgement rather than arrogance.

As for his alleged impetuosity, his speed in reaching a conclusion was more often the result of working things out in advance, than of acting on impulse. Certainly the examples of impetuosity usually quoted, such as his headlong charges in battle, were the product of reflection and experience over a period of years. He was well aware of the problems of control, which he tried to get over by expedients such as leaving a proportion of his force in reserve under a reliable commander, or later, by himself commanding the reserve, but he continued to rely on breaking the enemy's resistance by physical impact rather than by firepower, because it almost always worked. Another reason for the accusation of impetuosity was that his exceptional courage often took him to the forefront of a battle. But even this would have been done for a reason, that is to say to find out what was happening, to inspire the soldiers and to drive on those that faltered. Throughout his life Rupert planned his actions by relating knowledge of facts to the achievement of his aim. It was the speed of his thought processes and the energy with which he put his decisions into effect, together with his bad temper and abrupt manner, that gave the impresson of impetuosity.

One of Rupert's early mistakes was to have alienated a number of the King's older advisers, because when the council of war met to consider his plan for grabbing London before Essex could get there, the various factions that he had offended closed ranks against him. Digby's father, the Earl of Bristol, playing on fears engendered by Rupert's forceful behaviour at Leicester, claimed that if he was let loose on London, his troopers would loot the city and burn it to the ground. The peace party, led by Falkland and Hyde (though Hyde was not at the time a member of the council of war), wanted the King to open negotiations rather than attack London, because they thought that Parliament would be in the mood for a settlement on terms favourable to the King, and that this would give a better chance of satisfactory government in the long term than would an outright victory. No one objected to Rupert's plan on the grounds that it was unworkable from a military point of view and subsequent events, such as the fact that Essex did not reach London until 8 November by which time the whole of the King's army could have arrived, tend to confirm that it was sound.

But, for the first time since the setting up of the standard, the

King sided with Rupert's opponents on a major issue and vetoed a quick advance. It is suggested that Charles was shaken by the casualties in the battle, particularly the death of his cousin, a brother of the Duke of Richmond, who had been killed in the charge of the Royalist horse, to say nothing of the many officers and men of his life guard who had fallen around him. It is also suggested that Charles was convinced that his subjects would see for themselves the folly of opposing him.[19] Whatever the reason, his decision lost him the first and better of his two chances of winning the war militarily. By leaving his capital in the hands of the rebels, he was giving them the chance to exploit their long-term advantages. Rupert had offered the King a quick victory, but he had turned it down. It is ironic that one of the complaints being made about Rupert by the civilians was that he wanted to prolong the war for his own enjoyment and advantage.

6

INFORMING GENIUS

Two DAYS AFTER the capture of Banbury the King occupied Oxford, which was to be his capital for the rest of the war, while Rupert captured Abingdon and Aylesbury and scoured the country-side for arms and forage. Rupert then established himself at Maidenhead and tried to capture Windsor and Kingston, but both were too strong for him. On 4 November the King occupied Reading.

In a bid to gain time, Parliament offered to negotiate: it also asked for a 'cessation of arms' during the negotiations, which the King seems to have neither accepted nor refused. On 11 November, while the King was discussing the preliminaries for negotiation with Parliamentary representatives at Colnbrook, Essex's army, together with the London trained bands under the command of the Parliamentary Sergeant Major General of Foot, Philip Skippon, moved against him.

Skippon, who was the son of a plain Norfolk gentleman, had served as a volunteer in Sir Horace Vere's contingent in the Palatin-ate at the same time as Essex and Hopton; he later spent several years in the Dutch service. He was a thorough-going professional who rendered faithful service to Parliament throughout the war in the same way as his Royalist counterpart, Sir Jacob Astley, served the King. He missed Edgehill because he had been left behind to prepare the London trained bands for war.

The King responded to Essex's advance by pushing his outposts towards Brentford; then, realising that he would be in a dangerous position if Essex established himself firmly in that town, he ordered Rupert to capture it. Brentford was held by two Parliamentary regiments, but Rupert caught them off guard by attacking under cover of fog. One of the enemy regiments ran away immediately and Rupert quickly annihilated the other. By this time Essex's army plus the trained bands and some regiments from around London, amounting in all to about 24,000 men, were three miles away at Turnham Green. The King's army was not strong enough to attack such a force and withdrew west along the Thames valley, covered by a rearguard commanded by Rupert.

In later years Hyde blamed Rupert for wrecking the negotiations that had been going on at Colnbrook, by attacking Brentford.[1] But failure to occupy Brentford would have jeopardised the safety of the whole Royalist army and in any case it was the King who ordered it. Furthermore Parliament, which might have settled with the King had he occupied London, was unlikely to do so now that Essex had established a superior force between London and the King's army. The trouble was that although the King genuinely wanted to achieve the official Royalist aim of defeating the enemy and reoccupying the capital, he was also encouraging the peace party in the hope that negotiations might divide the enemy and draw men to his side. This would have been all right had the King been strong enough to co-ordinate the activities of the peace party with the operations of his military commanders, but he was, as always, indecisive, following the advice first of one party and then of the other, thereby ensuring that the activities of each undermined the other. As Sir Philip Warwick put it, 'neither of them [the two parties] stood in awe of him and so the consequences were fatall.'[2]

Having extracted themselves from contact with the enemy, the Royalist army went into winter quarters in a number of garrisons centred on Oxford. Thus in Reading there was one regiment of horse, one of dragoons and six regiments of foot; in Wallingford, one of horse and two of foot; in Abingdon two of horse and one of foot; and in Oxford itself two troops of horse (King's life guard) and four regiments of foot. Other regiments were stationed in Faringdon, Burford, Brill, Banbury, Woodstock, Enstone and Islip.

From this time the war took on a different shape altogether. Hitherto all eyes had been focused on the movements and battles of the rival armies. Various developments had been taking place in other parts of the country, but they would have been irrelevant had the King occupied London, or had Essex succeeded in his official task of defeating the Royalist army and freeing the King from his evil advisers, i.e. carrying him back as a prisoner to London. In the event neither of these things happened. By the end of 1642 Essex's army had recovered from its defeat at Edgehill and was between the King and his capital, around which new and

extended fortifications were being built enclosing both Westminster and the city. Although the Royalists had established a
superiority over their opponents in terms of the quality of their
soldiers and the efficiency of their army, Parliament had built up
its strength to the extent that London could no longer be captured
by direct assault of the main Royalist army.

Under these circumstances there were two main options open to
the King. First, he could try and raise enough extra forces in those
parts of the country where he had support, to reinforce his army
sufficiently for an assault to be made on London. Second, he might
be able to force Parliament to surrender if he could get control of
enough of the country to restrict the flow of money, food, fuel and
merchandise to the capital. Whilst pursuing these two options there
would be no harm in trying to negotiate a settlement, playing on
the superior efficiency of the Royalist forces. Such negotiations
could be switched on and off to take account of events.

In the King's mind, large-scale reinforcement from Ireland
seemed to be the most likely way of swinging the military balance
in his favour and by the end of 1642 events in that country did
look more promising from his point of view. The Dublin government was in a weak position, some of its members supporting the
King, some supporting Parliament and all of them realising that
events in England would preclude further help being sent from that
quarter. Meanwhile the Catholic Confederacy under the presidency
of Lord Mountgarret had consolidated its position and claimed to
be governing Ireland in the name of the King. King Charles naturally had to disclaim any connection with it, but in the early days
of 1643 he sent instructions to the Earl of Ormonde, who was his
firmest supporter in the Dublin government, to arrange a ceasefire
with Mountgarret.

Meanwhile Parliament, which could no longer expect to capture
the King while the balance of the two armies remained as it was,
also set about getting control of as much of the country as it could,
in order to bring such pressure on the King as would force him to
accept terms agreeable to it. In the same way as the King worked
for reinforcement from Ireland, Parliament set about getting assistance from the Scots: indeed it had already sent an urgent request
for help to Scotland in the dangerous days after Edgehill. In the
settlement that followed the second Scots war, the King had
appointed a Scottish council in which power was shared between
genuine supporters of the King, such as Hamilton, and the hardline
Covenanters, such as Argyll. Although the King still thought that

Hamilton and Argyll were loyally acting together as his government in Scotland, Argyll was working towards the day when
he could offer help to whichever side would agree to establish
the Presbyterian Church in England which, in practice, meant
Parliament.

But reinforcements from Ireland and Scotland would not be
available for some time. Meanwhile the important thing for both
sides was to extend their influence over as wide an area as possible.
As a result, what had started by looking like a war between two
armies spread and took on the appearance of an insurgency campaign in which the King tried to regain the allegiance of those of
his subjects who had rebelled, while Parliament tried to attract the
support of the King's adherents. Both sides vied for the allegiance
of those who hoped to remain neutral. Townsmen usually favoured
the side which best represented the commercial or religious interests of the town concerned, but in the countryside, where most of
the people lived, the support of the major landowners should have
been sufficient to ensure the allegiance of their tenants and labour-
ers. This was often the case but, as Joyce Lee Malcolm points
out in her study of loyalty in the Civil War,[3] land enclosure and
improvement schemes, which had accelerated greatly during the
years leading up to the war, resulted in many of the common
people becoming ill disposed towards large landowners, including
the King, because of loss of commoner's rights. The extent to
which this feeling affected recruitment and the collection of money
depended on the extent to which local leaders had a free hand to
intimidate those who would not support them voluntarily.

The primary role of the forces being raised around the country
was therefore to enable local leaders to gain physical possession
of their area, thus helping them to attract prominent people to
their side by rewarding support and penalising opposition. The
role of each side's main field army was to destroy their opponent's
field army if possible, to assist local forces when necessary, and to
maintain communications between them.

To prosecute the war, the King had already established two
main regional commands. The first of these covered the whole of
England north of the River Trent; the second covered Somerset
and the counties along the south coast from Cornwall to Hampshire. The King himself looked after the country in between. There
was no Royalist command structure in London and the counties
to the south-east of it, or in such places as Essex, Suffolk and
Norfolk which remained dominated by Parliament throughout.

By the end of 1642 the Royalist commander-in-chief in the north was the Earl of Newcastle and in the south-west the Marquess of Hertford. Both of these men were immensely rich landowners with far-reaching influence in their regions. Both were in their early to mid-fifties and were accustomed to deference and respect.

Wiliam Cavendish, Earl of Newcastle came from a family that had built its fortune on the dissolution of the monasteries. Its main territorial possessions were in Derbyshire, Nottinghamshire and South Yorkshire, which was where he and his young cousin the Earl of Devonshire were brought up. William also inherited a barony and extensive estates in Northumberland from his mother, which was why he took Newcastle as his title when he was made an earl in 1628. He became governor to the Prince of Wales in 1638, a post he held until May 1641. He was a highly cultured man with a European reputation for horsemanship.

William Seymour, Marquess of Hertford was the great grandson of the Duke of Somerset, uncle of Edward VI who was made Protector during the early part of the reign and then executed for high treason, losing his titles in the process. Queen Elizabeth restored the Earldom of Hertford to the family but not the dukedom. King Charles made Hertford a marquess in 1640 and in the following year he succeeded Newcastle as governor to the Prince of Wales, in which capacity he was instrumental in preventing both the Prince of Wales and the Duke of York from falling into the hands of Parliament in the early months of 1642. Hertford, who was married to a sister of the Earl of Essex, was a contemplative, lethargic person, better known for his love of books than for more active pursuits.

Like the King, neither Newcastle nor Hertford had any worthwhile military experience at the start of the war. As commanders-in-chief their job was to tie together all the various strands of war-making, including the raising of money and the filling of civil and military appointments. Each gradually established a military chain of command employing professional soldiers to plan and fight their campaigns.

Parliament also set up regional commands which consisted of groups of counties known as associations, for example the Midland Association or the Eastern Association, but with the exception of the Eastern Association, which was not established until the middle of 1643, they usually disintegrated under Royalist pressure. By the beginning of 1643 Parliament had a commander for Yorkshire, one for the west and one in the Midlands.

The Parliamentary commander in Yorkshire, Ferdinando, Lord Fairfax, came from a line of landowners, long prominent in the county and in the country. His father had been offered a Scottish peerage by King James in Elizabeth's reign, but declined for fear of offending the Queen: instead he bought one from King Charles many years later. Ferdinando was the oldest of five brothers, all of whom went to the wars. He himself spent little time as a soldier and soon returned to Yorkshire, subsequently becoming a Member of Parliament. All four of his brothers were killed abroad, two of them whilst fighting for Rupert's father in the Palatinate. At the start of the Civil War Ferdinando was in his middle fifties. His formidable son Sir Thomas, who had also seen service with the Dutch, was his general of horse.

Initially the Parliamentary commander in the west was Henry Grey, Earl of Stamford; his son Lord Grey of Groby was commander in the Midlands. The Greys were very powerful during the Wars of the Roses and afterwards until Queen Mary destroyed their influence and stripped them of their titles following their involvement in two unsuccessful rebellions. Stamford revived the family fortunes and received an earldom from Charles I early in his reign. Neither the father nor the son had any worthwhile military experience.

When the Eastern Association was formed it was commanded by Edward Montagu, Earl of Manchester, a contemporary of the King and a large landowner in and around Huntingdonshire. His father, a prominent lawyer and statesman, was raised to the peerage by James I. In 1625 Edward married the Earl of Warwick's daughter, after which he became engrossed in Puritan politics. He was the only member of the House of Lords to be included on the King's arrest list when he made his attempt on the five members in January 1642. Early in the war he raised a regiment of foot which ran away at Edgehill and was subsequently disbanded.

From the time that the King returned to Oxford at the end of November, he set up his court at Christ Church and adopted a routine that enabled him to combine his duties as Captain General of the army with his wider responsibilities as ruler of the country. This meant that much of his time was spent dealing with such matters as collecting taxes and contributions, minting money, making laws and dealing with foreign affairs in the same way as he did during the eleven years of his personal rule. He also tried to persuade people throughout the country that, despite the claims of those members of the Lords and Commons remaining in London, he represented the true source of legitimate authority.

Rupert and his brother Maurice were quartered near the King. Although designated General of Horse, Rupert had in effect three separate jobs. First, he was still the King's main adviser on all things military, giving his views both in the war council and directly to the King. As C. V. Wedgwood so strikingly put it, 'Prince Rupert was the informing genius of the King's army.'[4] Second, he was in modern parlance the arms director for the cavalry, which meant that he had to see that the regiments of horse were kept up to strength, supplied, trained, armed, and equipped to the standard necessary for carrying out the tasks allotted to them. Third, he was from time to time given command of a mixed force of foot, horse, dragoons and artillery, with instructions to carry out a particular task: in modern terms he was used as a task force commander. As any assessment of Rupert as a soldier must rest to some extent on his success in carrying out these three functions, it is worth looking in more detail at what each involved.

Although Rupert was in practice the King's main military adviser, he was never the only one. Furthermore, even when the King made a decision after full consultation in the war council, he was liable to change it later as a result of a casual conversation. Rupert's problem was that his other two jobs required him to be away from Oxford for much of the time, which meant that decisions made under his influence were often overturned in his absence. On the credit side Lord Forth, the new Lord General, consistently represented and supported Rupert's views, and the Duke of Richmond did his best to defend him from court intrigue.

Against this background it is easy to see that no long-term concept of operations was likely to bear fruit. Nonetheless long-term plans were discussed at Oxford in the last days of 1642 and some of the views expressed by Rupert are recorded.

At this time Rupert must have been concerned by the fact that, although the Royalists had been able to raise and train regiments of horse that were far superior to those raised by Parliament, the foot lagged behind, partly because of the shortage of weapons and partly because of the reluctance of many of the common people to support the King and the major landowners. Knowing that it was unsound to plan a campaign based on fighting set-piece battles with too few foot regiments, inferior in terms of numbers and equipment to those of the enemy, he advocated a policy of fortifying selected towns and strong points throughout the country which would dominate the surrounding areas. His idea was that Parliamentary armies would be forced to wear themselves out in siege warfare and dissipate their forces, thus making them and their supply convoys vulnerable to raids by Royalist detachments composed mainly of horse: a concept formerly used successfully by the Dutch against the Spaniards. But he made the point that the ancient defences of most of the towns that would have to be secured were greatly decayed if not non-existent. The cost of fortification would therefore be great. If the money could not be found, the best alternative was to get some high-class infantry from abroad, for example the four English regiments currently serving with the Dutch.[5]

Some historians suggest[6] that the Royalists adopted a long-term plan thought up by Prince Rupert, for a concentric assault on London by the armies of the King and the Earl of Newcastle, with Hertford's forces advancing through the southern counties to cut the Thames below the city. If such a plan was made, it must have been for the distant future, as in December 1642 Newcastle was fully occupied fighting Fairfax and Hertford hardly had an army at all: perhaps 3,000 men in Cornwall and some regiments of foot under training in South Wales. Furthermore such a concept hardly accords with the proposals made by Rupert, described above. Perhaps the concentric advance was designed to follow the period during which Parliamentary forces were ground down besieging the strong points which he advocated.

In the first few months of 1643, the job that took up most of Rupert's time was the day-to-day running of the horse, dotted around in the various garrisons. Over the past months these regiments had picked up a lot of experience, but they now needed to be systematically trained in accordance with an accepted tactical doctrine. The wide variety of weapons and armour that had been collected had to be sorted out and standardised: worn-out and unsuitable animals had to be replaced and schooled. A degree of conformity was essential with regard to the horses, since the performance of a body of horsemen was limited by the stamina, speed and weight-carrying ability of the worst of their mounts. Finally regiments had to scour the countryside for food and forage, not only for themselves but for the army as a whole. And all these activities had to be conducted in the intervals between raiding Parliamentary outposts and countering infiltration by detachments of Essex's army.

Rupert had no time to prepare a manual governing the conduct of the Royalist horse and in any case this was not necessary because a number of such works already existed, copies of which would have been in the possession of many of the professional officers on both sides. The one most favoured at the time was *Militarie Instructions for the Cavallrie* written by John Cruso and published by the printers to the University of Cambridge in 1632.[7] This was a comprehensive document which described how mounted forces should be raised, officered and trained and how their horses should be exercised and schooled. It discussed the use of guides and spies, how marches should be organised, quarters and camps established and how scouts, outposts and sentinels should be employed. It also covered the tactics of beating up the enemy in their quarters, of laying an ambush, of mounting a charge, of attacking enemy infantry and of defending against enemy attack.

But this manual had been written in accordance with the conditions prevalent in the Stadholder's army of the 1620s, which were different in some respects from those prevailing in the Royalist forces. For example the manual envisaged an army containing heavily armoured lancers and cuirassiers as well as the lightly armoured harquebussiers, and it described how they should be used to complement each other. But the Royalist horse consisted entirely of harquebussiers. Also, although many of the procedures and tactics described by Cruso would have been taken for granted by Rupert, he had himself invented and demonstrated a totally different system for charging the enemy which he was determined to make standard throughout the Royalist horse. Rupert therefore had to work out regulations for the Royalist horse which could be based on existing works, but which made his wishes plain where they differed from previously accepted procedures. He also had to ensure that his instructions were carried out, which would have been no easy matter in an army where many of the colonels and captains liked ordering things in their own way.

As usual Rupert's way of carrying out his task was to move endlessly from one regiment to the next, sorting out problems as he went, pursued by letters from his commanders bewailing the badness of their billets, or the shortage of food, forage or other necessities. These letters are all written in terms of intense personal devotion, but clearly show the pressure that the writers were under. For example on 10 December Sir John Byron writes begging that his regiment may be moved from Reading to prevent it breaking up altogether from want of accommodation and all things necessary for its subsistence, and on 19 December the lieutenant colonel of Rupert's own regiment, Dan O'Neale, says that, because of disputes within the garrison of Abingdon, he would rather be the Prince's groom than occupy his present position. On 27 December the Earl of Northampton, Governor of Banbury, asks for a regiment of horse and 300 dragoons to disperse numerous rebel detachments that are despoiling the country round about. On 31 December a letter from Sir Lewis Dyves, who had, on the promotion of Wilmot to lieutenant general of horse, become commissary general, asks for money to clothe his men's nakedness and get boots for their feet.

In the course of going round his regiments, Rupert was also overseeing the work of the garrisons themselves with particular regard to their defences. Throughout the country both sides were fortifying towns and castles, some of which were needed for stationing troops, some for controlling traffic along main roads and rivers, some for interfering with their opponent's trade and money-raising activities and some for controlling the ports. A few of these fortifications, such as the ones being erected at Oxford by Rupert's engineer de Gomme, were on a large scale, and required much time and money to complete, but even less elaborate works involved rounding up labour and collecting materials from the surrounding country before work could begin. Rupert's knowledge of fortification and siege warfare must have been in great demand at this time.

On four occasions in the first seven months of 1643, Rupert commanded sizeable detachments of the King's army in pursuit of specific objectives. In February he captured Cirencester and in April he captured Birmingham and Lichfield. In June, he raided Parliamentary forces east of Oxford and won a small victory at Chalgrove, killing the influential Parliamentary leader, John Hampden, in the process. In July he captured Bristol. In each case he had to plan and execute the operations concerned whilst carrying out his other two functions.

The capture of Cirencester was planned primarily as a measure to help the Royalist position in the south-west, but it was also designed to damage Parliament by interfering with the wool trade. The Marquess of Hertford received his commission as the King's lieutenant general in the south-west in July of 1642 and soon afterwards appointed Sir Ralph Hopton as his general of horse. These two were unable to establish themselves in Dorset or Somerset and retreated to Minehead on the Bristol Channel where they separated. Hertford went by boat to Wales in order to raise forces there in country held for the King by the octogenarian Marquess of Worcester and his son Lord Herbert. Hopton, together with Sir John Berkeley, William Ashburnham, two weak troops of horse and a few dragoons, rode on into Cornwall. In Cornwall opinion was divided amongst the gentry as to the relative legality of the King's commissions of array and Parliament's Militia Ordinance, so it was decided to test the matter at the Quarter Sessions, Hopton appearing in person to put the Royalist case. At about the time that Rupert was fighting the battle of Powick Bridge, the jury found for the King.[8] In the ensuing months, Royalist regiments of foot were raised by four men prominent in the area, Sir Bevil Grenville, Sir Nicholas Slanning, John Trevannion and William Godolphin. Three more regiments were raised later.

In November and December Hopton, with his newly raised

force, marched into Devon to meet up with the Royalists there. But both Plymouth and Exeter were too strong for him and, hearing that the Earl of Stamford was coming from Gloucester to help the Parliamentary forces in Devon, he retreated into Cornwall, arriving at Launceston early in the New Year. He then fell back to Braddock Down near Lostwithiel where on 19 January he fought and destroyed a large enemy detachment that had been sent after him from Plymouth. Afterwards he returned into south-west Devon to confront the Earl of Stamford who had by then arrived.

In the weeks following Edgehill the Parliamentary garrisons in Hereford and Worcester had been withdrawn and concentrated at Gloucester. Although Stamford left a garrison at Gloucester when he went into Devon, the Parliamentary presence in the area was much reduced, which enabled Hertford with his newly raised regiments of foot to cross the Severn at Worcester and move through the Cotswolds to Burford. But Parliament held Cirencester as well as Bristol and Gloucester, which meant that Hertford was cut off from his forces in the south-west. The Parliamentary presence at Cirencester also prevented the King from extending his influence westwards from his garrisons around Oxford. From both of these standpoints it was important that the Royalists should capture the town.

To this end Rupert arranged to meet up with Hertford and mount a joint attack. On 6 January he left Oxford and, marching by night through a terrible thunderstorm, arrived next morning to find that Hertford had not appeared, as a result of which the operation had to be delayed. Luckily the storm was followed by heavy snow which prevented Parliament from reinforcing the town. Two weeks later Rupert set out again with about 4,000 men as though to capture Sudeley Castle some fifteen miles north of Cirencester. He spent some days manoeuvring in this area and then, suddenly swinging south at great speed, joined up with Hertford and his men outside Cirencester on 2 February.

Luckily for the Royalists, some houses had been built over the years outside the walls which the Parliamentary garrison had failed to demolish. These offered the Royalists a covered approach right up to the walls themselves. Rupert's plan was that Wilmot should mount an attack from the north, which would draw as many of the defenders as possible in that direction, after which he himself would lead the main assault straight up the road from the south-west. The attack was pressed home with the utmost ferocity by foot, horse and cannon, the defenders resisting strongly, fighting from house to house and losing up to 300 men killed and around 1,200 prisoners. It took an hour and a half to clear the town, in the course of which some houses were inevitably destroyed. Unfortunately a number of Parliamentary supporters continued firing after the town had been taken which led to further burning and some looting by the infuriated Royalists. This was eventually brought under control, but in accordance with the rules of war the town was systematically stripped of everything that could be useful to the Royalist army, including large quantities of weapons, food and cloth together with some horses.

Royalist losses were negligible and the superiority of their forces was demonstrated to such good effect that Parliament withdrew its detachments from Tewkesbury, Malmesbury and Devizes as well as from Sudeley and Berkeley Castles. At a blow the King had extended his influence over most of Gloucestershire. The local gentry agreed to raise a regiment of foot to help defend the county and also to collect £4,000 a month for the Royalist cause.

Immediately after capturing Cirencester Rupert went with a detachment to Gloucester to see whether he could exploit the panic engendered by his recent success and take the town by a *coup de main*. But after having a good look round, he realised that it was too strong for him and withdrew. He then left garrisons in Cirencester and Malmesbury before returning to Oxford where the sight of his bedraggled prisoners made a healthy impression on a Parliamentary delegation that had recently arrived to negotiate with the King. In an attempt to exploit the fear that Rupert's presence inspired, the King got him and Prince Maurice to sit with him during some of the negotiations, but they took no part in the proceedings.

A month later Rupert took a detachment of the King's army to Bristol, where some Royalist sympathisers were plotting to deliver the city from within. But the plot failed and Rupert was not strong enough to besiege Bristol or take it by storm, so he returned to Oxford empty-handed.

The capture of Lichfield was designed to strengthen the Royalist position in the Midlands and to safeguard movement between the King and the Royalists in the north. The Queen's arrival in Yorkshire at the end of February made this a matter of importance as the King naturally wanted her brought safely to Oxford, together with the much-needed convoy of arms and munitions that she had collected in the Netherlands.

When the Earl of Newcastle moved south into Yorkshire at the beginning of December 1642, having secured Northumberland and Durham for the King, Parliamentary forces were containing the local Royalists in York. During December Newcastle established control of the north-east of the county and then pushed Fairfax back to the cloth-making towns of the West Riding. At the beginning of January he also improved his position in the south of his command by ordering Newark to be garrisoned. In January Fairfax counter-attacked and established himself as far forward as Tadcaster, but at the end of March Newcastle's horse won a minor victory which had the effect of pushing Fairfax back to Leeds and Wakefield.

Initially Newcastle employed Sir William Davenant, a poet with little military knowledge, as his lieutenant general, but in January the King sent Lord Eythin to fill the post.[9] Eythin, who had recently arrived from the Continent, was none other than the James King who had been Charles Louis's military adviser in the ill-fated expedition of 1638. King Charles had secured his services in return for a peerage and the promise of a pension of £1,000 a year. It would be interesting to know what Rupert thought of this arrangement and how he received Eythin at Oxford. At any rate, from Newcastle's point of view, Eythin was a great improvement on Davenant.

Another addition to Newcastle's army was Lord Goring, who had accompanied the Queen from Holland and who took over the horse from Sir Marmaduke Langdale. Goring was an experienced soldier and, at his best, a first-class operational commander; knowledgeable, quick-witted, brave and decisive. He had great charm and was popular with his soldiers. But he was utterly unprincipled and a compulsive gambler and drinker who was sometimes incapacitated for days on end, even when engaged on operations. During the early months of 1642 he was Member of Parliament and Governor of Portsmouth, but despite leading Pym to believe that he would hold it for Parliament, he declared for the King when the fighting began. He was soon besieged by Parliamentary forces whereupon he surrendered Portsmouth and escaped to Holland. Despite his questionable behaviour the Queen let him join her entourage, probably because he was the son of the Earl of Norwich, one of her favourite courtiers.

When in August 1642 the King left Nottingham for Shrewsbury, he took from the Midlands most of the leading Royalists and the troops that they had raised. This so weakened the local Royalists that Parliament was able to seize Nottingham and Derby. In December the King decided to restore the position and sent Henry Hastings, a leading Leicestershire Royalist and a long-standing enemy of the Grey family, back into the area with some horse and dragoons and authority to raise further troops as required. Hastings established garrisons south of the Trent in Stafford, Lichfield and Ashby de la Zouch, but in early March a Parliamentary detachment captured Lichfield and then, after joining up with some more troops from Cheshire under the command of Sir William Brereton, moved west to attack Stafford. In order to prevent this happening, the King sent the Earl of Northampton from Banbury to reinforce Hastings and on 19 March they won a battle at Hopton Heath, thus saving the town. Unfortunately the Earl was killed in the battle.

On 12 March Rupert, whose influence with the King was now at its peak and who was in effect directing operations in the whole area between the commands of the Marquess of Hertford and the Earl of Newcastle, received a letter from Charles. After saying that he did not mean to trust him by halves, the King authorised Rupert to appoint a governor for Shrewsbury and to include Cheshire within his sphere of influence.[10] Shortly afterwards Rupert, with the King's agreement, decided to join Hastings and capture Lichfield. With Stafford and Lichfield safe, Rupert hoped to spread Royalist influence through the Midlands as he had done in the Cotswolds after capturing Cirencester. After that he would be well placed either to push on to York and bring the Queen back to Oxford or, if absolutely necessary, to go to the assistance of Lord Derby in Lancashire who was sending urgent requests for help.

Rupert, accompanied by Lord Digby, left Oxford in the last week of March with a force of around 1,200 horse and dragoons, 700 ill-armed foot and six light cannon, probably sakers. On 3 April he arrived outside the small but hostile town of Birmingham. The inhabitants, who had captured some of the King's plate in the early stages of the war and had subsequently been intercepting Royalist messengers and manufacturing sword blades for the Parliamentary armies, foolishly refused Rupert entry, despite the fact that there was only a small detachment of troops from the Parliamentary garrison at Lichfield to defend them: probably one company of foot and a troop of horse.

Rupert set about taking Birmingham with his customary energy and determination. The enemy split their forces to block the main entrances to the town, erecting various barricades and obstacles, covered by fire. In this way they held off the Royalist attack for some time. But Rupert set fire to some houses near the barricades which enabled the Royalist horse to get off the road into some flooded meadows and thence back into the town through gardens and gaps between the houses. Once inside they rode through the streets beating down all opposition. At one moment the Parliamentary troop of horse mounted a charge which delayed the attackers for long enough to allow the enemy foot to withdraw from the town, after which the survivors of the charge also withdrew towards Lichfield.

It had been a brisk engagement while it lasted, the Parliamentary soldiers being reinforced by many of the local inhabitants. Amongst the Royalist casualties was the veteran Earl of Denbigh who had served as admiral in some of the naval expeditions of the 1620s and who was mortally wounded in the assault. His title and influence in his home county of Warwickshire passed to his son Lord Feilding who, to the distress of his family, fought for Parliament. As soon as Birmingham was secure Rupert had the fires extinguished, but next morning, as the Royalists were marching out towards Stafford, some soldiers, exasperated by the insults of the citizens and contrary to Rupert's expressed instructions, set more houses on fire thereby giving further opportunities to the Parliamentary propagandists in their non-stop attacks on the Prince.

At Stafford Rupert met up with Hastings and the new Earl of Northampton, who had assumed command of the troops brought by his father from Banbury. The combined force arrived at Lichfield on 8 April and Rupert called on the garrison to surrender. Although there was no proper wall round the town itself, there was an immensely strong one round the cathedral close, which was the area that the Parliamentary commander, Colonel Roweswell, decided to defend. In addition, according to Hyde, there was a broad and deep moat: it had probably been formed by joining together the meres that provided the town with water. Within these fortifications Roweswell had plenty of supplies and an adequate garrison, so he refused to surrender.

Rupert's problem was that the horse was ill suited to storming such fortifications and he was weak in foot and artillery. In theory he could have starved the garrison out, but it would have taken longer than he could afford. He had already heard from Sir Edward Nicholas, who was one of the two Secretaries of State, that Essex with his main army was planning to advance along the Thames valley when the peace talks broke down, as they were expected to do at any moment. He knew that he would have to rejoin the King when that happened. Further letters written by Nicholas on 6, 10 and 11 April convinced Rupert that there was no time to lose.

Rupert's plan was to withdraw most of the horse from the city, dismount them and use them as additional foot. As his cannon were too small to breach the wall he would have to undermine it, a process unknown in England at the time. For this purpose Rupert asked Hastings to get some miners from his estates nearby. Whilst they were being collected, Rupert got on with the job of draining the moat and building a bridge across the mud. It is recorded that officers and men joined in this perilous work with enthusiasm, Digby himself working waist-deep in mud until he was shot through the thigh. During this time the garrison sallied forth on several occasions causing casualties and taking prisoners, one of whom was Will Legge, the major of Rupert's regiment and his close friend and confidant.

Within seven or eight days the bridge was built and the miners started work, but by this time Rupert was getting letters written by the King himself, urging him to hurry. The first, written on 15 April, said that Essex had started to move and that Rupert should go north for the Queen as soon as possible. The next day another one arrived telling him to return to Oxford at once. Rupert decided not to wait for the miners but to try and capture the town using scaling ladders which he had been collecting from the surrounding countryside. This he attempted, but his attack was beaten off and the enemy unwisely hanged one of the prisoners from the wall, calling on Rupert to shoot him down. Rupert was furious and swore that the garrison should have no quarter, but by a coincidence that evening he received another letter from the King urging him to shed no more blood than was necessary and telling him that it was more important to capture the enemy's minds than their cities.[11] Although the wording is verbose and archaic, the argument contains sound advice for those involved in counter-insurgency and would be recognised as such today. Next morning Rupert went back on his threat to kill the garrison and offered them quarter if they surrendered, but they again refused, clanging the cathedral bells in defiance.

By this time the miners had burrowed under the walls, filling the cavity with barrels of powder. Next day, 20 April 1643, the first mine ever sprung in England blew a twenty-foot breach in an apparently impregnable wall. Although Rupert's initial assault was held, he brought up his cannon which fired through the breach until the enemy sued for terms, after which Hastings went into the close to negotiate the surrender. Rupert was so impressed by the gallantry of the defenders that he allowed them to march out with the honours of war, personally congratulating Colonel Roweswell on his conduct of the defence. But greater credit was due to Rupert himself for managing to take the town with such an unlikely force, especially as he lacked the heavy guns normally considered essential for such an enterprise. The capture of Lichfield was one of Rupert's most spectacular military achievements and stands as a memorial to his ingenuity and leadership.

Having retrieved the prisoners taken in the fighting, Rupert appointed Richard Bagot Governor of Lichfield which, with its gunpowder factories, brass foundries and food stocks, remained a valuable Royalist stronghold for the next three years. He then left Hastings to extend Royalist influence throughout the area as best he could, and hastened back to the King whom he joined at Wallingford on 25 April.

The situation that he found on his arrival was that Essex with the main Parliamentary army was besieging Reading where Sir Arthur Aston, the Governor, had been incapacitated by falling masonry. The command devolved on Richard Feilding who had gallantly commanded one of the foot brigades at Edgehill, but who had now decided to surrender Reading as he considered that the King could not possibly relieve it. Soon afterwards the King with nine regiments of foot tried to reach the besieged garrison by forcing a way across the Thames at Caversham Bridge, but was unable to make any impression on the Parliamentary forces that stood between him and the bridge. Meanwhile Rupert went down to the river and shouted across to Feilding that he should hold out as help was at hand. But Feilding told him that having agreed to terms he could not in honour go back on them. The terms permitted the garrison to march out with the honours of war, but contrary to Essex's orders some of the Royalists were attacked and their baggage plundered as they were leaving the town. Back in Oxford Feilding was stripped of his commission and condemned to death by a court martial, but Rupert, who sympathised with his predicament, persuaded the Prince of Wales to secure his pardon and he spent the rest of the war fighting as a volunteer.

Essex did not follow up his success at Reading by an advance on Oxford, because sickness was rife in his army and his men would not move until they were paid. Essex was therefore obliged to content himself with sending bodies of horse and dragoons into Royalist-controlled areas to strip the surrounding countryside of supplies. The Royalists responded by moving out of their garrisons and attacking Parliamentary detachments when they could be brought to battle, beating up their quarters at night and carrying out raids deep into areas controlled by Parliament.

In order to co-ordinate these Royalist ventures, Rupert reverted to his journeying between army headquarters at Oxford, the headquarters of the horse at Abingdon and the various Royalist garrisons, reinforcing first one and then another, so that each in turn could carry out operations against specific Parliamentary detachments according to current information. Rupert's correspondence for this period shows how Lord Crawford at Faringdon, on the basis of information gathered at Newbury, planned an operation against Parliamentary forces scattered between Reading and Malmesbury. How the young Earl of Northampton at Banbury attacked an enemy detachment of four troops of horse and 600–700 foot, killing or capturing most of the foot including all the officers and capturing large quantities of arms and ammunition for the loss of only three men. How Lord Wentworth and Sir John Byron took a detachment of horse and dragoons through Winslow to Buckingham, but failed to contact any worthwhile enemy forces and had to be content with taking arms from some hostile locals in the village of Swanburne. Some of these letters include apologies for excesses committed by the soldiers and undertakings to stamp them out, which implies that Rupert had been issuing orders to this effect.

On 10 June Essex started to move towards Oxford, establishing himself at Thame, twelve miles to the east of the city. On 17 June he sent a detachment of 2,700 men to secure the crossing of the Cherwell at Islip but was beaten back. A few days earlier Rupert had discovered from one of Essex's colonels, a Scots soldier of fortune called John Urry who had deserted to the King, details of the Parliamentary deployment, together with the fact that carts laden with money for their army were due to arrive in the early hours on 18 June.

On the strength of this information Rupert decided to make a raid through enemy lines to disrupt their army and, if possible, to capture the money. Accordingly he left Oxford in the afternoon

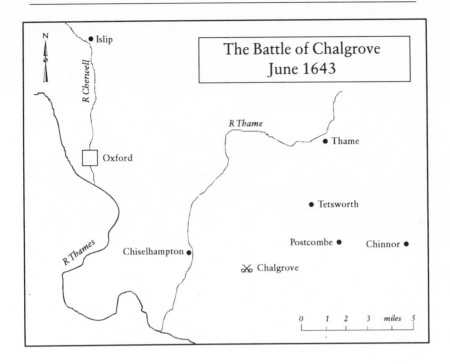

of 17 June with his own regiment of horse, the Prince of Wales's regiment and Lord Percy's regiment, together with 300 dragoons commanded by Lord Wentworth and Henry Lunsford's regiment of foot: in all about 1,800 men.

Rupert's force crossed the River Thame at Chislehampton, about four miles upstream of its junction with the Thames. He then pushed on and at 1 a.m. passed the strongly guarded village of Tetsworth, three miles south of Essex's headquarters at Thame. At 3 a.m. he reached Postcombe where he captured an officer and nine men and at 5 a.m. arrived at Chinnor up against the Chiltern Hills which was the most easterly of the Parliamentary encampments, i.e. he had passed right through Essex's army from west to east. At this village were 200 dragoons who had spent the whole of the preceding day in the saddle as part of the force that had tried to capture Islip. Rupert captured 120 of them and killed another fifty, but the noise of the engagement alerted the convoy with the money which hid in a nearby wood, thus avoiding capture.

By now it was light and Rupert turned for home, expecting that

Essex would send troops to intercept his withdrawal. In order to safeguard his retreat Rupert sent on the foot to secure the bridge at Chislehampton and the dragoons to line the hedges leading to the bridge in the hope of drawing his pursuers into an ambush. After a time he began to receive reports of enemy forces in the area and by 8 a.m. they were harassing his rearguard. An hour later Rupert halted his three regiments in a large cornfield near the village of Chalgrove. By this time he was being closely pressed by eight troops of Parliamentary horse who, thinking that they were pursuing a retreating foe, had become careless and disordered. When Rupert halted, they pushed some dragoons forward to a hedge which cut the field in two and started firing at the Royalists.

Some of Rupert's officers now suggested that it was time to move towards the bridge, thus drawing the Parliamentary horse into the lane lined by the Royalist dragoons, but Rupert was concerned that the enemy was too close and would throw his rearguard into confusion if he tried to withdraw. At the same time he could see that the enemy were not properly together and were therefore vulnerable to attack. He therefore told O'Neale to take his regiment and the Prince of Wales's regiment along the hedge to the left and thence round the bottom of it and so attack the enemy. As these two regiments moved off, Rupert, remarking on the enemy's insolence, rode straight at the hedge with his life guard and jumped into the field beyond, killing some of the enemy dragoons and dispersing the remainder. By this manoeuvre Rupert placed himself and his life guard on the left flank of the Parliamentary horse who had formed up facing O'Neale's men as they came round the bottom of the hedge. As soon as O'Neale's men attacked the enemy, Rupert charged into their flank which started to crumble. By now Percy had got his regiment through the hedge to reinforce Rupert and, as the enemy broke, he pursued them off the field, killing many as they fled.

Rupert then withdrew in a leisurely fashion to Oxford, arriving at about 2 p.m. with his prisoners. During the twenty-four hours that he had been away, he had covered more than forty miles and had passed through Essex's army from one side to the other and back again. He had taken over 100 prisoners and killed many others: his own losses amounted to no more than twelve men all told.

A further consequence of the raid became apparent a day or two later when information was received that John Hampden had been severely wounded. He had set off from his quarters when he heard

Prince Rupert (right) and his brother Charles Louis, about 1637, by Van Dyck

An engraving of Sir Jacob Astley

Charles I in 1628, by Honthorst

An engraving of the Earl of Essex

Prince Rupert, about 1642, attributed to Honthorst

Mary, Duchess of
Richmond, by Van Dyck

Prince Rupert's brother
Prince Maurice,
by Honthorst

An engraving of Lord Goring, from a painting by Van Dyck

Lord Digby, by Egmont

Thomas Fairfax,
by Robert Walker

of Rupert's raid and had arrived at Chalgrove just as the Parliamentary horse were breaking in the face of the Royalist attack. He tried to rally them but was almost immediately wounded in the shoulder, from which he died six days later. During the period leading up to the outbreak of war Hampden's opposition to the King was second only to that of Pym himself, but his apparent sincerity and attractive personality made him liked and respected by many of his opponents as well as his friends. Although he had no military experience he became colonel of a regiment of foot at the start of the war. He missed most of the battle of Edgehill because his regiment was guarding the artillery train, but he arrived in time to help check the rout. He carried great weight in Essex's army, because of his political position and his ability to present his views convincingly. He also used his diplomatic skills to reinforce Essex's blunt demands for resources, becoming in effect Essex's main link with Parliament. In the last six weeks of his life it was rumoured that he was going to take over command of the army from Essex, who was being widely criticised for his lack of drive.

Although Essex may have held the strategic initiative in the centre since taking Reading, the Royalists had continued to assert their superiority in the series of offensive raids mounted by Prince Rupert, which continued unabated in the weeks following the battle at Chalgrove. By the end of June Essex's army was thoroughly demoralised and the citizens of London itself were suffering from Royalist raids which denied them the produce of much of the surrounding countryside. There was further criticism of Essex in the Commons as a result of which he tendered his resignation, but it was refused.

At the end of June a Royalist plot to take control of London from within was discovered which, despite its failure, added to Parliament's nervousness. At the same time the Earl of Newcastle completely defeated Lord Fairfax and his son at Adwalton Moor a few miles south-east of Bradford, which more than compensated for a setback which he had suffered six weeks earlier when Goring was captured in a skirmish outside Wakefield. The time was now ripe for another attempt to get the Queen, who had moved to Newark earlier in the month, to Oxford.

On 3 July the Queen left Newark with 3,000 foot, 1,000 horse and six cannon. The plan was that Hastings, now raised to the peerage as Lord Loughborough, would prevent interference from Parliamentary garrisons in Lincolnshire and Leicestershire while Rupert moved north from Oxford to hold off any attack that might be mounted by detachments of Essex's army. On 1 July Rupert moved to Buckingham and early next morning, whilst shaving, heard that a number of enemy groups were concentrating nearby to attack him. Without waiting to finish shaving, he collected a few troops of horse and charged the enemy before they had time to deploy, scattering them completely. Thereafter he received no further interference from Essex, although it is said that he so harassed the detachments that were screening his advance that they were 'wearied of their lives'. The Queen, who had come via Ashby de la Zouch and Burton-on-Trent, met Rupert at Stratford-upon-Avon on 11 July. Two days later they joined the King on the battlefield at Edgehill and together they returned to Oxford.

Rupert's next task, the capture of Bristol, must be viewed against recent events in the south-west. Soon after Rupert took Cirencester, Parliament appointed Sir William Waller, in the absence of Lord Stamford in Devon, to take control of their interests in the counties between Somerset and Shropshire. In his youth Waller had been with Essex, Skippon, Hopton and Richard Grenville in Sir Horace Vere's force in the Palatinate and later in the Netherlands. On his return to England he became MP for Andover and held a minor position at court. In the early months of the Civil War he operated in Hampshire and captured Portsmouth from Goring before joining Essex for the battle of Edgehill.

On being sent into the west he established himself in Bristol, recaptured Malmesbury, defeated Lord Herbert's Welshmen outside Gloucester and occupied Ross-on-Wye, Monmouth and Chepstow. At this point Prince Maurice was sent from Oxford to restore the situation and, after some energetic manoeuvring, defeated Waller at Ripple Field on 13 April. But, like Rupert, Maurice was recalled when Essex moved on Reading and Waller was able to extend his influence northwards.

In the south-west Hopton, with his small Cornish army, lost a battle at Stourton near Okehampton towards the end of April, but won a decisive victory at Stratton near Bude on 16 May which virtually destroyed Lord Stamford's forces. Hopton immediately led his men to Chard in Somerset where on 4 June he met up with the Marquess of Hertford and Prince Maurice who had come from Oxford to join him. Hertford now had at his disposal a sizeable force of 4,000 foot, mainly from Cornwall, 2,000 horse, mainly from Oxford, 300 dragoons of the Cornish army and about fifteen cannon.[12] His orders were to push past Waller and join the King's main army around Oxford.

When he heard that Hopton had joined up with Hertford, Waller, who was besieging Worcester, moved rapidly south, gathering reinforcements from Bristol as he went, and engaged Hertford's army in a three-day running fight around Bath. This culminated on 5 July in a ferocious attack by the Cornish foot on Waller's position on top of Lansdown Hill, a few miles north of the city. Waller was dislodged but the Royalists suffered heavy casualties, including the loss of Bevil Grenville and the destruction of most of their horse. Next morning an ammunition wagon exploded, temporarily blinding and paralysing Hopton himself.

Despite being turned out of his main position, Waller suffered less than the Royalists and, after summoning further reinforcements from Bristol, followed them closely when they marched to Devizes. On arrival he drew up his army on Roundway Down to the north of the town, inviting a renewal of the battle, but the Royalists were short of ammunition and in no shape to attack. Next day Waller started to encircle the town prior to besieging it, but during the night, before the encirclement was complete, Hertford and Maurice escaped with the remainder of the horse to get help. They arrived at Oxford on 11 June, the same day that Rupert was meeting the Queen at Stratford-upon-Avon. In an amazingly short time regiments of horse were on the move to an assembly area at Marlborough where they arrived next day. On 13 June 1,800 horse commanded by Wilmot set off to rescue Hopton who was still holding out in Devizes.

As soon as Waller heard of Wilmot's approach he withdrew his men from Devizes and deployed them on Roundway Down with his 2,500 foot in the centre and his 2,000 horse split between the two wings. He had a massive superiority over Wilmot, but was concerned to get the battle fought before Hopton's foot could intervene. Wilmot, realising that he could not afford to be attacked by Waller's army, decided to take the initiative and rout the two wings separately. First he led an attack on the Parliamentary left and chased it from the field. Sir John Byron then attacked their right and, after a fierce struggle, drove them back over a precipice; many horses and men were killed in the process. Both then turned on the Parliamentary foot, but could make no impression until the Cornish regiments arrived from Devizes, after which all the enemy were taken prisoner or killed. Waller's army was destroyed.

Wilmot's victory at Roundway Down again demonstrated the

astonishing superiority of the Royalist horse and bore witness to the value of Rupert's ideas and training methods. Great credit is due to Wilmot for assembling the force so quickly and fighting the battle so well: it was the high point of his career. Waller escaped to Gloucester and later to London, where he blamed his defeat on Essex for not pressing the King more strongly which, he claimed, allowed the Royalists to reinforce Hopton. Essex, who grudged the resources diverted to Waller, blamed him for losing such a fine army. After the battle Hertford's men occupied Bath.

Rupert arrived back in Oxford with the King and Queen on 15 July and left three days later determined to exploit Waller's defeat. He took with him fourteen regiments of foot, most of which were very under strength, a reinforced regiment of dragoons and an indeterminate number of horse divided into two parts, described as wings. He also had eight siege cannons and was accompanied by his engineer, de Gomme, and his munitions expert, La Roche. It is estimated that his force numbered around 5,500 all told, which shows how under-recruited the foot regiments must have been.

Rupert marched first towards Gloucester but abandoned the idea of besieging it when he heard that Waller with 500 survivors of the battle of Roundway Down was inside. But by threatening the place he prevented reinforcements being sent to Bristol which, as the second city in the kingdom and a major port, was a more important prize. He now swung south, masking Gloucester and arriving on the high ground to the north-west of Bristol on Sunday 23 July. Meanwhile Hertford moved his army from Bath to a position to the south-east of the city: Maurice himself, who was Hertford's lieutenant general, joined Rupert on his march from Gloucester to co-ordinate the action of the two armies. As soon as they arrived the two brothers went out together to reconnoitre the defences.

The city of Bristol was built on land between the River Avon and its tributary the River Frome and, because of the course these two rivers took at the time, was almost completely surrounded by a natural moat. An ancient castle covered the gap between the two rivers where they diverged at the easternmost corner of the city. But many houses had been built beyond the rivers and the city was overlooked along its western side by a range of hills which, for part of the way, were no more than a quarter of a mile distant; in other words, if an attacker could establish himself along the crest, he could fire directly into the city below and smash it to bits, together with ships tied up alongside the quays.

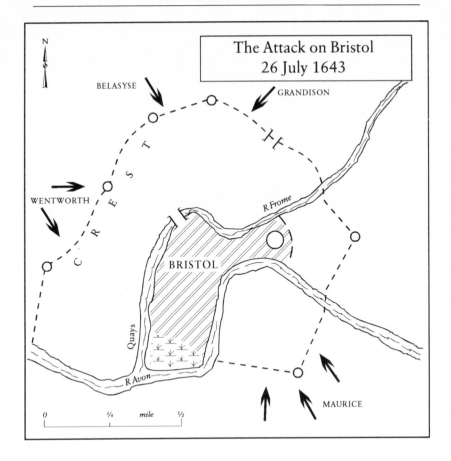

The Attack on Bristol
26 July 1643

N

BELASYSE

GRANDISON

WENTWORTH

C R E S T

R Frome

BRISTOL

Quays

R Avon

MAURICE

0   ¼   mile   ½

In order to defend Bristol, a ditch and earthworks, interspersed with small forts, had been erected along this crest and thence from its most northern point across the flatter ground to the east and south of the city. This defensive line effectively prevented an attacker from firing into the city itself or from closing, under cover of the houses that had been built outside them, with the inner defences. These consisted of the two rivers backed in places by an ancient wall. The outer line constituted a formidable obstacle, but de Gomme considered that in some places the ditch was too narrow and that the earthworks and forts were less well made than the ones that the Royalists had built around Oxford. Another draw-back from the point of view of the defence was that a large number of people were needed to man this extensive perimeter and Waller had reduced the garrison by about 1,200 during his operations round Bath. But the Parliamentary commander still had 1,500 foot and 300 horse together with 100 cannon of various sizes and plenty of powder, shot and victuals. He could also call on townsmen to bolster up his force.

On the Monday morning both Rupert and Hertford drew up their armies in such a way that the defenders could see them. Rupert then summoned Fiennes to surrender the city, which he refused to do. It was now clear to Rupert that the broken ground in front of the earthworks along the crest of the hill offered better lines of approach for an assault than the flatter ground to the east, and the rest of the day was taken up in placing cannon where they could fire on the forts and deploying the foot. The foot, which was commanded by Grandison, was deployed in three brigades (tertias) along the crest: one under Grandison himself in the north, one under Belasyse in the centre and the third under Wentworth in the south. During the night the enemy patrolled out from the defences on several occasions and a great deal of fire was exchanged.

On the Tuesday further adjustments were made, cannon being moved here and there as better positions were found for them. Meanwhile Rupert and some of his officers crossed the Avon to attend a council of war at Hertford's headquarters: Hertford did not himself attend, telling Maurice that as he knew nothing of the business, he left it to him to make what representations he thought fit.

At the council, Maurice's Cornish officers favoured a formal siege rather than an immediate assault, on the grounds that it was more certain and would save lives. They felt that as there was no chance of relief, the enemy would surrender when the siege works put them in an impossible position. But Rupert could not afford to wait: he had already received a letter from Nicholas and two from the King saying that Essex had advanced to Aylesbury and asking him to send back some of his horse. Rupert therefore argued for an assault, pointing out that the defenders were in a state of shock following Waller's defeat, that they should not be given time to regain their confidence and that in any case there were no commanders of experience in the city capable of organising an effective defence. The vigour with which he presented his case, and the total disregard for danger felt by all present, won everybody to his side. As one of Maurice's officers recorded afterwards, 'Rupert's very name was half a conquest'.[13]

The plan decided on was that Rupert's three brigades would attack the outer defences along the crest, while Maurice's regiments

attacked to the south of the city. It would not be possible to undermine the walls of the forts because of rock in front of Rupert and
bog in front of Maurice. It would therefore be necessary to assault
the forts and scale the earthworks at selected points. As soon as
the line was breached, the gap was to be enlarged so that both
foot and horse could pour into the area between the outer defences
and the city itself. It was not thought that the inner defences would
pose much of a problem, as the Frome was easily crossed and the
ditch in front of the wall was largely filled with rubbish: in any
case most of the defenders would be manning the outer ring. The
attack was to start at daybreak next morning, 26 July, the signal
for the assault being the firing of a cannon.

In the event Maurice's Cornish foot regiments were so keen to
get at the enemy that they launched their attack at 3 a.m. without
waiting for the signal. Furthermore they had failed to get the fag-
gots needed for crossing the ditch in front of the earthworks, which
was particularly deep in the place where they made their assault.
Believing that valour could achieve anything, they found themselves forced back with heavy loss. Of the four colonels who had
originally raised Hopton's army in Cornwall, Godolphin and Bevil
Grenville were already dead and the other two, Slanning and Trevannion, were lost in this attack. The survivors fell back to some
nearby hedges and continued firing at the defenders. Although
unsuccessful, the attack had at least prevented Fiennes from switch-
ing men to face Rupert's assaults which were now developing on
the other side of the city.

As soon as Rupert realised that the Cornish had jumped the gun,
he gave the signal for his three brigades to attack. For a time all
the assaults were beaten off with considerable loss, Grandison and
one of his regimental commanders becoming casualties as they led
an attack on the fort at the northern extremity of the line commanded by Robert Blake, the future admiral. Belasyse's brigade
was also unsuccessful in its attack on the fortifications.

When Wentworth's brigade attacked, some of his assaulting
troops found a section of the earthworks that was out of sight of
the forts on either side of it, because it lay in a dip in the ground.
Wentworth himself and Colonel Washington who was commanding the dragoons, together with a handful of other officers and
soldiers, managed to force their way across at this point. While
some held off the enemy, others made a gap in the earthworks
with their swords, halberds and hands so that in a short time there
was a gap through which both foot and horse were able to enter.

An immediate and badly co-ordinated counter-attack was quickly driven off, as also was a more serious attempt shortly afterwards. Fortune continued to favour the bold as some exposed men running for cover in the face of the enemy's counter-attack came upon another enemy fort that was behind their main lines. The occupants, thinking that they were being attacked, abandoned it and ran.

Rupert was visiting Grandison's brigade in the north when he heard from Legge that Wentworth had breached the earthworks. Telling Lieutenant Colonel Moyle, who was acting as Grandison's brigade major, to collect together what men he could and lead them into the city, he went to collect his life guard and as he was riding towards them his horse was shot through the eye. It is recorded that 'without even so much as mending his pace he marched off on foot leisurely till another horse was brought him'.[14] It is hard to imagine the conditions that must have existed at that time, with flame belching out of the cannons fired from the forts a few yards away and flashes from the muskets still showing up clearly in the early morning light.

Once through the breach, Wentworth's brigade swung right and advanced to the quays along the bank of the River Frome. From there they sent a message to Rupert, who had himself moved into the breach, suggesting that they should set fire to the ships tied up there, as the flames would spread to the inner city, obliging the enemy to surrender. But Rupert refused as he wanted to capture the city intact: the last thing he wanted was a pile of smouldering rubble. Meanwhile Belasyse's brigade had followed Wentworth's through the breach and had closed up to the river backed by detachments of Grandison's men led by Moyle.

Contrary to expectations, the enemy continued to resist strongly, sallying out from the inner city through the Frome gate and firing at the Royalists from the walls and from houses outside them. On the other hand the men in the forts along the earthworks fired very little as, being cut off from the city, they were frightened of being put to the sword if they interfered too vigorously. Rupert now sent a message to Maurice on the other side of the city, to bring round 1,000 of his Cornish foot as reinforcements, but just as the first of them were arriving with Maurice himself, some men of Grandison's brigade forced their way through the Frome gate into the inner city. Rupert therefore told Maurice to attack the largest of the forts on the earthworks and directed Wentworth's brigade to cross the Frome from the direction of the quays so as to enter the city further to the south. At this moment Colonel Fiennes called for a parley.

It is difficult to work out exactly how long the battle lasted, but it is known that the fight around the Frome gate went on for nearly two hours. Royalist losses at this time were considerable. Amongst the senior officers, Moyle and one of Belasyse's colonels called Henry Lunsford were killed and Belasyse himself was wounded. Throughout this desperate time Rupert moved from place to place where his presence was most needed, directing and encouraging some and leading up others. An eyewitness records, 'Generally it is confessed by the commanders, that had not the Prince been there, the assault through mere despair, had been in danger to be given over in many places.'[15]

Altogether Royalist losses were about 500, a heavy price to pay. But the rewards of capturing Bristol far outweighed the loss. Under the terms of the surrender Fiennes and his officers were allowed to march out with their arms and baggage but the soldiers had to leave their weapons behind. The Royalists therefore took possession of them, together with all the enemy's cannon, a large quantity of powder and shot and £100,000 in cash, on top of which the city undertook to raise £140,000 in return for not being sacked. A further prize came in the form of eighteen merchant ships and four ships of the Parliamentary navy, all of which changed sides thus providing the nucleus of a Royalist fleet. Many of the defeated garrison also joined the King's army.

Another result of capturing Bristol was that soon afterwards Dorchester and Weymouth fell to the Royalists and the Parliamentary garrisons in Berkeley Castle and Corfe Castle also surrendered. On a personal level, Rupert took over as colonel of Lunsford's regiment, which meant that he would now have a regiment of foot to look after as well as his regiment of horse.

Two incidents marred Rupert's conquest. The first was that the Parliamentary garrison, which under the terms of the agreement was required to leave the city at 9 a.m. the following day, moved out one hour early, before Rupert was ready. As a result the Parliamentary column was subjected to insults and attack by unruly Royalist soldiers. When Rupert heard about it, he and Maurice, together with some other officers, rode amongst the offenders slashing at them with their swords and driving them off. Fiennes subsequently exonerated Rupert in his report to Parliament and praised him for his efforts, but the incident left a bad taste.

The second incident was, at least partly, Rupert's fault. He and

Maurice had jointly conducted the operations to capture Bristol and in the heat of the moment had paid scant attention to Hertford, who took umbrage. As a result, when Bristol fell, Hertford appointed Hopton to be the Governor without consulting Rupert. At the same time Rupert, forgetting that Bristol was just inside Hertford's area of responsibility, and knowing nothing of Hopton's appointment, asked the King to make him Governor, which the King did.

When the King realised what had happened, he acted with speed and tact to avoid a rift amongst his senior commanders. First he wrote to Hopton saying that although he greatly valued his services, he could not cancel Rupert's appointment. He then went to Bristol in person where he suggested to Rupert that he should appoint Hopton deputy governor which Rupert was delighted to do. The King then made a great fuss of Hertford, saying that he badly needed him to be part of his inner council at Oxford and appointing Prince Maurice to be the General in the south-west in his place. Maurice took the Cornish army back to Devon and soon captured Exeter and all the ports that had remained in Parliament's hands when Hopton had left the county in early June, except for Plymouth. Hopton stayed in Bristol to recover from the wounds he had received outside Bath on 6 July.

In the nine months following the battle of Edgehill, Rupert conducted a wide variety of military operations including one withdrawal, i.e. the withdrawal from Turnham Green, and the capture of five towns, i.e. Brentford, Cirencester, Birmingham, Lichfield and Bristol. In addition he organised a series of raids on Essex's army in the period following the loss of Reading which prevented Essex from exploiting his strength and which virtually paralysed his army. As part of this programme, he personally commanded the biggest and most damaging of the raids, in the course of which, at Chalgrove, he demonstrated an unerring instinct for timing and the use of ground.

But it was in the capture of built-up areas that he showed his greatest skill, in particular at Lichfield and Bristol. In both cases he was faced by a determined enemy, well armed and well prepared. Also, in both cases, he was under pressure to conclude the business quickly, because of events elsewhere. At Lichfield he overcame a shortage of siege artillery and foot soldiers by the flexibility of his approach and by his mastery of a technique unknown to his opponents, i.e. the springing of a mine. At Bristol his success was due in part to the efficiency of his system of command which enabled him to attack on a wide front and then concentrate to exploit success. To a greater extent it was due to his ability to get his army to slog it out in a set-piece battle. Bristol may seem less satisfying in terms of military artistry than Lichfield, but sooner or later every commander has to prove his ability to fight it out with his fists, so to speak. Bristol was the one occasion in Rupert's career as a land force commander when he had to do this, and he did it most effectively.

Throughout this period Rupert inspired the complete trust of his officers and soldiers. None of those who worked with him had any doubt that he was a complete master of his trade and that he had the personal qualities needed to command them in battle. From time to time they may have been astonished at his daring, as when he placed himself and his life guard on the flank of the enemy's line at Chalgrove, but they had complete confidence that he would somehow contrive to beat the enemy whatever the odds. For some months to come it would seem that the enemy continued to share that opinion.

7

LOSING GROUND

ON THE SURFACE, the situation from the Royalists' point of view at the beginning of August seemed to be highly favourable. Not only had the whole of the west and south-west, with the exception of Gloucester and Plymouth, come under the King's control, but Yorkshire was also firmly in his hands following the victory won by Newcastle at Adwalton a month earlier; only Hull held out. The King therefore controlled a larger area than he had done before and was well placed to add to the number of his adherents and to increase economic pressure on London. At the same time both Houses of Parliament were greatly discouraged and a strong faction existed which wanted to negotiate an end to the war.

But it is doubtful whether Charles was in a position to take London by force. His own army was scarcely strong enough to defeat Essex and assault the extensive defence works around the capital on its own and Newcastle, for all his successes, was not prepared to bring his army to join the King whilst Parliament retained Hull. Indeed Sir Philip Warwick, whom the King had sent to sound Newcastle out, was of the opinion that he dreaded the thought of merging his army with that of the King or Prince Rupert.[1] Likewise Prince Maurice with the Cornish foot was needed to consolidate the Royalist position in the south-west and would be in no position to reinforce the King's army for some time: certainly not until Plymouth was captured.

The King was therefore obliged to continue with the policy decided on at the start of the year, i.e. first, to enlarge his armies and continue to extend the areas under his control and second, to negotiate when military success or economic pressure put him in a strong enough position to do so.

From the King's point of view the pursuit of this policy presented problems. For one thing the Queen and her circle were openly opposed to making concessions to rebels which not only undermined efforts to negotiate a settlement, but also made it harder to get prominent Parliamentarians to change sides. Another problem was that gaining adherents and negotiating successfully depended on countering Parliamentary claims that the King relied heavily on Roman Catholics, was sympathetic to them and was planning to introduce hordes of Roman Catholic Irishmen into the country to fight for him. The presence of the Roman Catholic Queen and the fact that there were a number of Roman Catholic officers in the King's army tended to give weight to this claim. If Parliament could lay its hands on firm evidence regarding the King's plans for Ireland, his cause would suffer a considerable setback. He was therefore obliged to restrict knowledge of his intentions in this matter to a small circle which even excluded one of his two Secretaries of State, Nicholas, and his Chancellor of the Exchequer, Hyde.[2]

Partly for this reason and partly because it suited his temperament, the King became ever more inclined to deal with different groups of advisers for different aspects of his business, very few people being privy to all his activities. There had always been an abundance of intrigue amongst the Royalists as individuals strove to outmanoeuvre one another and it increased significantly after the Queen's arrival at Oxford. Not only could she be used to gain favours from the King, but she also provided a focus for those who wanted to undermine the influence of Falkland and Hyde on the one hand or of Rupert on the other, in order to promote their own interests.

On the face of it Rupert's position as effective leader of the Royalist army seemed impregnable after his string of victories but, close as he was to the King, he was only directly concerned with one aspect of the King's business. Throughout the summer Rupert had continued to alienate certain individuals, in the same way as he had continued to add to the large number of his devoted followers. But as the scope for intrigue at Oxford increased so did his enemies become better able to undermine his influence. As his influence waned, so did the fortunes of the Royalist army.

Opinion in the Royalist camp immediately after the capture of Bristol was divided. One group, consisting of some of the King's civilian advisers strongly supported by the Queen, wanted to exploit the despondency and divisions in Parliament by an immediate advance on London. Another group, which included some of the senior army officers, wanted to capture Gloucester so as to eliminate the threat to their rear, open communications along the Severn between Bristol, Worcester and Shrewsbury, give direct access to the iron foundries in the Forest of Dean and facilitate the movement of men recruited by Lord Herbert in South Wales to the King's army.[3] Rupert does not seem to have been enthusiastic about either of these alternatives: he felt that the army should be concentrated around Oxford and that an advance against Essex should follow a short period of reorganisation. But he was pre-pared to back the capture of Gloucester provided that the job was done quickly.

At Bristol on 3 August the King presided at a council of war at which the decision was made to take Gloucester, partly at least because it was thought that there would be little resistance. The Parliamentary Governor, Edward Massey, formerly the lieutenant colonel of Lord Stamford's regiment, was a young professional soldier who, although a Presbyterian, was not thought to have any strong commitment to Parliament. In the past he had served under Will Legge, to whom he sent a message to the effect that he would probably surrender if the King appeared in person outside the city with a sufficiently strong force. He also sent pessimistic messages to Parliament saying that the weakness of the garrison and the delapidated state of the defences made it unlikely that he could hold out for long and that a relief force should be sent at once if Gloucester was to be saved. But Massey was a fine commander who exuded confidence and inspired both the garrison and the citizens. It is not now clear whether his overtures to the Royalists were genuine, or whether they were merely designed to gain time, but when the King summoned the city to surrender, he was firmly rebuffed.

It was now essential to take Gloucester as quickly as possible, that is to say by storm, but the King, distressed by the losses at Bristol, decided on a regular siege. Rupert, who wanted to reassert his grip on the Royalist horse, declined to take command of the siege, as a result of which Lord Forth was brought in to do the job. In the event, although Rupert made one or two brief visits to the garrisons around Oxford, his interest in the siege and his desire to get the job finished ensured that he spent much of his time there. It is recorded that he took part in the initial reconnaissance and that soon afterwards he spent the night in the trenches that were being pushed forward towards the walls. It is also recorded that on one occasion he was narrowly missed by a grenade and that on another he was hit on the head by a stone hurled down from the walls, having returned from visiting Oxford with the King early that morning.

There were two reasons for this visit to Oxford. Ostensibly the King went there to discuss the situation in Scotland with those of his advisers who were not with the army besieging Gloucester. A few days earlier Montrose had arrived outside Gloucester with news that Argyll and other leading Covenanters had decided to throw in their lot with the English Parliament and send an army into England. Montrose rode to Oxford with the King and Prince Rupert, but in the discussions that followed the King discounted his information as it ran counter to the assurances given earlier to the Queen by the Duke of Hamilton to the effect that he would be able to keep Scotland neutral, at least until the end of 1643.[4]

The other reason for the visit was for the King to reassure the Queen that Rupert was not trying to undermine her influence with him, as she had been led to believe. In the event the result was the opposite of that intended. A few days earlier three prominent Parliamentary supporters arrived in Oxford to make their submission to the King. They were the Earl of Holland, a brother of the Earl of Warwick, the Earl of Bedford, who in the early months of the war had been, in name at least, the Parliamentary General of Horse, and the Earl of Clare. To gain the adherence of those supporting Parliament was a prime Royalist objective and in this context the arrival of the three earls was a major event. It was important that the King should receive them warmly and harness their influence to his cause. But the Queen was opposed to him even seeing them. Rupert was determined that he should do so and personally brought the earls into the royal presence to make their submission, which Charles accepted with obvious reluctance. This event, above all else, turned the Queen's resentment of Rupert's influence into outright hostility.

In London depression resulting from the loss of Bristol was easing, thanks largely to Pym's resolute leadership. Soon there was a move to put Waller in charge of a force to relieve Gloucester. Despite his defeat at Roundway Down, Waller retained the support of a number of influential people who were inspired by his optimism and activity which were in such marked contrast to the attitude of Essex. But Essex, who was jealous of his own authority and wary of Waller's over-confidence, decided to lead the relief force himself.

As early as 2 August Essex had redeployed some of his army to the north-east of Oxford, a fact that had been reported to Rupert by Wilmot at the time. At the end of the month Essex took five regiments of foot and one of horse from the London trained bands to reinforce his army which, together with some smaller reinforcements collected during the ensuing march, brought it up to about 15,000 men. With this force he moved in a wide sweep north of Oxford to Brackley and then west through Stow-on-the-Wold to Cheltenham. Although Wilmot harassed him from the rear and Rupert tried unsuccessfully to cut off and destroy his advanced guard in the hills between Stow and Cheltenham, the Royalists made no serious attempt to bring him to battle: they were reluctant to do so while Gloucester remained in enemy hands behind them. As Essex arrived at Cheltenham the King ordered the abandonment of the siege and moved his army to Painswick, about six miles to the south-east. Essex marched into Gloucester on 8 September.

The arrival of Essex's army in Gloucester opened up a new opportunity for the Royalists, who were once again well placed to get between Essex and his London base as they had been in the days before Edgehill. If they could bring him to battle and defeat him, London would genuinely be at their mercy, as Essex had most of the London trained bands with him. All would depend on the King's ability to outmanoeuvre and fight him under favourable circumstances. It was a time for quick decisions and resolute, energetic action.

Essex was well aware of the danger. On 12 September he left Gloucester, moving north along the west bank of the River Severn in the hope of persuading the King that he intended to return to London via Stow and Brackley as he had come, or possibly even to take Worcester. The King responded by moving his army north into the country between Evesham and Pershore so as to be in a position to bring Essex to battle whichever of these two courses he adopted. But although the King's move was sensible, he was depressed by his failure to take Gloucester[5] and lethargic as a result of the cold wet weather: he showed no signs of being elated at the chance of striking a decisive blow. In short his mood was neither energetic nor resolute.

On the afternoon of 15 September, Essex was at Tewkesbury and sent some men to the north as though to move on Worcester. But as soon as darkness fell he crossed the River Severn and moved

his army as fast as possible in a south-easterly direction through
the Cotswolds. Despite pouring rain, his leading regiments reached
Cirencester early on 16 September, where they surprised and captured the Royalist garrison together with a large quantity of food,
powder and shot that had been moved there from Bristol for the
use of the King's army. Essex's plan was to move along the axis
Swindon–Newbury and thence down the main road to London.

Early on the morning of 16 September Rupert got wind of
Essex's move and sent to the King for permission to set off in
pursuit. But the King, who had heard nothing to confirm Rupert's
information, was not yet prepared to sanction the move. Meanwhile Rupert ordered the Royalist horse to concentrate on Broadway Down, some six miles south of the main Royalist army. At
this time Rupert would also have started to plan the pursuit, working out lines of march for each of his brigades and allocating
priorities between them at bottlenecks such as the centres of towns
or bridges and fords over rivers. The commissary general was
responsible for collecting guides to travel with each of the columns,
as the few maps that existed were of too general a nature to be
useful for navigating across open country. It was the job of brigade
and regimental commanders to arrange for detachments to scout
ahead of their columns to discover the whereabouts of the enemy
and to prevent unforeseen attack.[6]

To start with, there must have been much movement in the
assembly area at Broadway as the regiments arrived and moved to
where they would be best placed to start the pursuit. Gradually
the men would have settled down to rest their horses and prepare
meals, with perhaps the leading regiments in each brigade remaining saddled up in order to get off to a flying start. All ranks would
have been impatient to get moving as they waited uncomfortably
in the mud and rain.

By 6 p.m. Rupert, who realised that every hour's delay made it
less likely that the Royalists would be able to bring Essex to battle,
could contain himself no longer and set off with one officer and a
page to look for the King: for some reason he had not been told
where the King intended spending the night. Eventually in the dusk
he saw a light in a house window and cautiously approached to
discover whether the inmates could give him directions as to where
the King was staying. Looking through the window he saw the
King himself sitting at a table playing cards with Lord Percy, the
General of Artillery, while Lord Forth looked on.

The contrast between the intense sense of urgency felt by Rupert and the apparent lack of interest shown by the King must have tested Rupert's temper to the full. He insisted that the horse should move at once, through the night, to make contact with Essex, in order to delay him and give time for the rest of the army to arrive. Both Forth and Percy maintained that this was too dangerous, although their reasons are not recorded. They may have felt that part or all of the horse might bump into the whole Parliamentary army and suffer severe casualties, or possibly that Essex might double back and confront the King who, without the horse, would be unable to beat off his attack. In the end the King agreed with Rupert's proposals and gave orders that 1,000 musketeers should move ahead of the main body to support the horse. Within minutes Rupert was on his way back to Broadway and the pursuit of Essex's army began.

Something of Rupert's urgency must have communicated itself to the King because, once on the move, the Royalist foot made good time despite the awful weather. By the evening of 17 September Rupert, who was moving parallel to Essex and about ten miles to the east of him, reached Stamford-in-the-Vale some four miles beyond Faringdon. Essex, despite the initial speed of his march, had only got to Swindon: he had been obliged to slow down to give his army a chance to forage for food as they had already used the rations captured at Cirencester on the previous day. That same evening the King, with the main body of the Royalist army, moved into the area around Burford.

Next morning Rupert heard from a scouting party led by Sir John Urry that Essex was moving down the road from Swindon to Newbury, which he intended to reach that evening. Riding with Byron's brigade, which was leading the advance, he came on Essex's column in the vicinity of Aldbourne Chase some five miles to the north-west of Hungerford. At this time Essex had about 4,000 horse and 10,000 foot with him but they were strung out on the line of march and apparently unaware of Rupert's close proximity. Rupert, who had about 5,000 horse with him, decided to attack at once and launched his forward brigades at the rear of Essex's column, leaving the rear brigade under Charles Gerrard to bring on his 1,000 musketeers as soon as possible. Although taken by surprise, the Parliamentary foot and horse worked well together and eventually beat off Rupert's attack although not without considerable loss. But the attack had the desired effect in that it delayed Essex, who decided to close on Hungerford for the night and advance on Newbury next morning keeping the River Kennet

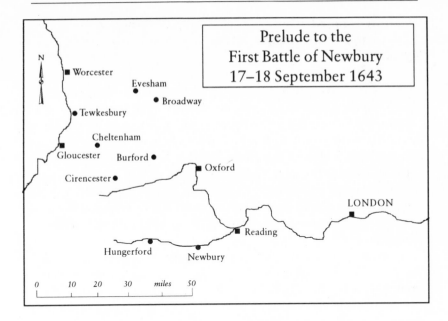

Prelude to the
First Battle of Newbury
17–18 September 1643

between himself and Rupert's marauding horse. He also pushed some troops of horse together with quartermasters and billeting parties forward to Newbury so that his sodden troops would be accommodated under cover when they arrived next day.

Meanwhile the King had reached Wantage. On the morning of 19 September Rupert, who had collected his brigades together during the night, rode with his whole force into Newbury, scattering the Parliamentary troops of horse and capturing some of the billeting parties in the process. He was now in a position to hold off any advanced guard that Essex could get to Newbury until the King arrived. Essex was cut off from London and would have to fight a battle or starve. For the moment all he could do was to move forward with his senior commanders and work out how to deploy his army to the west of the town when it arrived. Rupert must also have considered how the King's army should deploy when it arrived.

Newbury lay along the banks of the River Kennet. To the south of it, the ground rose gently in a series of small fields and hedges for about a mile until it reached a plateau. In places on the plateau such as Wash Common and Endbourne Heath the ground was relatively open. On the northern edge of the plateau, a mile and a half west of the town, a small ridge or spur jutted northwards into the lower ground. This has been known by historians as Round Hill because of the impression that it gave to those on the lower ground below.

Because Essex was advancing from Hungerford along the south bank of the river, the Royalist army was pushed through Newbury as it arrived during the afternoon of 19 September and was deployed in the small fields about a mile to the west of the town on a line from north to south between the river and the plateau. At some stage during the afternoon Rupert sent a body of horse on to the plateau to keep enemy patrols away and to give warning of any attempt by the enemy to occupy it, but it seems that little emphasis was placed on this area, presumably because the Royalist leaders were expecting that the battle would be fought over the lower ground to the north.

Essex's army consisted of fourteen regiments of horse amounting to 4,000 men, divided into two wings under Sir Philip Stapleton and Colonel John Middleton. His 10,000 foot consisted of his own four brigades together with the London trained bands and auxiliaries which constituted half of the total. Philip Skippon was Essex's major general of foot and the man responsible for preparing the trained bands for war. Essex had about twenty guns in his artillery train.

The Royalist army, which had been reinforced from Oxford during the past few days, consisted of some 6,000 horse and 8,000 foot. The horse were organised into five brigades under Rupert, Wilmot, John Byron, the Earl of Carnarvon and Charles Gerrard. The foot, which consisted of a large number of under-strength regiments, was divided into four brigades under Nicholas Byron, Belasyse, Gilbert Gerrard and William Vavasour. It is thought that the Royalists had about the same number of cannon as their opponents.

There was a meeting of the war council on the evening of 19 September at which Rupert recommended that Essex should be left to launch the attack. He argued that the Royalists could be replenished from Oxford and Wallingford and had in any case captured the supplies collected by the people of Newbury for the Parliamentary army, whereas Essex's army would either have to fight its way through the strong positions that the Royalists were preparing, or break up in search of food. In addition the Royalists were short of powder and shot and should if possible wait until further supplies were received from Oxford. But Rupert's view was opposed by many of those present who had a low opinion of the

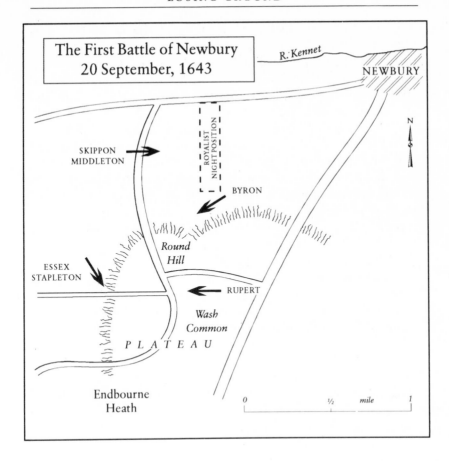

The First Battle of Newbury
20 September, 1643

enemy and who considered that they would collapse in the face of a determined attack. One authority maintains that the Queen had joined the King at Newbury and strongly supported this contention and that the King overruled Rupert.[7] Others maintain that the King decided to wait for Essex to attack.[8]

In the event it was Essex who dictated the way in which the battle would be fought. As soon as he saw the Royalist army drawn up in the fields to the south of the Kennet he realised that he would not be able to batter his way through to Newbury. Instead he planned to get up on to the plateau, thereby turning the Royalists' left flank and putting himself in a position to continue his advance to Reading along the lanes to the south of the river even if he failed to win an outright victory over the King's forces. He accordingly gave Skippon Middleton's horse and two brigades of foot who were to deploy opposite the Royalists in the fields below the plateau. Their task was to hold any attack in that area and also to capture the spur known as Round Hill. Essex would command the other two brigades which, with Stapleton's horse, would advance on to the plateau itself. The London trained bands and auxiliaries would be held in reserve.

As it was getting dark the Parliamentary forces noticed that the Royalist horse on the plateau had not physically occupied Round Hill, and during the night Skippon pushed forward most of his right-hand brigade with two light guns on to that position. At 5 a.m. the two brigades under Essex also moved forward and established themselves on the plateau at Wash Common.

As it got light on 20 September, the Royalists realised that they had no option but to attack in order to restore the situation. Sir John Byron was given the task of turning Skippon's men off Round Hill with two regiments of horse and Sir Nicholas Byron's brigade of foot. Rupert was given the task of attacking Essex's two brigades on Wash Common with most of the remaining horse and 1,000 commanded musketeers: probably the ones that had been allotted to him when he left Broadway Down.

Accounts of the ensuing battle are so diverse and contradictory as to make any reliable description of it impossible. Because of the broken nature of the ground, no one could see much of what was going on, with the result that eyewitness accounts do not tally and even people like Hyde and Warwick, who tried to write down what happened in the lifetime of many of those involved, failed to produce a coherent account of events.

In outline it would seem that Rupert succeeded in pushing Essex's two brigades back from the open ground on Wash Common into the small hedged fields on the edge of the plateau, but despite innumerable assaults he was unable entirely to break through and disperse their pikemen. He also occupied the area of Wash Common leading to Round Hill and established a battery of guns which caused many casualties to the Parliamentary forces there. Byron also mounted many assaults on Round Hill, but was unable to evict the enemy. Although his own two regiments behaved with the utmost gallantry they were badly supported by his uncle's brigade of foot. Nothing is known of events in the close country to the north of the plateau except for the fact that at one stage Skippon tried unsuccessfully to get some men across the Kennet in order to turn the Royalists' northern flank.

When darkness fell it was clear that most of the advantage lay with the Royalists, who had pressed the enemy back on both flanks and gravely weakened him in the centre despite the fact that they had not captured Round Hill. Both Rupert and Byron were of the opinion that if the King held his ground throughout the night, he would find Essex too exhausted to renew the fight in the morning.[9] But the Royalists were down to their last ten barrels of gunpowder and the King gave way to Lord Percy and others who urged him to break off the battle. During the night the Royalist army withdrew through Newbury towards Oxford. In the morning Essex was amazed to find them gone and was able to continue his journey towards Reading.

Rupert himself must have had a frustrating battle as the terrain prevented him from mounting the great whirlwind charges that had always hitherto broken the enemy's resistance. Instead he had to organise a series of assaults on Stapleton's horse who resisted strongly and retreated behind positions manned by pikemen when the pressure became too much for them. At the same time Rupert had to dislodge the enemy foot as best he could with his horse and such musketeers as he could muster. Right across the battlefield the Parliamentary foot fought stubbornly, especially the London trained bands who were moved forward to reinforce the line as required. As usual Rupert, who was in the thick of the fighting all day, seemed to bear a charmed life. At one point he was standing with a group of officers when a lone Parliamentary horseman rode up and fired at him at point blank range, the bullet glancing off his helmet. It transpired that his assailant was Sir Philip Stapleton in person, who also in some mysterious manner survived the encounter.

A number of other leading Royalists were less fortunate, including the Earls of Carnarvon and Sunderland who were both killed. Even more significant was the fact that Lord Falkland was missing. Although one of the King's Secretaries of State, he had insisted, as at Edgehill, on riding as a volunteer and had attached himself to Byron's regiment of horse. In the first assault on Round Hill he had charged at a gap in a hedge in a most reckless fashion and was not seen again. When darkness fell, Rupert, who had sent a message to Essex asking for news of him, heard that he was dead. Afterwards the rumour went around that Falkland had been seeking death because he was upset with the inability of the two sides to reach an agreement, but Hyde, who was his great friend, maintained that his determination to expose himself in battle was designed to show that his efforts to negotiate an end to the fighting had nothing to do with a reluctance to hazard his person.

Despite intense fatigue, Rupert stayed in the saddle during the night following the battle, collecting together a body of horse with which to harass Essex's army. Next morning, as the bulk of the Royalists trudged north to Oxford, he sprang an ambush near Aldermaston which succeeded in killing a considerable number of the enemy. But Essex continued to Reading, which he evacuated when he moved on to London. Rupert finally returned to Oxford, leaving a garrison in Donnington Castle just north of Newbury as he went.

There can be no doubt that the battle of Newbury was as decisive a defeat for the Royalists as Edgehill had been for Parliament. Although the capture of Bristol had greatly increased the strength of the Royalist hand in terms of negotiating a settlement, it did not of itself enable the King to dictate terms to his opponents. By heading off Essex at Newbury, Rupert had given the King an opportunity to win a battle that would have decided the war. In retrospect we can see that it was the King's last chance of winning an outright victory.

But the circumstances prevailing at Newbury were not as favourable as those at Edgehill from a military point of view. The Royalist horse was superior to the Parliamentary horse both in terms of quantity and quality, but the ground gave the advantage to foot soldiers and in this respect Essex's army had the advantage. Furthermore the initial Royalist failure to extend their line to the south and secure the plateau enabled Essex to turn their flank and obliged the King to withdraw men from his main position and commit them piecemeal to attacks on this important ground. The King undoubtedly made a second error in abandoning the contest after the first day. Although his powder was low, he had won an advantage in the fighting and, given the nature of the ground, could almost certainly have held Essex until more powder arrived. Even if Essex had broken through to Reading during the second day, the King would have been no worse off.

The fact is that the conduct of the campaign after the capture of Bristol lacked drive. It could be argued that the King was so confident of negotiating a satisfactory settlement that his chief interest was to save life and minimise risk, but it is more likely that the pressure of court intrigue caused him to listen to even more views than usual and dulled his ability to decide between them.

Rupert's performance was also less impressive than usual. Had it not been for his unnecessary dispute with Hertford after the capture of Bristol, the King need never have become so closely involved with the operations of what was still Rupert's task force: Rupert could probably have taken Gloucester or returned direct to Oxford as he pleased. By declining to take charge of the siege of Gloucester when the King overruled his recommendation that it should be carried by storm, he gave the King no alternative but to summon Forth and Percy from Oxford and take command of the army himself. When Essex relieved Gloucester and then gave the King the slip on his way home, Rupert restored the situation by a fast and well-organised pursuit. Against this he must, as the first senior officer to arrive at Newbury, bear a share of the responsibility for the Royalists' failure to secure the plateau, in the absence of evidence that he wanted to do it and was overruled. Needless to say, his performance in the battle itself was first class, as also was his assessment of the situation afterwards and his energetic follow-up next morning.

An unusual aspect of the campaign was that both Essex and his army operated with uncharacteristic efficiency. His strategy was well thought out and executed with drive. Furthermore his foot and his horse co-operated well together and both fought with a determination that had not been seen in Parliamentary armies up to that time. For once Essex deserved the enthusiastic reception that he got on his return to London.

While failure to overcome Essex at Newbury had destroyed the King's chances of defeating his enemies at a blow, a number of other events were taking place that would have equally harmful effects on Royalist fortunes in the long term.

The first of these was the entry into the war of the Scots on the side of Parliament. This followed an agreement reached between the English Parliament and the Scots under which the Scots undertook to send an army into England on condition that Parliament reformed the religion of England in accordance with 'the word of God and the example of the best Reformed Churches'.[10] This agreement had been worked out in Edinburgh by a Parliamentary delegation headed by Sir Henry Vane, whose father had been ambassador to Gustavus Adolphus in the winter of 1631–2 and later one of the King's Secretaries of State. It was ratified in London on 25 September when both Lords and Commons swore to uphold the Covenant. Although the Scots took the agreement to mean that Parliament would enforce the Presbyterian religion on England, the Independents, of whom Vane was one, took it to mean that all versions of the reformed religion which excluded bishops would be permitted. These events confirmed the warning brought to the King outside Gloucester by Montrose which the King had at that time rejected.

In detail the agreement stipulated that the Scots would provide an army of 18,000 foot together with 3,000 horse and an artillery train. The sixty-three-year-old Alexander Leslie, now Earl of Leven, was once again appointed to the chief command. His general of horse was David Leslie, who was also a veteran of Gustavus Adolphus's army and the younger son of a Fifeshire knight, unrelated to Leven. The English Parliament agreed to pay £30,000 a month to keep this army in the field. To direct the war a 'Committee of Both Kingdoms' was set up consisting of fourteen members of the Commons, seven members of the Lords and the Scots Commissioners in London led by Lord Maitland. This superseded the old Parliamentary Committee of Safety which had previously been the link between Parliament and its commanders in the field and which had been dominated by Essex's Presbyterian supporters such as Denzil Holles. The English component of the Committee of Both Kingdoms was led by Vane and the Solicitor General, Oliver St John, who as Independents were more critical of Essex.

While negotiations were going on to get the Scots into the war, developments were taking place in England's eastern counties that constituted a second adverse development so far as the King was concerned and would in the end exercise an even more harmful influence on his fortunes than the intervention of the Scots. From the end of 1642 Parliament, acting initially through the Earl of Warwick and his son-in-law Manchester, had been taking measures to gain control of the rich eastern counties in order to secure their wealth, farm produce, wool and fish for Parliament.

On 20 July the Parliamentary commander in Lincolnshire, Lord Willoughby of Parham, captured Gainsborough, thus threatening Newcastle's communications with Newark and the southern part of his command. Newcastle immediately ordered Sir Charles Cavendish to recapture it, but Parliament, conscious of its strategic importance, sent Sir John Meldrum from Nottingham to relieve it, which he did on 28 July, killing Cavendish in the process. Two days later Newcastle himself arrived at Grantham, defeated the Parliamentary forces and recaptured the town: he then took Lincoln and returned to Hull where Lord Fairfax had been bottled up since his defeat at Adwalton Moor.

As a result of these operations Parliament became acutely aware not only of the vulnerability of the eastern counties themselves, but also of the danger that Newcastle might pass through them and, in conjunction with the King's main army, threaten London. In August the Earl of Manchester was appointed General of the Eastern Association with orders to take under his command all forces operating under local commanders throughout the area and to raise such extra regiments as were necessary for its defence.

Initially Manchester was obliged to remain in Norfolk where he was besieging a pocket of Royalist resistance at King's Lynn but, not needing his horse for this purpose, he sent them into Lincolnshire under one of the regimental commanders, Colonel Cromwell.

Oliver Cromwell had been MP for Huntingdon in the Parliament of 1628 and for Cambridge since 1640, and was a firm supporter of Pym. Even before the King set up his standard at Nottingham, Cromwell had distinguished himself by seizing the plate of the Cambridge colleges which the King was moving to York to prevent it from falling into the hands of the rebels. Although he had no military experience and was already forty-three when the war started, he set about raising a troop of horse which was part of Essex's regiment at the time of Edgehill. Accounts vary as to Cromwell's involvement in that battle, but it would seem that his troop only arrived in time to witness the flight of most of the Parliamentary horse, which convinced him of the need to recruit better men than were to be found in most of the Parliamentary regiments at that time and to train them with care. In January Cromwell received a commission to raise a regiment of horse, which he did whilst vigorously helping Manchester to gain control of the eastern counties. He had five well-equipped and mounted troops by March and ten by September, by which time he had made a reputation for himself as a tactician in a number of small battles, including the operations around Grantham, and as a first-class trainer of men.

On his arrival in Lincolnshire Cromwell moved up to the Humber and, taking advantage of Parliament's command of the sea, pushed much-needed supplies into Hull, which was being besieged by Newcastle. At the same time Lord Fairfax shipped his son Thomas together with his surviving regiments of horse to join

Cromwell in Lincolnshire. Soon afterwards Manchester, who had succeeded in capturing Lynn, moved north to join them, bringing with him the foot regiments of the Eastern Association. On 11 October Manchester and Fairfax defeated a Royalist force from Newark at Winceby, but shortly afterwards Newcastle abandoned the siege of Hull and re-established control over the northern half of Lincolnshire, thus ensuring Royalist possession of Grantham and Newark. None the less Parliament retained firm control to the south and had, in the rapidly expanding Eastern Association army, a force that succeeded in defending the eastern counties for the rest of the war.

Like Oliver St John, who was his cousin, Cromwell was an Independent. The Independents were Puritans to the extent that they were Calvinists who wanted to do away with bishops, but they did not support the authoritarian and exclusive arrangements favoured by the Presbyterians: they wanted freedom for all Puritans to worship as they liked. But although in one sense they were more tolerant than the Presbyterians, they tended to be more earnest about their religion. In modern parlance the Presbyterians were the establishment Puritans whereas the Independents were of the charismatic or 'born again' variety. Partly as a result of Cromwell's influence, the Eastern Association horse, and to a lesser extent the Eastern Association army as a whole, developed a degree of religious commitment bordering on fanaticism that was completely different from the outlook of the officers and men in the armies of Essex or Waller. This undoubtedly made the Eastern Association forces more formidable, but as the war progressed it embittered relationships between the two sides and made a negotiated settlement more difficult to reach.

The third event which hurt the Royalists as a whole, and Rupert in particular, was the appointment by the King of George Digby to replace Falkland as one of the two Secretaries of State. The King's first choice was the Chancellor of the Exchequer, Sir Edward Hyde. Hyde declined, partly because he felt that he was insufficiently distinguished to hold such an important post and partly because he felt that his dislike and suspicion of everything French would have made his position impossible with the Queen and therefore ultimately with the King. Instead he recommended that the King should give the post to Digby who was at the time a close friend and also the Queen's first choice for the job.[11]

It is difficult to understand how someone of Hyde's good sense could have recommended a person whose judgement was to say the least mercurial and who was by nature attracted to intrigue as his preferred way of getting things done. Furthermore Digby was a firm supporter of the strong line and diametrically opposed to the policy of searching for a fair and honourable settlement with Parliament which had been consistently followed by Falkland and Hyde himself.

The fourth factor adversely affecting the Royalist position was Prince Maurice's inability to capture Plymouth in the face of a Parliamentary fleet of twenty-two ships which, from September until the end of the year, not only kept the town supplied, but also guarded it from an assault across the Tamar estuary. As a result of being tied down in the far west, Prince Maurice was unable to bring his army to support the King, so a new Royalist army under Hopton was formed to oppose Waller who, from the beginning of November, was operating independently of Lord Essex in Surrey, Sussex and Hampshire. Hopton's army consisted of about 1,500 horse and 3,000 foot.

It is doubtful whether the King's outlook in the autumn of 1643 was affected by these setbacks to any great extent. In the first place, although he must have understood the seriousness of the Scots entry into the war, he would not at that stage have recognised the menace that was building up in the Eastern Association nor would he have foreseen the havoc that Digby was destined to wreak on the Royalist war effort. Furthermore there was a piece of good news that might ultimately outweigh the damage done by Scotland's intervention. This concerned Ireland.

By mid-September Ormonde, now promoted Marquess, had succeeded in reaching an agreement with the Confederacy in accordance with the instructions given to him by the King. There was to be a ceasefire for a year during which a permanent agreement between the two sides was to be worked out. In the intervening period the authorities in Dublin would garrison the Pale with English troops while most of the rest of the country would be garrisoned by the Confederacy. The Confederacy also agreed to provide £30,000 for the use of the King.[12]

Almost immediately units of the English forces in Ireland started to return to fight for the King under whose authority they had been sent there. For the most part these were veteran regiments of foot under competent officers and were of great value to the Royalist army. Because of the threat posed by Parliament's navy, they sailed piecemeal to Royalist ports in the west of England, the majority landing between October and the following March in

Cheshire, Wales or Bristol, although two regiments landed on the south coast at Weymouth where they were incorporated into Hopton's new army, and 2,000 other men landed as far north as Carlisle.

It is difficult to know how many arrived during this period. An analysis of the principal Irish forces in England based on many contemporary sources, which lists the units concerned and the ports of arrival, reckons that the total was 12,000[13] but it does not rule out the possibility of other arrivals. Another source based on departures from Ireland[14] gives a total of over 20,000 but includes some intercepted by Parliamentary ships and a contingent of 1,600 that went to Scotland. Professor Kenyon's estimate of around 17,000[15] is probably pretty near the mark. Whatever the number, these units constituted an immensely valuable addition to the Royalist order of battle. The King himself looked on them as the advanced guard of a much larger force of Confederate Irish who he hoped would swell his ranks once a permanent peace could be secured.

When Rupert returned to Oxford after the battle of Newbury he resumed the sort of life that he had been leading before he left for Bristol. In October Essex, having rested his men and recalled some of the trained bands that had been stood down after Newbury, prepared to recapture Reading, intending to leave London on 18 October. But he was pre-empted by Rupert who left Oxford three days earlier for Northamptonshire and Bedfordshire. Sir Lewis Dyves was soon established in Newport Pagnell, which constituted a serious threat to Parliament as it cut the direct line of communication between London and Yorkshire and provided the Royalists with a jumping-off point for future operations against the Eastern Association.

This caused Essex to abandon his advance on Reading and lead a strong detachment to recapture Newport Pagnell. By this time Rupert's men had also occupied Towcester and Rupert himself was waiting at Buckingham to carry out raids against enemy detachments attacking Dyves. Unfortunately at that moment Dyves received an order from Oxford to abandon Newport Pagnell and the whole operation was called off, much to Rupert's fury. Rupert naturally demanded to know who had ordered Dyves to withdraw and it eventually turned out that it was the result of a misunderstanding of something said by the King. The King smoothed matters over by saying that in future he would be more careful when issuing orders, but from Rupert's point of view it was just one more example of courtiers frustrating his efforts. A few days later Rupert recaptured Cirencester, which had fallen to Essex on his return from Gloucester.

As the second winter of the war closed in, it is worth taking a closer look at the way business was being conducted in Oxford in order to reassess Rupert's position in the Royalist hierarchy. The war council, which the King some months later described in a letter as Rupert's council, still met regularly, dealing mainly with short-term matters of limited importance. It seldom considered overall strategy and from the middle of 1643 the King increasingly took the advice of a small group of Privy Councillors, including Digby and Richmond, which gradually superseded the war council as makers of policy. Rupert was a member of this group and when he was with the King his views carried the greatest weight.

In September the King set up another small group of advisers, including Richmond, Hyde, Culpepper and Nicholas, which met at Oriel College under the chairmanship of Lord Cottington to advise the King on the civil administration of those parts of the country under Royalist control and on foreign affairs.[16] This group did not include Rupert. Cottington had for many years been a professional diplomat and had later played an important part in the administration of the country during the eleven years of the King's personal rule. A. L. Rowse describes him as being very unfanatical, cool and good-tempered, patient, persistent and hard-working with a sly sense of humour.[17] He was a member of the war council, but spent most of his time dealing with civil adminis-tration, including the handling of the personal finances of the King's and Queen's households. This group played an important part in prosecuting the war and was not much influenced by faction and intrigue, nor did it ever deliberately exercise its influence against Rupert's designs.

In addition to these official bodies, the Queen still put pressure on the King directly and also through her supporters, many of whom were using her influence to further their own ambitions. The Queen's favourite at this time was the commander of her life guard of horse, Lord Jermyn, who played a large part in making her influence felt. He was an affable forty-year-old, who was unprincipled in pursuit of comfort and wealth, but loyal to the Queen throughout the war and during her subsequent exile. As the months went by the Queen's resentment of Rupert seems to

have cooled down, but Rupert remained suspicious of her intentions and took no trouble to ingratiate himself with her.

Rupert's concern that the King would alter plans agreed between
them as soon as his back was turned, was at this time accentuated
by the growing hostility that he felt existed towards him. Some
authors have suggested that he was developing a persecution complex,[18] but there is no doubt that he had grounds for his misgivings.
Digby was only one of a group which included Wilmot, Percy and
the Paymaster General, John Ashburnham, all of whom were hostile to him to the extent of undermining his influence and making
life difficult for him when they could. Also some of the older men,
such as Culpepper and Hertford, strongly objected to his roughshod ways and Hyde still thought of him as a warmonger despite
the fact that the Queen and her circle criticised him for being too
conciliatory. Finally there was opposition to him from a few of
the more senior regimental officers who felt that he demanded too
much of them considering the lack of money and supplies under
which they laboured.

But Rupert received more help from his friends than damage
from his detractors. Next to the King himself his most important
supporter was the Duke of Richmond who, with the exception of
a few weeks at the end of 1643 when he was on a mission in
France, was always close to the King and diligent in countering
any hostility towards Rupert in court or council. And in this he
was backed by his wife, who was equally devoted to Rupert's
interests. Another influential friend was Digby's fellow Secretary
of State, Sir Edward Nicholas, who was as constant in his friendship as Richmond himself. Surprisingly perhaps, in view of the
difference in their outlook, Rupert had another friend in Jermyn
who was probably instrumental to some extent in abating the
Queen's hostility.

Within the army Rupert retained a solid core of supporters
amongst the senior officers including Forth, Astley, Hopton, the
Byrons, the Gerrards and Aston, and virtually all the junior officers
were fervent admirers. Of all his officers, the one he most relied
on and who had already become his closest friend, apart from his
brother Maurice, was the major of his regiment, Will Legge. Sir
Richard Crane, in command of his life guard, was another constant
and trusted companion. Finally the shared dangers, privations and
hardships of his frequent journeys around the country would have
brought him close to the inner circle of officers, pages and troopers
who attended him personally, despite normal social barriers. The

comradeship of these people should not be underestimated, as any-one who has experienced such conditions must know. They would have provided him with an inner sanctum into which he could escape from the irritations of high command.

With such strong support any logical assessment would have shown him that his position was secure. But logic alone could not free him from the emotions generated by the pressures of his immensely demanding job. For a man who was still only twenty-three it was natural to feel resentment towards those who carped at him despite the consistent soundness of his military advice and the success that had attended all his operations. Nothing like this had happened to him in the past. Throughout his early campaigns he had been petted and fêted by his own side, and when he was released from his long captivity he was openly admired by his enemies from the Emperor downwards. Now after fifteen months of herculean effort and continuous victory he found himself criti-cised by those who had most reason to praise him. Perhaps he had not realised that military success and the ability to inspire intense devotion can also arouse jealousy.

And there were more respectable reasons for complaint. For example, in the early days of the war Rupert was one of the few people in high places who knew much about the mechanics of making war, as a result of which his views were accepted without much question. Now every nobleman who had raised a regiment and taken part in a few skirmishes thought that he knew at least enough to have his opinion heard. But Rupert was always in a hurry, paying scant attention to their ideas and making no con-cession to their desire to contribute towards his plans. All he wanted was obedience to his well thought out instructions. A dif-ferent sort of person might have realised that some at least of those who were sniping at him would have responded enthusiastically had he turned to them for help. As it was, their hostility merely made him more remote.

To add to Rupert's worries, Prince Maurice fell ill outside Ply-mouth in October and nearly died. Rupert sent his own physician to look after him. The story goes that one day word was brought to Rupert of Maurice's death, but that he refused to believe it. Shortly afterwards reports started to arrive that Maurice was on the mend and by the end of the month it was clear that he was going to recover.

It would seem that at about this time Rupert added to his per-sonal difficulties by falling in love with the Duchess of Richmond.

Unlike many of his contemporaries, Rupert was very discreet about his love life, but there can be little doubt of his devotion to this beautiful and strong-willed creature who was three years younger than himself and who had been brought up by the King and Queen after the murder of her father, Buckingham. On the other hand there is no evidence to back the contention, put about by Parliamentary propagandists and others, that she became his mistress. Rupert remained firm friends with both the Duke and the Duchess throughout the war and it is most unlikely that, with his exaggerated sense of honour, he would have carried on a clandestine affair with his friend's wife. Furthermore it is most unlikely that he could have done so without being discovered, as the Duchess was as indiscreet as Rupert was careful. Certainly, if the utterly strait-laced Richmond had discovered such a thing, he would have broken off all personal contact with Rupert. The likelihood is that Rupert was in love but managed to control himself. If true, this would have added considerably to the pressures under which he was working.

Altogether Rupert was probably not enjoying himself much as the nights drew in that winter. But he was as busy as ever, organising raids against Essex's outposts and arranging for the reception of the troops from Ireland as well as carrying out his business as General of Horse. One of the decisions reached by the King at the end of October, with which Rupert concurred, was that Lord Byron with another detachment of troops from Oxford should take over command in the north-west from Lord Capel, who was based at Shrewsbury but who had been notably unsuccessful against the local Parliamentary forces. Byron was to secure the north-west and cover the deployment of the troops from Ireland. As Rupert had been given responsibility for this area following his capture of Lichfield the previous March, it fell to him to issue Byron's commission and draw up his instructions.

A number of important events took place in the final weeks of 1643 and the early days of 1644 which must be mentioned before describing Rupert's next venture. The first concerns Hopton's force, which started well by occupying Alton in Hampshire and Arundel Castle in Sussex. But Hopton over-extended himself and in December Waller surprised and defeated a Royalist detachment at Alton and recaptured Arundel so that by the end of the year Hopton was back where he started, having suffered significant losses. In order to restore the situation he was sent further reinforcements from the Oxford army together with Lord Forth to help him, as he was still not fully recovererd from the wounds he had received the previous summer.

The next significant event was the death of John Pym whose dominance of Parliament passed into the hands of St John and Vane despite the fact that, numerically speaking, the Presbyterians remained in the majority.

The third event was the arrival at Oxford from Scotland of the newly promoted Duke of Hamilton who was expecting to be thanked for trying to keep Scotland out of the war. But the King had at last realised that Hamilton had been running with the hare every bit as strongly as he had been hunting with the hounds so he committed him to prison. Charles now turned to Montrose who, with the backing of the Earls of Aboyne and Antrim, both of whom were with the King, made a plan for the recovery of Scotland. This plan required Montrose to raise troops in the north of England and to take them into south-west Scotland where he would be joined by 10,000 of Antrim's Macdonnells shipped over from Ireland. Even if this combined force proved too weak to achieve its aim in full, it might at least bring about the withdrawal of some units of the Scottish army when it moved into England. It is difficult to know what part Rupert played in the planning of this enterprise, but he would certainly have been involved in the raising of troops for Montrose, especially as they included a regiment of horse.

Finally, in the north-west Byron started well by defeating the Parliamentary commander Brereton at Middlewich. Brereton fled to Manchester leaving most of his men beseiged by Byron in Nantwich. But early in the New Year Sir Thomas Fairfax, who had recently recaptured Grantham, made a spectacular sortie across the country for the purpose of relieving Nantwich. This place was strategically important to Parliament because forces based there could interfere with the deployment of Royalist troops from Ireland landed at Chester. Fairfax joined Brereton at Manchester and together they marched through deep snow to Nantwich. On 25 January, assisted by a sortie from the besieged town, they inflicted a disastrous defeat on Byron who only managed to extricate his horse. All his foot, which included two complete regiments recently arrived from Ireland, were killed or captured. Amongst the prisoners was Colonel Monk who spent the rest of the war in the Tower of London. As these operations were taking place the Scots army crossed the border and pushed into Northumberland.

It was now essential for the Royalists to restore the position in the north-west. Only if the whole area could be made safe for the arrival of troops from Ireland, and for the raising of recruits from Wales and the western counties, would it be possible to build up forces strong enough to reinforce Newcastle and contain the Scots. By the end of January the King decided that Rupert was the only person capable of carrying out this task.

Earlier in the month Rupert had come near to being captured when told by a spy that the Parliamentary Governor of Aylesbury was prepared to admit his troops into the town. Rupert took some men from Oxford and was met outside the town by a young guide who told him to come in at once as the Governor was ready for him. But Rupert was suspicious as he had stipulated that he should be met by the Governor's brother. Having talked to the boy for some time he discovered that it was a trap. He sent the spy under guard to Oxford to be hanged, but Digby arranged for him to be pardoned.

At about this time the King made Rupert Duke of Cumberland and Earl of Holderness so as to give him a seat in the House of Lords. For propaganda reasons Charles had recently arranged for a duplicate Parliament, consisting of those members loyal to him, to meet at Oxford. When it was decided that Rupert should take over in the north-west, he was also made President of Wales which gave him authority over the Marquess of Worcester and Lord Herbert in the south, as well as over Capel and Byron in the north. In addition he was given a new commission as Captain General of Cheshire, Lancashire, Worcestershire and Shropshire with power to appoint commissioners to recruit and raise taxes. Rupert left Oxford early in February on the same day that Montrose left for York *en route* for Scotland. Rupert established his headquarters at Shrewsbury a few days later.

8

NORTHERN VENTURE

RUPERT TOOK WITH HIM to Shrewsbury his life guard, his regiment
of horse and his regiment of foot, and immediately set about building up a worthwhile army. Historians have always credited Rupert
with being good at attracting recruits and preparing his units for
battle[1] and on this occasion he excelled himself in the speed and
energy with which he went about the business. Within a few weeks,
by dint of much travelling and his usual combination of threats
and encouragement, he had resuscitated the remains of the units
formerly commanded by Byron, the majority of which had come
from Ireland, and visited many of the Royalist garrisons in the
process.

For some weeks before leaving Oxford, Rupert had been corre-
sponding regularly with Ormonde over the despatch and reception
of troops from Ireland. The closeness of their co-operation, which
was made easier by the fact that they shared an Oxford agent,
Arthur Trevor, now increased despite a mischievous letter sent by
Digby to Ormonde suggesting that Ormonde rather than Rupert
should have been given the command in the north-west, an option
that the King had considered before appointing Rupert. But
Ormonde replied that he thought Rupert best fitted for the appointment and he continued to push across to him every man that he
could spare.

Parliament naturally objected to the Royalists being reinforced
in this way, and insisted on describing the men in the units that
had been in Ireland as Irish, even though most of them were English. None the less there must have been a number of Irishmen
amongst them who would have been recruited initially to bring
the units up to strength and later to replace those lost over the
months from wounds, sickness and death. That this number represented a significant proportion of the regiments concerned can
be seen from the fact that the total returning to England was in

excess of the numbers that left these shores in the first place. Certainly many of the King's civilian supporters objected to the arrival of the Irishmen almost as strongly as the Parliamentarians, so great was the prejudice against them as a result of the atrocity stories that had been circulating since the uprising.[2] By contrast some Royalist military commanders, including Rupert, found them to be more reliable than the Englishmen in the units, many of whom would have preferred to fight for Parliament and some of whom deserted at the first opportunity.

Parliamentary propagandists naturally made good use of the arrival of the Irish units to discredit the King, whilst their ships intercepted as many as they could on passage, casting men they regarded as Irish into the sea to drown. To discourage those that did arrive from fighting for the King, Parliament decreed that all members of Irish regiments were to be hanged out of hand if captured. As a result, in early March, the Parliamentary Governor of Nantwich hanged thirteen of Rupert's men in defiance of all the rules of war. Rupert immediately hanged thirteen of his prisoners as a reprisal and sent a fourteenth with a letter to Essex saying that in future he would kill two for every one of his men hanged. Essex replied, asking whether he had any authority for this, to which Rupert said that he did it as a soldier and not by any particular direction. Although Parliament did not rescind their order, most of their commanders ceased to involve themselves in such an infamous procedure and much blood was thereby saved.

During this period Rupert was receiving urgent requests from Lord Derby to move north into Lancashire to restore the situation there. Although Derby had managed to contain the Parliamentarians in Manchester up to the end of 1643, Fairfax and Brereton had turned the tables on him since their victory at Nantwich. Derby was particularly worried about his wife, a cousin of Rupert's, who was being beseiged at Lathom House. But a more serious threat developed at the end of February when the Parliamentary commander for Nottinghamshire, Sir John Meldrum, with a force of 2,000 horse and 5,000 foot, laid siege to Newark. Hastings, now Lord Loughborough, was still the Royalist commander in the Midlands, but he had been obliged to weaken his garrisons in order to send reinforcements to the Marquess of Newcastle in the face of the Scots invasion. He was therefore unable to put together sufficient men to attack Meldrum and save Newark, which was of great importance to the Royalists as a link between Oxford and the north.

On 7 March the King asked Rupert to do what he could to help as soon as possible; Rupert sent some preliminary instructions to Loughborough, asking him amongst other things to send 700 horses to Bridgnorth to assist in the rapid movement of some musketeers when the time was ripe. On 12 March the King wrote again, telling Rupert to collect together what forces he could and to march to the relief of Newark without delay. Rupert was at Chester when this order reached him late on Wednesday, 13 March and he immediately sent Legge to Shrewsbury to collect as many musketeers as he could from the garrison there and despatch them to Bridgnorth. Rupert himself, with his own regiment of horse, a contingent from another regiment and three pieces of artillery, met up with these musketeers at Bridgnorth on 15 March. There were 1,100 of them, commanded by Colonel Henry Tillier, a veteran professional who was colonel of one of the foot regiments from Ireland. The speed with which they got to Bridgnorth was due to the fact that Legge had despatched them down the Severn in barges.

Rupert marched via Wolverhampton and Lichfield to Ashby, collecting additional men from the garrisons through which he passed, so that by the time he arrived his force had grown to 3,400 men. At Ashby on Monday, 18 March he met up with Loughborough who had a further 3,000 men with him. The combined force consisted of around 3,300 horse and 3,000 foot together with a small artillery train. At this time Meldrum knew that Loughborough was moving forces around in the area, but he did not suspect that a sizeable army under Rupert was descending on him at speed, even though Essex had been told of Rupert's initial movements and had sent out a detachment of horse to discover what was going on.

In order to speed up his advance and lessen the chance of being detected, Rupert had arranged with Loughborough to have wide gaps cut in the hedges on a direct cross-country route from Ashby to Newark so that the army with its guns and wagons could move as quickly as possible with the least chance of being detected by the enemy, who would naturally be watching the roads. On 19 March Rupert and Loughborough reached Rempstone and by the following evening were at Bingham, a mere ten miles from Newark. Not wanting Meldrum to escape in a north-easterly direction towards Lincoln, Rupert decided to make an early start

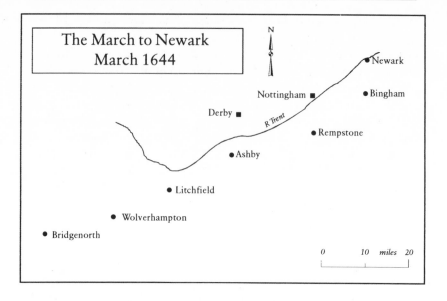

The March to Newark
March 1644

N

Newark

Nottingham ■

Bingham

Derby ■

R Trent

Rempstone

Ashby

Litchfield

Wolverhampton

Bridgenorth

0   10   *miles*   20

next morning and take his men round the south of the town so as to launch his attack in such a way as to cut off Meldrum's retreat.

Late in the evening of 20 March Meldrum received a message from the Governor of Nottingham telling him that Rupert was definitely making for Newark, and he decided to concentrate his men along the right bank of the Trent to the north-east of the town so as to be well placed to withdraw to Lincoln should he find that Rupert was too strong for him. Word of this concentration reached Rupert while he was still asleep and it is said that as he woke up he told Legge that he had dreamed that the enemy was beaten. Fearing that Meldrum was about to withdraw, Rupert set off at 2 a.m. with Loughborough and an advanced guard consisting of several troops of horse, intent on holding Meldrum in place until the main body could arrive.

Just upstream of Newark the Trent divides, the town lying to the south-east of the right-hand branch of the river. Downstream of the town the two branches of the river rejoin, thus forming an island between them which is two and a quarter miles long and a mile and a half wide. In order to lay siege to the town Meldrum had surrounded it and occupied the island. He had also fortified a derelict medieval hospital called the Spittal which lay just outside the town on the right bank of the river and built a bridge of boats next to it in order to give himself access to the island. About a mile due east of the town is a long kidney-shaped feature called Beacon Hill.

Rupert reached Beacon Hill just before dawn on 21 March, chasing away some of Meldrum's horse who were occupying it in the process. As it got light Rupert could see Meldrum's foot and guns moving around near the river bank with the bridge of boats behind them. In front of the foot were drawn up two considerable bodies of horse estimated at about 1,500 men.

Rupert decided to see what could be achieved by a quick attack and formed his horse up in three lines, the first led by himself, the second by Loughborough and the third by Gerrard. At about 9 a.m., while the main body was still arriving, he set off down the hill at a good pace, breaking into a fast canter at the bottom so that he hit the enemy's line with colossal force. Once again this tactic proved too much for the vastly superior Parliamentary horse, most of which was dispersed by the impact. But two of their regiments put up a fight and even started to launch a counter-attack, during which Rupert and a few of his troopers were surrounded. Three of the enemy attacked Rupert himself and for a moment it looked as if he would be killed. But he managed to cut down one of his attackers with his sword and his French attendant Mortaigne shot another with his pistol. At that moment the third assailant, who had grabbed Rupert by the collar, had his hand cut clean off by Sir William Neale. Rupert then got together a number of his own men and led another furious charge which finally dispersed the counter-attack and took Rupert right up to the Spittal. Meldrum evacuated the remains of his horse over the bridge of boats on to the island, leaving his foot supported by some artillery pieces to fight from the fortified Spittal.

By now Rupert's main body were ready and Tillier was sent right-handed from Beacon Hill with a body of musketeers to work his way along the bank of the river and capture the bridge of boats. But in this he was unsuccessful because the bridge was too well covered by the fire of Meldrum's musketeers and artillery. Rupert had by this time brought up enough men to contain the enemy in the Spittal but was reluctant to risk the casualties that would be sustained in assaulting it.

During the course of the afternoon Rupert managed to get 500 of his horse on to the island to the west of Newark. Soon afterwards the Governor of Newark, Sir Richard Byron, led a sally from the town across the island and captured a fort on the far side that was guarding Meldrum's exit to the north. By the evening Meldrum's

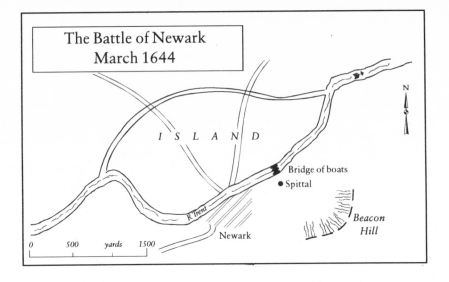

The Battle of Newark
March 1644

ISLAND

N

Bridge of boats
• Spittal

R Trent

Beacon
Hill

Newark

0   500   yards   1500

position was hopeless and he sued for terms. He was permitted to march away with his swords, pikes and colours next morning, leaving behind eleven brass cannon, two mortars and 3,000 muskets. As so often happened, the withdrawal of the vanquished was accompanied by disorder on the part of the victors who grabbed, amongst other things, some of their colours. Rupert did his best to restrain his men, riding in amongst them with drawn sword and personally returning the colours to one of their officers.[3]

Rupert lost about 100 men in the battle, which not only relieved Newark but also caused Parliament to abandon Lincoln, Gainsborough and Sleaford. In all probability Rupert could have taken Nottingham and Derby at this time had he attacked them, but he was anxious to get back to Shrewsbury in order to build up a sizeable army with which to assist Newcastle against the Scots. Furthermore on his march to Newark he had denuded the garrisons of the towns through which he had passed and it was important to restore their defences quickly.

Rupert's relief of Newark was recognised at the time as a remarkable feat of arms and he was congratulated on all sides in the most extravagant terms. Historians, from those writing a few years after the event to those of the present day, have tended to regard the operation as little short of a miracle. The combination of surprise, speed and economy has rightly been singled out for comment and lies behind the wonderment expressed by Hyde in the sentences quoted in Chapter 4 above;[4] Richard Ollard's description of the operation as elegant stems from an appreciation of the same three factors.[5]

From the point of view of assessing Rupert's capability as a commander, it is interesting to see how he set about planning and executing the operation. In this respect the first thing to notice is that, from the start, his aim was not just to relieve Newark, but also to destroy Meldrum's force and thereby prevent the enemy from reinvesting the town as soon as he departed. Rupert's whole plan was made with this in mind, his central calculation being to balance the need to keep the force small for speed of movement against the need to have enough on arrival to defeat Meldrum and his 7,000 men. An interesting aspect of the business was Rupert's assessment that he could not take a large enough force from his own units in the north-west and move it to Newark without Meldrum realising, as soon as he started, that Newark was the likely target. The moment Meldrum recognised the danger he would send for reinforcements which would certainly arrive ahead of Rupert. Rupert naturally understood that the Parliamentary garrisons close to his line of march would know that something was going on, but he bargained on the fact that his having so few men with him in the early stages would prevent them from suspecting that he intended to tackle Meldrum. In the event Parliamentary opinion about his target was split as between Nottingham and Leicester until the very evening before the attack went in.

The next most important factor was logistics. Stocks held in the garrisons along the route would not have been sufficient to support the move of a large army unless it dispersed each evening to forage, or alternatively moved with a sufficiently large baggage train to keep it supplied. Either way the distance covered daily would be cut down and the chances of surprise reduced. By taking very few of his own men from Chester and Shrewsbury and picking up detachments from the various Royalist garrisons as he went, the logistic burden would be reduced and movement speeded up, but at the expense of having to fight the battle with units that he had neither trained nor worked with before. Another danger was the weakening of the garrisons from which the units were drawn for the time that they were away.

There can be little disputing the fact that Rupert's concept for the operation was as clever as it was elegant, but success came from the way in which he put it into effect. In the event he must have pushed himself and his men to the limit. With his original contingent, he covered 130 miles from the time he left Chester late on 13 March until arriving at Bingham on 20 March, an average of eighteen miles a day: other parts of the force covered less ground, but at the end of it they all marched the ten miles from Bingham to Newark on 21 March and then totally destroyed a slightly superior enemy force for negligible loss. In the battle Rupert combined rapid appreciation of the ground with extreme boldness and a wonderful sense of timing. And his opponent Meldrum was a professional soldier with experience in Ireland and the Low Countries who had proved himself as a brigade commander at Edgehill and in numerous smaller engagements in the East Midlands. It was indeed a remarkable performance.

Not the least surprising aspect of this operation was the way in which Rupert planned it and made the necessary preparations at a time when he was fully employed restoring the remains of Byron's army and harrying those Parliamentary detachments still active in his area. Indeed, on the day before the King wrote his first letter about Newark, Rupert with his life guard had ridden through the night to catch up with a force of 700 Parliamentary troops outside Drayton which he chased into some buildings, holding them there until his regiment caught up with him, after which he attacked them, killing or capturing the lot. Rupert had no staff in the modern sense to help him, and he must have made his calculations and issued his instructions while riding between one place and the next. Despite the disappointments and frustrations of the previous autumn, Rupert was on the top of his form at this time.

Those wishing to point the finger at Rupert's greatest success have a number of operations to choose from and might well select the relief of Newark. Those wishing to point to his greatest disaster need only look at the battle of Marston Moor. Fourteen weeks and five days separate Newark from Marston Moor and events taking place in a number of different areas during this period affected the way in which Rupert approached this battle. It is therefore necessary to project Rupert's activities against these other happenings in order to discern the pressures that caused him to act as he did.

Rupert's eagerness to get back to Shrewsbury from Newark arose from the fact that there was an immense amount to be done before he could move against the Scots with a sizeable force. It was not just a question of preparing the troops, but also of establishing an organisation throughout his area capable of supporting them in the field. As Warburton points out, he had to reconcile hostile interests, conciliate powerful families, regulate port dues, fortify harbours, ensure that contributions raised from the various places were fairly assessed and that the necessary commissions were distributed. In addition recruits had to be obtained, trained, clothed, armed and paid, as far as possible with money, credit and supplies provided from within his own command. He also had to set up an army commissariat and persuade Percy to send him powder and shot from Oxford and Ashburnham to supplement his meagre financial resources so that his troops could be paid.[6]

In furtherance of these aims Rupert was at Conway Castle in North Wales on 29 March. On the same day Waller beat Hopton, who had been reinforced by Lord Forth and a detachment of troops from Oxford, at Cheriton near Alresford in Hampshire. As a result Forth and Hopton were withdrawn to Oxford together with their troops and the whole area south of the Thames passed under Parliamentary control with the exception of a few fortified strongholds such as Basing House. These events so upset the King that he sent for Rupert to return to Oxford with all the troops that he could muster but, realising that this would mean abandoning all hope of restoring the situation in the north, he soon cancelled the order. At this time Rupert sent Legge to Oxford to convey his views to the King: Legge was rewarded for past services by being appointed a gentleman of the King's bedchamber. On 10 April an assembly of the various detachments of the Oxford army took place and it was found to consist of 4,000 horse and a little over 5,000 foot. Waller and Essex each had armies of about 10,000 men.

A further misfortune overtook the Royalists in the north-east when, on 9 April at Selby, the two Fairfaxes and Meldrum beat that part of Newcastle's army left behind to hold Yorkshire. As a result Newcastle was obliged to retreat to York where he arrived on 18 April with 6,000 foot. Not wanting his 5,000 horse to be cooped up in a siege, he sent them to Newark where they found their former general, Lord Goring, who after ten months as a prisoner had been exchanged for the Earl of Lothian. Two days later the Scots joined forces with Fairfax at Tadcaster and on 22 April the siege of York began.

In the south-west Prince Maurice had emerged from winter quarters and was laying siege to Lyme on the Devon/Dorset coast in an attempt to complete a line of interlinking Royalist positions stretching from Bristol to the English Channel. The capture of

Lyme would give him complete control of land traffic into and out of his area. Sir John Berkeley with a small force was left to isolate Plymouth from the rest of Devon.

In view of the worsening situation the decision was now taken to move the heavily pregnant Queen to Exeter where she could give birth to her next child in comparative safety. Although her departure would involve a further detachment from the Oxford army, it would at least reduce the harmful influence that she exerted on the King and it would also mean that the King could leave Oxford at short notice if he needed to do so. It is interesting to note that when discussing where she should go, the Queen herself suggested that it might be safer for her to place herself under Prince Rupert's protection in Chester than to move to Exeter, an indication that her hostility to him had declined since the previous autumn. In the end the King chose Exeter and she left on 17 April. On the same day, with her full approval, the King made Rupert Master of the Horse in place of the disgraced Duke of Hamilton.

One week later Rupert, who was then at Hereford, rode to Oxford to take part in a meeting of the war council which was being held to discuss the deteriorating situation. In addition to the King, those attending included Forth, Wilmot, Hopton and Astley together with Richmond, the two Secretaries of State, Nicholas and Digby, Hyde and Culpepper. Hyde's description of Forth and Hopton as they were at this time is worth recording. Forth is described as having been a very good soldier in his day, but now 'much decayed in his parts with the long custom of immoderate drinking, dozed in his understanding which had never been quick and vigorous'. Furthermore he had become very deaf, 'often pretending not to hear what he did not want to contradict but afterward thought fit to disclaim'. Hyde describes Hopton as having total integrity, a good understanding, clear courage, an ability to work hard and unlimited generosity. But in debate he took longer in making up his mind and was more apt to change it than was agreeable in a commander-in-chief. Hyde's verdict on the King was that he judged the counsel put forward by his advisers more on the basis of what he thought of the person than of the counsel itself and that he 'trusted less to his own judgement than he ought to have done which rarely deceived him so much as that of other men.'[7]

At the meeting Rupert recommended that while he was away trying to restore the position in the north, the main garrisons around Oxford, including Reading which had been reoccupied after the battle of Newbury, should receive reinforcements of foot and be firmly held. He suggested that most of the horse should be concentrated near Oxford and used to harry Parliamentary forces attempting to lay siege to any of the garrisons, the rest being sent to Prince Maurice in the west in order to hasten the reduction of Lyme and safeguard the position of the Queen in Exeter. He also recommended that the main arms factories and powder mills be moved to Bristol from where they could continue to supply the various Royalist armies even if Oxford itself became cut off. This course of action was agreed and during the next ten days Rupert accompanied the King on a tour of the main garrisons around Oxford and secured some additional powder and other supplies for his own forces.

Rupert arrived back at Shrewsbury on 6 May, which was the same day that Lord Manchester and the army of the Eastern Association recaptured Lincoln on their way to join Fairfax and the Scots outside York. Ten days later Rupert left Shrewsbury, collecting up his regiments from the various garrisons as he went, so that when he crossed into Lancashire he had with him 2,000 horse and 6,000 foot. He left Legge behind as Governor of Chester.

For the most part Lancashire supported the King, but Parliament held Liverpool and Manchester which had recently been reinforced by Meldrum. Bolton also supported Parliament and was known as the Geneva of England because of its Puritan sympathies. Rupert had three reasons for going to Lancashire before moving on York. First, he wanted to re-establish Royalist control of the county so as to be able to use it as a source of men, money and supplies. Second, he wanted to secure the port of Liverpool in order to prevent Parliamentary ships based there interfering with traffic from Ireland, and also so that troops and supplies from Ireland designated for his use could be landed there. Third, he wanted to reduce the chances of Parliamentary forces in Lancashire raiding into Cheshire and Wales while he was away.

Rupert set about these tasks with his customary energy. Travelling via Whitchurch, he reached Knutsford on 23 May, where he met and defeated a small Parliamentary detachment. Two days later he took Stockport by storm and on the same day, skirting round Manchester to the west, relieved Lathom House, thus freeing Lady Derby who had held out there for so long against heavy odds. The beseiging force, commanded by Colonel Rigby, fled to Bolton. On 28 May Rupert, accompanied by Lord Derby, closed up to

Bolton which was held by a force of about 5,000 foot. During the early stages of the attack one of Rupert's men was taken prisoner and hanged from the walls on the grounds that he was an Irish Papist. Nothing could have been better calculated to infuriate Rupert, whose anger knew no bounds. Dismounting from his horse, he led attack after attack against the town until it was overrun and sacked. Accounts differ as to the fate of the defenders. According to the rules of war, having summoned the town to surrender, Rupert would have been within his rights to order that no quarter be given, but it is not entirely clear whether a formal summons was issued, or whether Rupert gave the no quarter order. All that can be said is that about one-third of the garrison were killed, some of whom may have been trying to surrender. Rupert's diary records that a great slaughter was made of the enemy, but adds that Rupert accepted the surrender of 700 men who had taken refuge in the church.[8]

Two days after the capture of Bolton, Rupert was joined by the 5,000 horse of Newcastle's army which Goring had brought from Newark together with 800 foot. They laid siege to Liverpool on 5 June and it fell four days later. In London the Committee of Both Kingdoms, fearing that the Parliamentary position in the north-west was about to collapse, sent Vane to urge the commanders of the allied armies besieging York to despatch a detachment into Lancashire to oppose Rupert. But the commanders wisely decided to keep their forces together in order to continue with the siege and to be in as strong a position as possible to fight Rupert when he turned to relieve it. At the same time Rupert decided not to attack the town of Manchester, probably because he could not afford the loss of men and powder that such an assault would entail, but also because he must have assumed that Meldrum, with a large part of the garrison, would be called back to the allied armies outside York as soon as he started his eastward move and would not therefore pose any threat to Cheshire and Wales. Instead Rupert decided to rest his army and reorganise it so as to absorb the forces brought by Goring and additional detachments gathered in from Lancashire, Derbyshire and Cumbria which more than offset the casualties sustained in the recent fighting.

But although Rupert's arrangements were progressing well, disaster struck the King's army around Oxford. Soon after Rupert had left Oxford in early May, arguments arose concerning the plans agreed at the council of war on 25 April. As a result King Charles abandoned Reading on 19 May, which left the armies of Essex and Waller free to approach Oxford. The next day Essex met Waller at Henley-on-Thames to co-ordinate the move of the two armies. Essex moved via Wallingford while Waller moved on a converging course to the west of him. On the same day that Rupert was storming Stockport, the Royalists evacuated Abingdon, which was promptly occupied by Essex: by this time Waller's army had reached Marcham, about four miles to the west. The loss of Abingdon was a major blow to the King as it was one of the inner ring of Oxford garrisons and the headquarters of the horse. Furthermore the evacuation took place without the King hearing of it until it was complete. The King blamed Wilmot and there were even suggestions of treachery. In fact the executive order for the evacuation came from Lord Forth, although he may well have been acting on Wilmot's advice.

During the next few days Essex's army crossed the Thames from west to east at Sandford and worked its way around the east side of the Oxford defence works, finally arriving at Islip to the north. Meanwhile Waller closed up to the Thames to the south-west of the town. By the afternoon of 3 June it looked as though the King and his army would be besieged in Oxford where they could only be expected to hold out for about two weeeks before their supplies ran out, a period too short for a relief to be mounted by Rupert. One suggestion made to the King was that he should surrender to the rebels, to which he replied that 'possibly he might be found in the hands of Essex but he would be dead first'.[9]

Instead the King decided to escape with the Prince of Wales that night, passing between the armies of Essex and Waller. Leaving 3,500 of his foot in Oxford with instructions to make a feint against Abingdon to divert Waller's attention, he slipped out on the Banbury road with 2,500 musketeers joining up with his 5,000 horse outside the town. Once clear he turned west, passing a few miles to the south of Essex's outposts at Woodstock, and then made his way via Burford, Broadway and Evesham to Worcester, where he arrived on 6 June. By this time Waller, whose army had reached Stow-on-the-Wold, was summoned to meet Essex at Chipping Norton. At this meeting Essex announced his intention of taking his army into the south-west to relieve Lyme, telling Waller to pursue and defeat the King.

Next day the King wrote to Rupert informing him of these developments and saying that his chief hope for the future lay with him.

He went on to say that had Rupert stayed with him, or had he followed Rupert's plan agreed on 25 April, he would not now be in such a bad state. He concluded by saying that he reckoned to be able to defend himself until Rupert beat the Scots and returned to his assistance provided he did not take too long about it.[10] At the time of writing the King did not know about Essex's intention to move into the south-west, which would relieve the pressure on him to some extent. It is not clear when this letter, together with a more detailed letter written by Digby, reached Rupert, but it was probably a day or two after he captured Liverpool.

With no foot other than musketeers and with no artillery, the King could not expect to hold Worcester against Waller. He therefore moved with his musketeers to Bewdley, just to the west of Kidderminster, sending the horse on to Bridgnorth to give Waller the idea that he was moving to join Rupert, which was one of the options being considered at the time. Waller moved rapidly to Stourbridge to head him off. For two days at Bewdley a special committee of the council of war considered whether the King should try to fight his way through to Rupert, or double back to Oxford to collect the remainder of the foot that had been left there. On 14 June this second option was agreed and Digby drafted a letter for the King to send to Rupert.

This fateful letter, which led directly to the battle of Marston Moor, started by congratulating Rupert on his successes in Lancashire and went on to explain why the extra powder that he needed could not come from Oxford, although some might be forthcoming from Ireland or Bristol if not already beseiged. The rest of the letter is of such importance that it must be quoted in full:

> But now I must give the true state of my affairs, which if their condition be such as enforces me to give you more peremptory commands than I would willingly do, you must not take it ill. If York be lost I shall esteem my crown little less; unless supported by your sudden march to me; and a miraculous conquest in the South, before the effects of their Northern power can be found here. But if York be relieved, and you beat the rebels' army of both kingdoms, which are before it; then (but otherwise not) I may possibly make a shift upon the defensive to spin out time until you come to assist me. Wherefore I command you, by the duty and affection that I know you bear me, that all new enterprises laid aside, you immediately march according to your first intention, with all your force to the relief of York. But if

that be either lost, or have freed themselves from the besiegers, or that for want of powder, you cannot undertake that work, that you immediately march with your whole strength, directly to Worcester, to assist me and my army; without which, or your having relieved York by beating the Scots, all the successes you can afterwards have must infallibly be useless unto me. You may believe that nothing but an extreme necessity could make me write thus unto you; wherefore in this case, I can no ways doubt of your punctual compliance with

Your loving and most faithful friend, Charles R.[11]

Despite the alternative courses of action suggested, this letter left Rupert with little room for manoeuvre. Although the King started by saying that the loss of York would be a disaster unless Rupert joined up with him immediately so that together they could win a miraculous victory in the south, it continued by saying that only three circumstances were to prevent him from going to York: i.e. if the city had already fallen, or if Newcastle's army had beaten off the besiegers, or if Rupert could not obtain enough powder to carry out the task. As none of these circumstances applied, the option of Rupert joining the King instead of relieving York was ruled out. The King was also adamant that success involved 'beating the rebels' army of both kingdoms' as well as relieving York, which further limited Rupert's options. It is interesting that Culpepper, who had taken part in the deliberations of the council of war but who had not been involved in the drafting of the letter, went to the King when he saw the draft to ask whether it had been despatched. When Charles said that it had, Culpepper's reply was, 'Why then before God you are undone, for upon this peremptory order he will fight, whatever comes on't.'

Rupert was at Lathom House when he received this letter, probably on 16 June, and he started his move to York six days later. There has been speculation, based on a letter written to Ormonde by Arthur Trevor, Rupert's agent in Oxford, that the delay was caused by a threat by Rupert to resign his command, because he had heard that some of those around the King were being highly critical of him, even to the extent of saying that it would make no difference in the long run whether the war was won by Parliament or by Prince Rupert. According to this source, Rupert was only persuaded to keep going by one of his friends, supposedly Richmond.

In fact it is more likely that he needed the extra six days to complete his preparations and to obtain the powder without which he could not start. None the less his distrust of Digby, Wilmot, Percy and the rest would have remained as strong as ever, especially as he would have held them responsible for causing the King to abandon Reading which was the immediate cause of the flight from Oxford.

Rupert's army moved first to Preston and then up the Ribble valley via Clitheroe and Gisburn to Skipton where he arrived on 26 June; a distance of fifty-two miles in four days. At this point he halted for three days in order to send messengers to York and gather intelligence about the allied armies, before making his final approach to the city. No doubt he also needed to replenish his stocks of food as he was moving a much larger force than he had taken to the relief of Newark.

It is difficult to know exactly how large Rupert's army was at this time. Of the original force with which he had entered Lancashire, he still had five regiments of horse, one of which was from Ireland, and seven regiments of foot, five of which came from Ireland. From levies raised in Lancashire and Cumberland he had a further two regiments of horse and three of foot, and from Derbyshire, two of horse and three of foot. In addition there was a regiment of horse from Dudley Castle. The difficulty arises in knowing how strong these regiments were. The 5,000 horse and 800 foot of Newcastle's army that Rupert had with him were made up of the remnants of forty separate regiments, each of which must have been very under strength, and this certainly applied to the Derbyshire contingent as well. The Governor of Liverpool reported to Ormonde that Rupert departed for York with 7,000 horse and 6,000 foot, but this is now thought to have been an underestimate and takes no account of an artillery train of between sixteen and twenty cannon. Altogether Rupert's army must have topped the 14,000 mark.[12]

Because Rupert's army was made up of the remains of several other armies and because so many units were under strength, there was a higher proportion of officers to men than was usual. Some weak regiments had to be amalgamated in order to make up worthwhile fighting units and several of the brigades were no stronger than full-strength regiments. On the other hand a few regiments, such as the two of which Rupert was colonel, were fully recruited. There was also much variation of quality between Rupert's and Goring's veterans on the one hand and the recently recruited levies on the other who scarcely knew how to handle their weapons.

Many commanders would have been reluctant to engage in any but the simplest of operations with such a force, but Rupert was getting used to cobbling together armies one day and fighting with them the next. Furthermore, if he could relieve York before having to fight the combined forces of his enemies, he would be able to strengthen his army with some of Lord Newcastle's experienced foot regiments.

The only other possible source of reinforcements was the small force led by Montrose which was near the town of Newcastle. After leaving Oxford at the beginning of February, Montrose recruited 1,300 men in mid-April and occupied Dumfries to await the Macdonnells who were supposed to be joining him from Ireland. But no Macdonnells arrived, many of his soldiers deserted and the Covenanters chased him out of Dumfries. Montrose withdrew into England where, assisted by Colonel Clavering, he wasted no time in rebuilding his force. He then moved across the lines of communication of the invading Scottish army that had by this time moved south into Yorkshire and on 10 May attacked one of their garrisons in Morpeth. His first attempt was unsuccessful, but after collecting some cannon from Newcastle, which was still in Royalist hands, he returned and took Morpeth on 29 May. He went on to take South Shields, but was repulsed when he attacked Sunderland after which he set about passing supplies into the town of Newcastle to build it up against a siege. At this point he received orders to join Rupert.

As mentioned earlier, Rupert gave a high priority to the gathering of intelligence and before leaving Lancashire he would undoubtedly have known a great deal about the commanders and units in the three opposing armies. What he could not have known then, and what he was trying to find out while at Skipton, was how many of the enemy's units were present outside York, how many had been left to garrison various towns around the country and how many were involved in containing Royalist garrisons that were still holding out.

How much of this he succeeded in discovering remains unknown, but records show that the Scots army outside York consisted of six regiments of horse, one regiment of dragoons, fifteen regiments of foot and thirty to forty field guns. Altogether, of the 21,500 men that had entered England from Scotland, about 15,000 were at York. Information about Lord Fairfax's Northern army is less exact, but it is thought that he had ten very weak regiments of horse amounting to about 2,000 men, and seven or eight regiments of foot amounting to about 3,000 men. There is no record of dragoons or cannon. Manchester's Eastern Association army had five strong regiments of horse and a regiment of dragoons amounting to 4,000 men, and six foot regiments amounting to a further 4,000 men.

The allied armies surrounding York consisted therefore of 8,000 horse and dragoons and about 20,000 foot soldiers and artillerymen, altogether about twice the number that Rupert had with him at Skipton. It is interesting to notice that the Scots army considerably outnumbered the combined strength of Fairfax and Manchester, but that these two between them contributed a preponderance of the horse. Furthermore, in terms of quality, i.e. armament and training, the four Eastern Association regiments of horse outstripped the rest. They were commanded by Oliver Cromwell who had been made Manchester's Lieutenant General in January. Opinions differ as to whether the Eastern Association's horse were fully armoured cuirassiers like Haselrigg's regiment in Waller's army, or whether they were just unusually well-equipped troopers on good heavy horses.[13] Undeniably they had been trained to a high standard and had proved themselves in the small Eastern Association battles of 1643.

Unlike Rupert, the allied armies could expect to receive significant reinforcements within the next few days: Meldrum was marching to join them from Lancashire and Lord Denbigh was bringing a further contingent from Staffordshire. According to a letter sent by the Committee of Both Kingdoms to Meldrum, Denbigh had 2,000 horse and at least 2,000 foot.[14] On 23 June Vane, who was still with the allies outside York wrote to the Committee of Both Kingdoms saying that the reinforcements coming from Lancashire, over and above Denbigh's contingent, were 4,000 horse and 4,000 foot.[15] Whether the allied commanders were expecting as many as 12,000 reinforcements to arrive is perhaps questionable, but they were certainly expecting a large number, because they hoped that they would be able to face Rupert without raising the siege of York, provided that Meldrum and Denbigh appeared before he did.

But on 28 June they heard that Rupert's army had already reached Skipton and, realising that Meldrum could not join them until 3 July at the earliest, they raised the siege and concentrated their forces in a defensive position astride the road from Knaresborough to York, behind the River Nidd about two miles north of the village of Long Marston. In order to move those of their troops

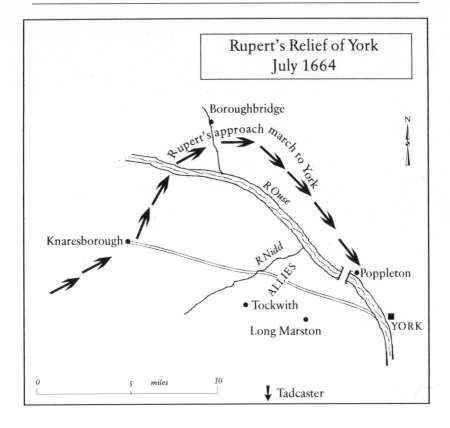

Rupert's Relief of York
July 1664

Boroughbridge

Rupert's approach march to York

R Ouse

N

Knaresborough

R Nidd

ALLIES

Poppleton

• Tockwith

Long Marston

YORK

0   5   miles   10

↓ Tadcaster

that were to the north of York to their new positions and to enable
them to withdraw back to the east side of the Ouse in an emer-
gency, they built a bridge of boats across that river at Poppleton,
about four miles upstream of York. They left small detachments
in the trenches to look after their siege guns and the large quantities
of ammunition and other stores that they had not time to move.

Rupert's army arrived at Knaresborough on 30 June. Not wishing to confront the allied armies until he had linked up with Newcastle's forces, he decided to make a detour round their right flank
and move on York from the north. Early next morning he sent a
strong contingent of his own horse out of Knaresborough along
the York road to give the allies the impression that he was about
to attack them. But while the allies were drawing up their armies
in expectation of battle, Rupert led the rest of his force northwards
to cross the River Ure at Boroughbridge, thence east across the
River Swale at Thornton Bridge and finally down the east bank of

the Ouse towards York, a march of no less than twenty-two miles. So great was the surprise achieved by this manoeuvre that he even managed to capture the bridge of boats at Poppleton intact. He immediately pushed some of his regiments of horse across the river to reconnoitre the rear of the allied position and to cover the deployment of his main body whilst others chased the enemy detachments out of their siege works. York was relieved and during the night the detachment of horse that Rupert had sent to confront the allied armies rejoined him.

Rupert's own movements during the evening and night of 1 July are not known in detail, but it is probable that he crossed the bridge of boats and rode forward to get a look at the ground between his screen of horsemen and the allied army before it got dark. He would then have had to prepare an outline plan for the next day's operations, after which he must have issued instructions for the reception of his units as they arrived at the end of their long march. They would have moved into holding areas from where they could be brought up to cross the river, either by the bridge of boats, or at a ford that had been discovered nearby, in the right order with regard to the requirements of the next day's operations. Finally Rupert would almost certainly have had a meeting with his senior commanders to brief them on the situation and explain his intentions for the next day.

At some stage in the proceedings Rupert sent Goring into York to make contact with Lord Newcastle, whom he asked to join him with as many of his foot as possible at 4 a.m. next day: he had already received an extravagant message of thanks from Newcastle for relieving his besieged force. It is recorded that Rupert slept briefly on the ground in the Galtres Forest between York and Poppleton, but he would have been fully occupied until late and would have wanted to be up as soon as it got light at about 3.15 a.m., so he could not have rested for more than an hour or two.

There has been much speculation as to why Rupert was so keen to bring on a battle immediately after his exhausting march to York and before he had integrated Newcastle's regiments into his force, or even consulted Newcastle regarding future plans. Had he done so he would have discovered that Newcastle was opposed to offering battle at this juncture, because he believed that the allied commanders would fall out amongst themselves if given time.

Rupert, on the other hand, had good reasons for seeking a quick result. In a strategic context he was conscious of the need to reach a decision in the north as fast as possible so as to get back to rescue the King. Although by now he would have received a letter written by Digby on 22 June saying that the King had succeeded in reuniting his small force with the foot regiments left in Oxford, he could not have known that on 29 June the Royalists had repulsed an attack made on them by Waller at Cropredy Bridge. Rupert would certainly have thought that the King was still in grave danger, which was indeed the case, since at that very moment the defeated Waller was being reinforced by a further 5,000 men under Browne raised from counties in the Eastern Association. Consideration of the King's position alone made it certain that he would have to fight a battle in the near future since, having relieved York, he could hardly return south leaving the allies to renew the siege. It was for this reason that the King had expressly commanded Rupert to fight in his letter of 14 June.

But there were also two overriding tactical reasons that made it essential for Rupert to fight the allies at once. First, the allies were in a state of complete disorganisation, being drawn up to fight an enemy approaching from the opposite direction. It would be impossible for the enemy commanders to select a new position and for such a large number of troops to occupy it during the short summer night. If next morning Rupert could sweep down on them from behind, he would catch them at a serious disadvantage which would go some way towards compensating him for his numerical inferiority. The second pressing tactical reason was to fight before the arrival of Meldrum and Denbigh. Even when joined by Newcastle's regiments, Rupert would be heavily outnumbered; he could not afford to have the odds against him increased. To have thrown away the opportunity presented by his successful outflanking movement, for no better reason than a hope that the enemy commanders might fall out amongst themselves, would have been the height of folly and it is surprising that historians have been so slow to recognise the tactical imperatives that drove Rupert on.

In fact the allied commanders decided on the evening of 1 July that it would be better for them to retreat south to Tadcaster rather than turn about and fight in their present position north of Long Marston. At Tadcaster they would also be well placed to join up with Meldrum and Denbigh and to intercept Rupert were he to strike south into Lincolnshire to draw them away from York, a worry that Rupert had fostered by sending a detachment of horse south from York soon after reaching the city. In consequence of their decision, the allied foot started their march to the south early on 2 July, the Scots foot leading, followed by the English foot and with the artillery train bringing up the rear. A little over half of the allied horse, under the command of Sir Thomas Fairfax accompanied by both Cromwell and David Leslie, deployed along a ridge of high ground south of the road that runs between Long Marston and Tockwith, in order to cover the withdrawal. Between the ridge and the road was a wide expanse of arable land. North of the road was moorland: Marston Moor.

The distance between Marston Moor and the bridge of boats at Poppleton was about five miles. In the early hours of the morning Rupert heard that the allies intended to retreat to the south and he sent a body of horse to reconnoitre: between 8 a.m. and 9 a.m. they appeared on the moor opposite Fairfax's position, but soon moved away. Shortly afterwards, hearing that the leading elements of the Scots foot had almost reached Tadcaster, Fairfax started thinning out his regiments from the ridge. In due course he began to move southwards himself and had almost reached Bilton before he realised that the moor behind him was rapidly filling up with Royalist horse. By 9 a.m. about 5,000 horse and dragoons had arrived and soon afterwards the first of the Royalist foot regiments started to appear. Fairfax was now concerned for the safety of the allied foot which was strung out along a number of lanes leading to Tadcaster, highly vulnerable to attack. He therefore brought back his horse to the original ridge and sent messages to the three allied commanders suggesting that they should return their troops at once and take up a proper defensive position.

During the night Newcastle had been unable to get his regiments moving, because as soon as the siege was lifted, they had surged out of the town into the abandoned allied trenches in search of food and clothing: many of them got drunk and some refused to march until they received their arrears of pay. Leaving Lord Eythin to collect them together as soon as he could, he set off with a troop of gentlemen to find Rupert. One account says that they met on Marston Moor at 9 a.m. Another maintains that Newcastle overtook Rupert on the road, which would have been rather earlier. Both accounts agree that Newcastle initially expressed doubts about the wisdom of rushing into a battle, saying that it would be better to wait for the reinforcements being brought along by Clavering which he optimistically put at 3,000 and which he claimed were due to arrive in a few days. This would also give the

enemy coalition a chance to break up. But when Rupert told him
that the King had ordered him to fight, he accepted the situation
without further objection.

At this point, Rupert, realising that Newcastle's foot would not
arrive for some hours, decided to forgo the opportunity of bringing
on a running battle to scatter the enemy's marching columns. If
things went wrong, as might happen if control was temporarily lost
for example, his own foot, unsupported by Newcastle's regiments,
would be vulnerable to a counter-attack. It may be that in reaching
this decision Rupert was influenced by past accusations of rashness,
or perhaps he just thought that a set-piece battle, when all the
Royalist forces were ready, stood a better chance of success. None
the less such caution was uncharacteristic of him and contrary to
his previous practice, which had invariably been based on carefully
calculated audacity.

The rest of the day was spent by both sides in deploying regiments into battle positions as they arrived. In the case of the allies,
who failed to realise that Rupert was handicapped by the late
appearance of Newcastle's foot, the priority was to build up their
line of battle as quickly as possible before he attacked. As a result,
their foot regiments got put down into the positions that most
needed occupying as they arrived, with little attempt made to divide
the battlefield up according to the command arrangements of the
three armies. Overall the allies laid out their men in the customary
way, with a large block of foot in the centre and with bodies of
horse on each wing.

The allied centre consisted of fourteen brigades of foot in four
lines; five in the front, four in each of the second and third lines
and one in the fourth.[16] Most of the brigades consisted of two
regiments. The first line consisted of two Scots brigades, two Eastern Association brigades and one brigade of Lord Fairfax's Northern army. The second line were all Scots. The third consisted of
two of Fairfax's brigades, two Scots brigades and one of Manchester's, and the fourth line consisted of another Scottish brigade.
Altogether there were around 11,000 men in the allied centre. It
is difficult to work out how command was supposed to be exercised
in this mass of foot, because brigades from one army in the second
and third lines were not necessarily behind their own brigades in
the front line. All that can be said is that Manchester's major
general, Lawrence Crawford, was in charge of the left of the front
line and that the Scots general, William Baillie, was in charge on
the right. It is also clear that Lord Leven's major general of foot,

James Lumsden, commanded the second line. Lord Fairfax and the Earl of Manchester seem to have stationed themselves in the third line, Fairfax on the left and Manchester on the right. Lord Leven, who was by far the most experienced soldier present, acted as commander-in-chief for the allied army.

The allied right wing consisted of three lines of horse with musketeers interspersed between troops in the manner favoured by Gustavus Adolphus and with a regiment of dragoons to cover the flank. The first two lines consisted of the 2,000 horse of the Northern army under Sir Thomas Fairfax, the third consisting of three Scottish regiments of horse amounting to a further 1,000 men commanded by the Earl of Eglington. The left wing, like the right, consisted of three lines of horse: the front two, from the Eastern Association, were commanded by Cromwell and were 3,700 strong; the third were Scots, commanded by the Scottish lieutenant general of horse, David Leslie, and amounted to another 1,000. As on the right wing, musketeers were interspersed between the troops and a regiment of dragoons covered the extreme left flank.

Virtually all of the twenty-five guns belonging to the allies were concentrated behind the centre, on a piece of slightly higher ground from where they could fire into the Royalist position over the heads of their own forces.

With the exception of Newcastle's foot, Rupert's army arrived on the moor well ahead of the allies as a result of which he was not obliged to deploy it piecemeal. From sketches made by Rupert's engineer, de Gomme, and by Leven's major general, James Lumsden, it is clear how the troops of both sides were laid out. From these sketches it can be seen that Rupert planned to offset the enemy's numerical superiority by making maximum use of such topographical features as existed and by holding a larger number of reserves than usual in order to be in a position to restore the situation in sensitive places should the enemy succeed in over-running them.

The area into which both sides were pouring their troops was a two-mile stretch between the villages of Tockwith to the west and Long Marston to the east, the two villages being joined by Marston Lane. Although the enemy had the advantage of slightly higher ground on their position, their men were drawn up in standing and sodden corn which, until it was trodden down, was both awkward and uncomfortable.

There were a number of terrain features that the Royalists could utilise, notably a deep ditch with a stiff hedge in front of it which

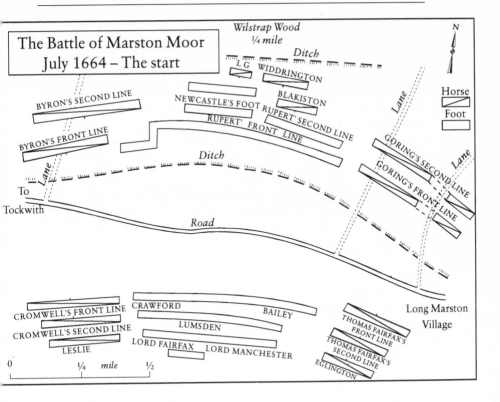

The Battle of Marston Moor
July 1664 – The start

By drawing up his army within cannon shot of the enemy, Rupert
ensured that the two armies would not sit watching each other for

ran 300–400 yards to the north of, and parallel to, Marston Lane
and which would inevitably break up the cohesion of the enemy's
attack as he scrambled across it in the face of the defenders. On
the other hand it would have made it correspondingly difficult for
the Royalists to have launched an attack from their positions
since they would have had to cross the ditch before starting their
assault. On the right of the Royalist position the ground behind
the ditch was boggy and behind that again were some rabbit
warrens that would further slow down attacking horsemen. Two
lanes at right angles to Marston Lane passed north on to the moor
between hedges through the left of the Royalist position and
another passed through the right of their position. About 700 yards
behind the ditch and parallel to it ran another shallower ditch, the
army being drawn up between the two ditches. Some 400 yards
behind the second ditch was Wilstrop Wood.

By drawing up his army within cannon shot of the enemy, Rupert
ensured that the two armies would not sit watching each other for

too long and it has been suggested that he did so in order to provoke the enemy into attacking him.[17] Such a theory fits in well with the way in which the army was deployed, with particular reference to the holding of large reserves. Furthermore it would be a logical response to the numerical superiority of the enemy. But it is also possible that he selected the position to give him security from enemy attacks until he was ready to launch an assault of his own. Later in the day Rupert was criticised by Lord Eythin for siting his position too close to the enemy but he could not have deployed his whole force behind the second ditch, because there was insufficient room between it and Wilstrop Wood, and the only alternative would have been to have placed his forward regiments in front of the second ditch and his second line regiments behind it. But this would have deprived him of the advantage of the forward ditch as an obstacle to the enemy's advance and would have turned the second one into an obstacle for his own second line troops when they moved to support the front line. In the light of all these considerations it seems probable that Rupert laid out his position primarily so as to be in as strong a position as possible if attacked, and that this is what he wanted to happen. But he also deployed his army in such a way as to leave him capable of attacking should the enemy refuse to attack him.

The Royalist right wing was commanded by Byron and consisted of 2,600 horse in two lines with 500 musketeers in gaps between bodies in the front line which, on the right, was close up to the rabbit warrens already mentioned.[18] Rupert's own regiment of horse, which was by far the strongest and most experienced of all the Royalist regiments, was on the inside of the second line from where it could go to the assistance of the front line or of the right flank regiments should the flank be turned. The Royalist left was commanded by Lord Goring with Sir Charles Lucas as his lieutenant general. It consisted of around 2,100 horse drawn up in two lines and 500 musketeers. Thus on the Royalist right Byron had 2,700 horse to oppose Cromwell's and Leslie's 4,700, whereas on the left Goring had 2,100 horse to oppose Fairfax and Eglington's 3,000.

The Royalist centre consisted of the foot regiments of Rupert's army under his major general Henry Tillier, deployed in divisions, i.e. units of two or more depleted regiments, laid out in two lines. Behind these two lines, on the right side of the centre, would be the 3,500 men of Newcastle's regiments of foot when they arrived, commanded by his major general, Sir Francis Mackworth.

Two strong regiments of foot, Rupert's and Byron's, were placed forward and to the right of the centre at its juncture with the right wing, to stiffen up the obstacle formed by the ditch which may have been weak at this point. A brigade of horse under Sir William Blakiston, probably about 600 strong, was placed close up behind the forward divisions of foot towards the left of the centre. It is possible that Newcastle's general, Lord Eythin, commanded the centre.

Rupert had a reserve consisting of his life guard, which at 140 men was as strong as some of the weaker regiments, and a brigade of horse under Sir Edward Widdrington, about 400 strong, in addition to which must be included Newcastle's own life guard. Because there was no high ground behind the Royalist position, Rupert's sixteen guns had to be spread out in the centre to fire between the various bodies of foot.

Clearly Rupert foresaw that the greatest danger was to his right flank, the whole of the Royalist layout being heavily weighted to repelling an assault from this direction. It is well attested[19] that he had instructed Byron not to advance beyond the rabbit warrens when attacked so that his attackers would have to negotiate the ditch lined with musketeers, the boggy ground and the rabbit warrens before reaching him, during which time they would be subjected to the fire of the musketeers drawn up between the bodies of his horse.

Rupert's concern for his right flank would have been based partly on the nature of the ground, the lanes, hedges and gorse making the left wing more difficult to attack, and partly because he had discovered during the morning that the more heavily armed and better trained Eastern Association horse were poised to assault his right wing. Great play has been made by historians of the fact that Rupert, when interrogating a prisoner in the morning, asked whether Cromwell was there, implying that he had a special interest in Cromwell as a person. It is much more likely that his question was related to the location of Cromwell's troops on the battlefield, the 'there' referring to the place of the skirmish where the man was captured, which was at Bilton Bream on the Royalist right.

Rupert's contacts with Newcastle and Eythin have also been the subject of comment. It is clear that Newcastle was upset that Rupert did not come into York during the previous night to discuss the situation with him and, as already mentioned, when he did meet him next morning, he started by being opposed to Rupert's intention to attack the allies. But he accepted Rupert's assurance that the King required it, and he went so far as to say that he would follow Rupert's instructions in all respects as if the King was present in person, adding that he had no ambition but to live and die a loyal subject of His Majesty. From 9 a.m. onwards he had been with, or near, Rupert on Marston Moor. He advised him against launching an attack in the morning before his own foot arrived and he must have been fully conversant with the details of the Royalist position and with Rupert's design for the battle. It is likely that when Rupert went round the position pointing out where the various brigades and regiments should place themselves, Newcastle accompanied him, after which he would probably have spent some time talking to the senior officers of his own regiments of horse whom he had not seen since the start of the siege and who were now spread around the battlefield; some with Goring on the left wing, some with Blakiston in the centre and some with Widdrington in Rupert's reserve. Rupert would certainly have kept in close touch with him in order to get the latest reports of the progress of his foot regiments on their march from York.

Eythin arrived with these regiments between 2.30 and 4.30 p.m., having had a difficult time getting them away from the enemy trenches and quietening their protests at being taken off to battle so soon after the lifting of a long and dangerous siege. Like Newcastle he was opposed to attacking the allies: as an elderly professional he had no wish to risk losing his lucrative job by fighting a battle that might well end in defeat. When he arrived he had not heard Rupert's reasons for wanting to fight, nor did he know that Newcastle had fallen in with them. When Rupert showed him a sketch of the position, he must have realised that the enemy was bound to attack it, whether Rupert meant them to do so or not, and he was rude enough to say that in deploying his men so far forward Rupert had made the same mistake as he had made at Vlotho. Miraculously Rupert did not lose his temper, even asking Eythin whether he thought that certain parts of the line should be withdrawn, although both of them must have known that it was too late to make such adjustments.

By the time that Newcastle's regiments were drawn up in position it was getting late. It had been a hot and clammy day with showers of rain from time to time and Rupert's men had been up and about since 4 a.m.: in some cases even earlier. For these reasons, and taking into account the reluctance of Newcastle and Eythin to fight a battle, Rupert announced his decision not to attack the enemy that evening. Orders were given for the regimental wagons to come forward and for the men to prepare their food. He also gave instructions for the chaplains to read prayers to their regiments. It seems clear that Rupert discounted the possibility of the allies mounting an attack on him so late in the day, especially as detachments were still arriving from the direction of Tadcaster. Newcastle is on record as asking the Prince whether he was certain that there would be no attack and only went to his coach when Rupert assured him that this was so. Soon afterwards Rupert himself went to the rear and dismounted to have something to eat.

When, late in the afternoon, Lord Leven reconnoitred the Royalist position, he would have had an opportunity to see the extent to which he outnumbered them and he would also have noticed that the Royalists were settling down for the night rather than preparing to assault his position. With a lifetime of war experience he must have realised that he had a chance to achieve tactical surprise by attacking in the last hours of daylight. It is even suggested that he ordered some of his own regiments to put down their arms and start cooking food in order to reassure the Royalists that he had no plans to attack that evening.[20] After making his decision he held a meeting with Manchester, Lord Fairfax, and Baillie to co-ordinate arrangements and to agree on a signal for the attack, for example, the firing of a salvo from the guns: it was important that the whole line should move forward together if maximum value was to be gained from their superiority of numbers. Leven then continued his careful watch of the Royalists in order to work out the best moment for signalling the attack.

Accounts differ as to the time that the attack was launched, but it was probably at about 7 p.m. which would have left a little under two hours before it got dark. Just as the allied foot in the centre jumped to their feet and started to advance, a thunderstorm broke over them which had the effect of causing many misfires amongst the Royalist musketeers manning the ditch. This reduced the casualties sustained by the allies as they crossed the 800 yards separating them from the ditch, which they passed after a brief struggle before moving on to engage the Royalist front line.

At the same time the allied horse attacked on both wings. On the Royalist left the allied assault was led by Sir Thomas Fairfax, whose men had a difficult time amongst the hedges, ditches and gorse where they were subjected to effective fire from the musketeers interspersed amongst Goring's regiments of horse. Although Fairfax himself with about 400 men managed to break through on the extreme left of the Royalist position, the remainder of his horse were thrown into disorder and, when charged by Goring at exactly the right moment, broke and fled. Carrying all before him Goring pursued the enemy across the road and chased them from the battlefield. Meanwhile Sir Charles Lucas, in charge of Goring's second line, did what Byron should have done at Edgehill and swung into the exposed flank of the allied foot, some of whom had already taken to their heels, having witnessed the flight of their neighbouring regiments of horse.[21] But although some of the Scots on the right of the front two lines had fled, others stood firm so that there was still oppositon in this part of the battlefield.

In the Royalist centre things were also going well. Here the allied foot had forced their way across the ditch and had become engaged with the front line of the Royalist foot who fought with them for some time, after which Newcastle's regiments, stationed behind them, pushed in to join the fray. As a result the allied foot gave ground, whereupon they were charged by Blakiston's brigade of horse which turned their withdrawal into a rout. Newcastle himself, with his troop of gentlemen, now joined in on Blakiston's left and together they swept across the road and pushed right through to the third line of the allied centre.[22]

By this time the whole of the allied right, together with all of the centre except for the two brigades on the left of it, was thoroughly disorganised, resistance being confined to individual regiments of foot grimly holding out against Royalist assaults. Leven, watching from the ridge and receiving reports from different parts of the battlefield, was convinced that he was defeated. He had kept no reserve with which to influence the battle so he fled to Leeds from where he doubtless hoped to collect together the remnants of his army. Lord Fairfax also left the field and made his way to Hull. Of the three allied commanders only Manchester remained and he was fighting with his own regiment of foot which, having started on the right of the third line, was now one of the isolated pockets of resistance, probably situated between the ridge and the road. Within about an hour of the battle starting it looked as if the Royalists had won a great victory, news of which was carried to York where the bells started pealing in triumph. Messengers even set off to carry the good news to the King.

But tidings of a Royalist victory were premature and took no account of events on the right of their line. When the allies moved forward at the start of the battle, Crawford led the two brigades of Manchester's foot that had been on the left of the allied front line across the ditch and engaged the two Royalist regiments of foot stationed close behind it. These regiments were forced back on the Royalist centre. As a result the Eastern Association horse led by Cromwell were able to get across the ditch without breaking ranks, since the Royalist musketeers manning it, assailed by Crawford's foot on one side and the enemy dragoons on the other, were unable to offer much resistance.

If Byron had stood fast behind the rabbit warrens and the boggy ground, giving his musketeers an opportunity to fire at the advancing enemy as Goring's had on the other wing, all might yet have been well despite the fact that Cromwell and Leslie outnumbered him by almost two to one. But once again Byron could not contain his impatience and launched his front line against Cromwell. In the ensuing struggle Byron's front line and possibly the right-hand regiments of his second line were defeated and one regiment at least fled the field. At this point Cromwell, who had been slightly wounded by a pistol shot that grazed the back of his neck, left the field to have it dressed and there seems to have been a break in the action while his regiments sorted themselves out before attacking what was left of Byron's second line.

At the time that the allies started their attack, Rupert was sitting on the ground having his supper. He immediately got mounted to watch the battle and to receive such reports as were brought to him by messengers from the different parts of the field. He soon realised that it was his right wing that was in danger and he led his life guard and Widdrington's brigade in that direction. Rallying what he could of Byron's men, he led them in a furious charge against Cromwell's horse. Although shaken, these men did not turn and run and for some time a fierce struggle took place. As one of Cromwell's men later recalled, they had a hard pull for it being charged in front and flank by Rupert's bravest men. This is corroborated by the Parliamentary magnate, Lord Saye, who stated that the enemy's horse, being many of them gentlemen, stood very firm a long while coming to a close fight with the sword and standing like an iron wall, so that they were not easily broken. But Rupert had no more men to throw into the fight whereas David Leslie's horse, which had followed Cromwell's regiments into the battle, were as yet uncommitted. At this point they charged into the flank of the Royalist line which broke under the impact and fled back across the moor, over the second ditch and on towards Wilstrop Wood, pursued by Leslie's troopers.[23]

By now, although the storm had passed, the sky was overcast

and once the sun set, which it did at about 8.30 p.m. the smoke of battle conspired with the gathering dusk to speed the onset of night. No one knows precisely what happened to Rupert at this time, but an eyewitness records seeing him trying to rally his own regiment of horse as they broke. Later he got separated from his life guard and the story goes that he had to hide in a beanfield to escape capture. It is not possible to work out where this incident occurred, but by the time he was able to elude his pursuers, it was too dark for him to play any further part in the contest. He is next heard of trying to collect his men together outside York some hours later.

With hindsight it can be seen that as darkness fell the battle still hung in the balance. Although the Royalist horse on their right wing had been forced from the field, their line in the centre still held, a new flank having been formed by Newcastle's foot regiments which now faced to their right thus extending the Royalist front line, angling it back to protect the centre (see Fig. 13). On the moor to their right the Eastern Association horse was busy collecting itself together, Cromwell having rejoined them by this time. On the left Goring was trying to collect up his men, some of whom had pursued the enemy horse for several miles from the battlefield and some of whom, under Sir Charles Lucas, had been involved in the attacks on the flanks of the enemy foot. By this time Lucas himself had been unhorsed and taken prisoner as also had Goring's commissary general, Sir George Porter, so Goring was short-staffed as he tried to assemble his men in roughly the same place as Fairfax's horse had occupied when the battle started. In the centre fighting still continued between the foot of both sides, the allies having to some extent recovered their cohesion as Lumsden plugged the gaps caused by earlier setbacks, with troops drawn from the third and fourth lines.[24]

It will be remembered that at the start of the battle Sir Thomas Fairfax had pushed through the extreme left of Goring's line and had for a time headed off towards York, causing what disturbance he could in the Royalist rear areas. At some point he returned into the area previously occupied by Goring's horse with two or three troops and there he met up with his second-in-command, Lambert, who had somehow escaped Goring's charge and who had also got two or three troops of horse with him. The area in which they found themselves was alive with Royalists so they removed from their hats the white ribbons which the allies were wearing that day to distinguish themselves from the Royalists, and rode round the

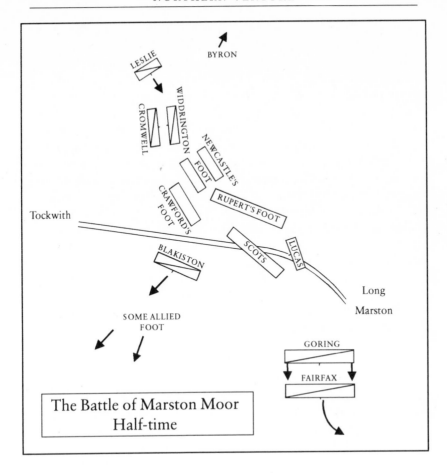

LESLIE

BYRON

WIDDRINGTON

CROMWELL

NEWCASTLE'S FOOT

CRAWFORD'S FOOT

RUPERT'S FOOT

Tockwith

SCOTS

LUCAS

BLAKISTON

Long

Marston

SOME ALLIED
FOOT

GORING

FAIRFAX

The Battle of Marston Moor
Half-time

rear of the Royalist position until they met up with Cromwell.[25]
It later transpired that part of Balgonie's regiment of Scottish
horse who had started the day with Fairfax had already joined
Cromwell.

Fairfax now explained what had happened on the other wing
to Cromwell and urged him to bring his regiments round the back
of the Royalist line to attack Goring and thereby dispose of the
last Royalist horse remaining in the field. Cromwell, with the
reinforcements provided by Fairfax, must have considerably outnumbered Goring when shortly afterwards they faced each other
on what had originally been the left of the Royalist position, Goring
attacking along the same axis as Thomas Fairfax had done at the
start of the battle. No details are available for this, the last clash

of horsemen in the battle, but Cromwell, with his well-disciplined and heavily armed troopers, smashed Goring's line and drove him from the field. He then led his men back to help in the destruction of the Royalist foot.

By now it was fully dark but the clouds had gone and a bright moon illuminated the scene. Under pressure from the Eastern Association foot on the Royalist right, the whole line had been pushed back so that, to keep contact with Newcastle's regiments, the remainder had been obliged progressively to withdraw and face towards the west. By the time Cromwell had finished with Goring the two sides were therefore lined up from north to south between the two ditches instead of from east to west as they had been when the battle started. From his position Cromwell was able to take the Royalists from the rear. Gradually gaps appeared in the Royalist line and some brigades and regiments were surrounded, others being withdrawn by their commanders and marched off towards York. After this the remainder either surrendered, or broke up and disappeared into the darkness. The last to continue resistance was Newcastle's own regiment at the extreme north end of the Royalist line. These tough men from Northumberland, dressed in their uniforms of undyed wool which had earned them the name of Whitecoats, would neither break nor surrender and continued fighting until they were all killed or wounded.

It was nearly midnight before the carnage ceased, by which time Rupert, Newcastle and Eythin had met up again outside York. Eythin asked Rupert what he intended to do, to which the Prince replied that he would rally his men. He then asked Newcastle what he would do; he said that he would go to Holland. Rupert asked Newcastle to stay and recruit more forces in the north, but he declined to do so. Next morning Newcastle left York in the care of its Governor, Sir Thomas Glemham, and made for Scarborough *en route* for the Continent with a party that included Eythin, Mackworth, Widdrington and ten other senior officers and notables. Rupert also left York for Richmond with about 6,000 horse that he had gathered up after the battle, and as many foot as he could mount on spare horses; possibly about 2,000. Glemham, with three complete regiments that had remained in the city on the previous day, together with the remains of some of the regiments that had fought in the battle, closed up the ports and prepared for a resumption of the siege.

*   *   *

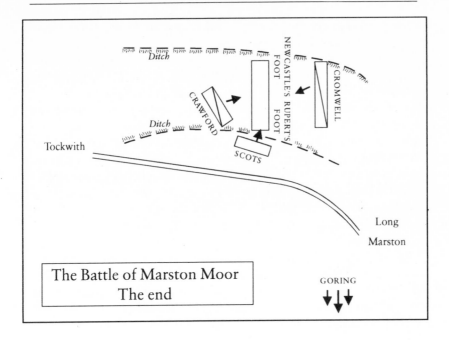

The Battle of Marston Moor
The end

Undoubtedly the Royalists had suffered a heavy defeat. No accurate casualty figures exist, but a contemporary account maintains that local people buried 4,000 bodies in the next few days in which case, bearing in mind the fact that many of those who died would have got beyond the battlefield before they did so, a total figure of 6,000 dead as suggested by another partici- pant might well be possible. Of these apparently around 2,000 were from the allied armies and 4,000 were Royalists, includ- ing one brigade commander and seven colonels. A further 1,500 Royalist prisoners were taken, including Rupert's major general, Henry Tillier, as well as the two subordinate generals of Goring's horse already mentioned. As a direct result of the battle, York was captured two weeks later and the north, which had been lost to the Royalists at the time of the Scots invasion, was controlled by Parliament for the rest of the war, with the exception of a few strongholds such as Newark and Scarborough.

This Royalist disaster can be attributed partly to errors made by Rupert and other Royalist leaders and partly to the strength of the allies and the tactical ability of their commanders. Marston Moor was Rupert's biggest battle and consequently his reputation as a general depends to a significant extent on his performance on this occasion.

From the time that Rupert left Lancashire to the moment that he relieved York in the late afternoon of 1 July, he had been on the top of his form. Indeed it would be no exaggeration to say that the operation up to that point was an even greater achievement than the relief of Newark, because he had gathered together and moved a much larger force in the face of an enemy that considerably outnumbered him and had so outmanoeuvred them as to have put himself in a position to fight them on advantageous terms. But he still had to defeat them in battle and for this he needed Newcastle's foot before he lost the tactical advantage.

Much has been written to explain why Newcastle's foot were not available early enough on 2 July. Some historians claim that the fault lay with Rupert for not going into York to confer with Newcastle when he arrived on 1 July, but the idea that he could have left his army and gone to see Newcastle at a time when he was closing up to a superior enemy, with whom he was about to give battle, makes no sense to anyone with an understanding of an army commander's duties at such a time. In any case Rupert sent Goring, who was fully acquainted with the strategic and tactical circumstances, to explain the situation to Newcastle and to ask him to send his regiments to join Rupert at 4 a.m. next day. If Newcastle was not convinced by Goring, he could have gone to find Rupert himself, or sent Lord Eythin to talk to him. In any case, even if Rupert had visited Newcastle in York during the evening of 1 July it would probably have been too late, because the garrison had already been allowed to surge out of the town to loot the allied trenches and once this had happened it would have been virtually impossible to get them ready to move in time.

There is little doubt that Newcastle and Eythin were put out by the momentum of Rupert's operation which gave them little opportunity for influencing a matter that was of great importance to them, but it was undoubtedly their duty to see that their men were ready to assist the relieving force in the same way as the Governor of Newark had assisted Rupert when Newark was relieved. Although Newcastle gave as his reason for leaving England after the battle that he would not endure the laughter of the court, it is more likely that he feared condemnation for failing to support Rupert at the critical moment. Newcastle had done well as commander-in-chief in the north in so far as organising his area in support of the King was concerned, and he had spent vast amounts of his private fortune in the cause. But he was no soldier, leaving the direction of operations to Eythin and his other senior officers and contenting himself with appearing on the day of battle when he conducted himself with becoming gallantry. On this occasion he was let down by Eythin, whose speedy departure to the Continent was undoubtedly the result of concern as to his fate at the hands of a court martial. Inevitably Eythin was suspected of treachery, but bloody-mindedness and an inability to cope with the speed at which the operations were developing seem a more likely cause of his failure.

Rupert on the other hand has been criticised for fighting at all on the grounds that had he avoided a battle after relieving York, as recommended by Newcastle, the allied army would, in Clarendon's words, have 'mouldered to nothing', because of 'irreconcilable differences and jealousies between the officers and between the nations'.[26] Undoubtedly there must have been differences of opinion amongst the allies as there always are in the early stages of a campaign, with particular reference to logistical problems and operating methods. In addition it is known that there was a specific bone of contention resulting from Vane's visit in June, when he suggested that, as negotiations with the King were never likely to succeed, consideration should be given to overthrowing him altogether and replacing him with someone else such as the Prince of Wales, or possibly with Rupert's brother Charles Louis. This idea was opposed by Leven, Fairfax and Manchester, but found favour with the Independents in the Eastern Association army.[27] It was reports of this dispute that made Newcastle believe that the allied armies would break up,[28] and later in the year, it was one of the main causes of the rift that grew up between Manchester and Cromwell and became of considerable significance in the prosecution of the war.

But the dispute about overthrowing the King was not one that divided the three army commanders, nor would it have caused the armies to separate in the period immediately following Rupert's relief of York. For purely military reasons the coalition could not have broken up in the face of the combined forces of Rupert and Newcastle, sitting as they were across the Scottish lines of communication. Neither the Scots nor Lord Fairfax's Northern army could have survived such a break-up and there is no evidence to support the idea that Manchester would have deserted them contrary to the orders he had received from the Committee of Both Kingdoms in London. In practice the allied armies would have been obliged to attack Rupert and Newcastle soon after Meldrum and Denbigh arrived, if only because the logistic situation would not have permitted them to do anything else. Once Rupert was defeated, the allied armies would no doubt have parted company, as actually happened after the fall of York on 16 July, when the Scots moved north to capture Royalist strongholds such as the town of Newcastle and to restore their communications with Scotland; when Lord Fairfax set about consolidating Parliamentary control in Yorkshire; when Manchester moved south to take part in operations against the King; and when Meldrum and Denbigh returned to their own areas of influence. Examination of these facts leads to the conclusion that Rupert was correct in planning to engage the enemy as soon as possible. His conduct of the operation up to the time that he met Newcastle on the morning of 2 July can hardly be faulted.

The next contentious issue concerns Rupert's decision not to bring on a running battle when the enemy was strung out on the road to Tadcaster. In order to attack the allied columns, the Royalist horse would either have to force back the screen of allied horse holding the ridge, or they would have to outflank them. In either case, as the Royalist foot arrived on the battlefield, they would have to be fed into a defensive position so that they could protect themselves against detachments of allied horse and at the same time provide a shelter behind which groups of their own horse could rally if necessary. If the Royalist horse were successful in their attacks, the foot would have to move forward and take up another defensive position further on for the same reasons. Throughout the day this forward movement of horse and foot would have to continue until the enemy broke up and dispersed, the foot moving forward by bounds, always ready to defend themselves and to provide shelter for parties of their own horse. This would have been a difficult battle to fight, especially with units that were unaccustomed to working together.

It is impossible to know whether such a battle would have worked, but if it was to be tried it would seem that 9 a.m. would have been the moment to launch the attack, when 5,000 of Rupert's horse were confronting Thomas Fairfax's rearguard of about 3,500. But even then the risks were considerable as most of Rupert's foot were as spread out as the allied foot. As the morning wore on, Rupert improved his position, but so too did the allies as more of their horse returned to the battlefield and the first of their foot regiments started to arrive. It is possible that in making his decision Rupert thought back to his assault on Essex's army as it marched between Swindon and Newbury the previous September. On that occasion, although his action had enabled the King to bring Essex to battle, he had inflicted little actual damage on the enemy. For better or worse Rupert decided not to bring on a running fight, concentrating instead on drawing up his forces in as strong a position as possible. Writing in the light of what happened later in the day it is easy to feel that this decision was wrong, a view that has been endorsed by the two modern historians of the Civil War with professional military experience, i.e. Brigadier Young and Colonel Rogers. But Rupert, bolstered as he then was by an unbroken string of victories, would hardly have discarded such an opportunity without the best of tactical reasons.

Rupert next had to decide whether to take advantage of the fact that his foot regiments were arriving more quickly than those of the allies. Had he launched a full-scale attack at about noon, most, if not all, of his own foot, excluding Newcastle's contingent, would have been present, whereas most of the allied foot would still have been some way from the field. It has been suggested that he did not do this because he thought that Newcastle's troops would arrive at any moment and he felt that it would be worth waiting the extra time before attacking. But Rupert must have known when Eythin's men were likely to arrive as he only had to send a horseman towards York to see how far they had got. He must have decided not to attack at midday, because he thought that the odds were too heavily stacked against him, but in making this decision he forfeited the last of the advantages gained by outflanking the enemy on the previous day. Certainly a noon attack would appear to have been a better bet than the running battle that he had discarded earlier, and a possible reason for his rejection of this option was that he had already decided that his best chance was to get the enemy to attack his position.

The layout of the Royalist position with its dependence on natural obstacles and the extensive use of reserves confirms the theory that Rupert was hoping to fight a defensive battle, whilst retaining the option of launching an attack of his own if necessary. By placing both his wings on ground that was difficult to attack, he was able to allocate one brigade of horse to act as a reserve for the centre and still have a second brigade as a reserve under his own hand. It takes nerve to weaken the front line in the face of a superior enemy in order to form such reserves, but they are essential in defence to offset the attacker's ability to concentrate on specific parts of the defender's line. Rupert's decision to allocate a brigade of horse to the centre followed Essex's use of Balfour's and Stapleton's regiments at Edgehill. Although in the event the battle was lost, Rupert's deployment seems to have made good use of the ground and of the resources available. Eythin's criticism that Rupert had drawn up his force too close to the enemy, was based on his realisation that it would cause the enemy to attack, which Eythin did not want. It also overlooked the fact that Rupert was there first and that it was the enemy who drew up too close to him, which incidentally caused complaint in the allied ranks. On balance there is little ground for criticism of Rupert's layout.

One definite error on Rupert's part was his conviction that Leven would not attack on the evening of 2 July and this resulted in his army being taken by surprise. It is hard to know how much advantage the allies gained from this misjudgement, but it must have reduced the casualties that they suffered in closing up to the ditch. It would be an exaggeration to suggest that this accounted for the Royalist defeat, but it further weighted the odds against them.

It is difficult to judge Rupert's conduct of the battle itself, because little is known of the part he played in it. All that can be said is that he made use of his reserve in the right place at the right time, and by personally leading the counter-attack he ensured that it was launched in the right way.

It could perhaps be argued that he should have stayed in his command post and allowed Widdrington to command the counter-attack, which would have had the advantage of ensuring that Rupert was present later on to reorganise loose parties of horse from either wing and direct them to the place where they were most needed. But at the time, the priority was to hold the allied attack on his right, and he was probably correct in supposing that his presence at that point outweighed other considerations. It is unfortunate that he was not able to get back to the battlefield after his counter-attack was defeated because, even at that late time, he might have been able to organise resistance to the move behind the battlefield of the Eastern Association horse and prevent them from taking the remains of his foot in the rear. Doubtless he would have returned to the fray had he been able to do so.

To sum up, it may be said that the main Royalist mistakes were the failure of Newcastle's foot to arrive on time, Rupert's error in thinking that Leven would not attack when he did and Byron's failure to blunt Cromwell's initial assault by staying behind his defences as ordered. In addition, Rupert might have done better to have brought on a running battle in the morning, or launched an attack of his own at midday before the arrival of Newcastle's foot. But despite these errors, it looked at one time as though the Royalists were going to win and it would be churlish not to acknowledge that their opponents' recovery was as much due to their own merits as to Royalist shortcomings. In the end their victory was due to a combination of Thomas Fairfax's tactical flair, the disciplined excellence of the Eastern Association horse raised, trained and led by Cromwell, and the competence of senior Scottish commanders such as Lumsden and David Leslie, to say nothing of the numerical superiority of the allies and the determination in adversity of some of their foot regiments. Had Rupert been opposed by the sort of armies that Essex and Waller normally led, he would probably have been victorious despite the Royalists' mistakes and their numerical inferiority.

As usual, Rupert took all the responsibility for the defeat on himself, refusing at the time to blame any of his subordinates, or even to give much credit to his opponents, his explanation for their victory being that the devil was looking after his own. In later life in conversation with friends, he went so far as to say that it was the superior strength of the enemy that brought about his downfall, but it is widely held that for the rest of his life he kept the King's letter of 14 June ordering him to fight, as a final justification for his action.

9

RETREAT AND RECOVERY

EARLY IN THE MORNING following the battle, Newcastle and Eythin left for their self-imposed exile. Rupert, whom in the words of Sir Winston Churchill, 'nothing could appal',[1] was left to pick up the pieces.

Certain strategic considerations were immediately apparent. First, the north, which had been lost to the King when the Scots invaded early in the year, had not been recovered and there was no prospect of the Royalists recovering it for the time being. Second, the army that Rupert had formed in the north-west to safeguard that region, and to recover the north, had lost many of its foot regiments and some of its artillery, as a result of which the north-west itself, together with the important recruiting area of North Wales, was at risk. The main threat to that area was posed by the Scottish army, but it was unlikely that it would move in that direction until it had cleared its lines of communication with Scotland. A secondary threat arose from local Parliamentary forces in the north-west reinforced by Meldrum. All of this, except for the details of his losses, would have been clear to Rupert on the morning after the battle. What he still did not know was the extent to which the King himself was in danger in the south.

In practice there was little that Rupert could do immediately to help the King and his first priority was to get as many of his men as possible back into the north-west so as to secure that vital area. Glemham was to hold York in order to keep the allied army occupied while Rupert got his men away. When obliged to surrender he was to take what men he could to Carlisle and hold that place for as long as possible in order to impede the lines of communication of a Scottish force operating against the Royalists in the north-west. Rupert intended to take the remains of his army back into Lancashire along a route to the north of the one he had followed during his advance and which he had already prepared.[2]

On 3 July Rupert was at Thirsk where he met Clavering with the advanced guard of Montrose's force; on the following day he met Montrose himself at Richmond where he stayed for two days collecting stragglers. He then moved to Castle Bolton taking Montrose's men with him. Montrose and a few attendants set off for Carlisle where he was to wait for an opportunity to intervene in Scotland.

After this Rupert moved rapidly west through North Yorkshire along the valley of the River Ure and thence south-west across the watershed to Ingleton where he arrived on 9 July. By 12 July he was at Garstang, between Lancaster and Preston. He then moved north again to Kirkby Lonsdale, probably to make arrangements for the future of the regiments of horse which had formerly been part of Newcastle's army and which had now arrived in that area. Even before Rupert set off to relieve York, the King had asked for their commander, Lord Goring, to be sent to him, as his services were urgently needed in the south, but Rupert could not spare him at that time. Now Rupert gave command of these regiments, which would subsequently be known as the Northern Horse, to Sir Marmaduke Langdale, a dour, strict and competent professional. Rupert was back in Preston on 21 July, in Liverpool on 22 July, in Chester on 25 July and finally, accompanied by Goring, at his headquarters in Shrewsbury on 5 August.

On 16 July York surrendered, Glemham having negotiated favourable terms under which the garrison was permitted to march out, escorted by a detachment of the Parliamentary army to within fourteen miles of Prince Rupert's forces. Having reached Knaresborough in this way, Sir Henry Slingsby records that Glemham and his three regiments marched off to Carlisle whereas 'those of the Prince's men that had been left in York, took the nearest way to go to the Prince'.[3]

It is difficult to know how many men Rupert had under him by the end of July, but the combination of the survivors of the battle, who had travelled with him and Goring, plus Montrose's men, plus the men who had rejoined him after the surrender of York, plus the regiments that had originally been left behind to garrison the north-west, must have amounted to a considerable army, albeit gravely short of weapons and powder. Certainly local Parliamentary forces made no attempt to interfere with him as he moved through the area.

There has been much speculaton regarding Rupert's frame of mind in the period following the battle with suggestions that he became totally demoralised, wandering aimlessly hither and thither with no set purpose. Doubtless he was disappointed with the outcome of his efforts to recover the north and he must have been sad at the loss of so many fine men, some of whom, such as Lord Grandison, brother of the Grandison lost at Bristol, were personal friends. He would certainly have been very upset by the loss of his dog Boy, the companion of his imprisonment in Linz and of his subsequent adventures, who had been killed in the battle to the great joy of the Parliamentary propagandists. In addition he may well have gone over the battle in his mind, questioning some of his decisions and cursing the inadequacies of his subordinates and allies, but if he did, he kept his feelings to himself and, initially at any rate, did not allow them to interfere with his performance. On the contrary, from the moment that the fighting stopped, faced by a mountain of problems and deserted by his principal ally, he made a series of quick and sound decisions which he energetically put into effect, so that within a month the position was, on the face of it, not greatly different to that prevailing when he set out for York. Only his reputation for invincibility had disappeared and that was a loss that the Royalists could ill afford.

But there is no disguising the fact that the underlying position in the north-west had changed for the worse. For one thing the flow of reinforcements from Ireland had slowed to a trickle and there would be no new regiments to make up for those lost at Marston Moor. Rupert could only set off on a new round of visits to raise money and recruit, but this time he met with prevarication and reluctance. He had always relied on threats as well as encouragement when reminding the civilian population of their duty to the monarch and now, with the failure of the northern venture gnawing at his morale, his demands became more forceful and his threats more menacing.

After repulsing Waller at Cropredy Bridge on 29 June, the King moved his army to Evesham, correctly assuming that Waller and Browne would not follow him so far to the west. Rupert probably heard of the King's victory during his march back to Lancashire, but the King was still uncertain of the outcome of Marston Moor when Digby wrote to Rupert on 12 July, although indications of defeat had already reached him, casting doubts on the first reports of a great victory. Soon afterwards the King's army moved to Bath from where Digby wrote again on 17 July.[4] From this it is clear that the King had received a letter from Rupert giving an account of the situation following the battle. Digby explained that, as the King could not reach Rupert in time to be of any assistance, he had decided to follow Essex's army into the west, intending to crush it between his own forces and those of Prince Maurice. The King's assessment of Waller was that if he tried to put together a large enough force to rescue Essex, he would arrive too late, whereas the force he could take with him at once would be too small to influence the outcome.

The King's campaign in the south-west was highly successful. Essex relieved Lyme and Maurice retreated as far as Barnstaple. Bypassing Exeter, from where the Queen had escaped to France a few days earlier, Essex moved on to relieve Plymouth and Sir Richard Grenville, who was besieging it, withdrew into Cornwall. On 26 July the King was at Exeter where he was joined by Prince Maurice: their combined force was around 16,000 strong. By this time Essex, who had decided to invade Cornwall, had reached Tavistock, his army having shrunk to about 10,000. The King moved rapidly via Launceston and Liskeard, arriving at Boconnoc on 4 August, a short distance to the east of Lostwithiel where Essex's army lay. Grenville's small army now closed up to the north, thus cutting off Essex's escape in this direction. Essex was effectively trapped between Lostwithiel and the sea in an area along the west bank of the River Fowey. Unless rescued by Waller his fate was sealed. But Waller, who had fallen out with Browne, could make his army march no further and settled down around Abingdon: he was not even strong enough to besiege Oxford. The best that Parliament could do for Essex was to send him a small force of horse and dragoons under Middleton, but they never got as far as Cornwall, being defeated by local Royalists in Somerset.

The King had no desire to sustain the losses of a battle and sent a message to Essex asking him to join him in ending the war on the basis of a constitutional settlement. This appeal was backed up by a letter signed by Prince Maurice, Lord Forth and other senior officers to the same effect. But Essex refused to negotiate, saying that if the King wanted to stop the war he should return to his Parliament.

While these exchanges were in progress, it transpired that Wilmot had made a treasonable proposal to Essex that the two of them should use force against the leadership of both sides to end the war.[5] The King, influenced by Digby who opposed Wilmot's expressed desire for an accommodation with Parliament, had been suspicious of him ever since the loss of Abingdon and had been waiting for a suitable excuse to replace him as lieutenant general of the horse. Goring, having left Rupert at Shrewsbury, arrived with the King on 7 August. Next day the King had Wilmot arrested at the head of his regiment and sent under guard to Exeter: Goring took over. At the same time Percy, who had been closely connected with Wilmot and who shared his views, resigned as general of the artillery, this post being given to Hopton.

The removal of Wilmot was unpopular with many of the officers of the horse and various protests and petitions to the King followed. In order to damp these down the King, on the advice of Digby who hoped thereby to damage Rupert's standing in the army, said that he had made the change at Rupert's request. It is difficult to know what role Rupert played in the handover, but he disliked Wilmot and had known about the King's suspicion of him since June. Whether or not he wanted Wilmot replaced by Goring is another matter. Rupert doubtless knew of Goring's questionable record in the opening stages of the war and of his reputation for drinking to excess, but he had done well at Marston Moor and in the subsequent withdrawal. Although Rupert fell out with Goring within a few months, he may well have thought him an improvement on Wilmot and in any case there was no one else available who was qualified for the post. On balance it is unlikely that Rupert raised any objections to the King's wishes in the matter, but it is equally unlikely that he played any part in plotting Wilmot's downfall despite Wilmot's conviction to the contrary. To avoid an open split in the army, Wilmot was not court-martialled, but allowed to withdraw to France where he continued his vendetta against Rupert.[6]

Soon after Goring's appointment Rupert received a letter,[7] unsigned but probably written by the Duke of Richmond, giving an account of the affair and making three other points. First, that the King was not in any way blaming Rupert for what had happened in the north. Second, that the King would be unlikely to get many of the Cornishmen now with his army to follow him out of the county once Essex was beaten and therefore Rupert should join him with such forces as he could muster without too much delay. Third, that it was being put about in the King's army that Rupert's own commanders in the north were criticising him for not listening sufficiently to their views. The letter was clearly intended to let Rupert know that the King still had faith in him, but that intrigue continued and that he should not stay away too long. On 15 August[8] Digby wrote again, describing the tactical situation and outlining arrangements for getting powder to Rupert's army. He also gave an account of Wilmot's replacement. Digby went on to say that the King intended to make Rupert 'Generalissimo' in place of Lord Forth as soon as a decent excuse could be found for doing so. For this reason the King wanted Rupert to put the north-west into a state of defence and move south towards Gloucestershire or Oxford with as many men as possible, so as to be ready to join up with him when he had disposed of Essex.

During the second half of August the King tightened the net around Essex's army, pushing it southwards towards Fowey and the sea. By the end of the month Essex had given up hope of being rescued by Waller and ordered Balfour to try and break out with the 2,000 horse, which he succeeded in doing during the night of 31 August. This disaster was put down to Goring being drunk, but it is more likely that the Earl of Cleveland, who was responsible for watching the sector where the break-out occurred, had too few men for the job and, although he chased the fugitives as far as Saltash, most of them made good their escape to Plymouth. On 1 September, with his army pressed on all sides, Essex too escaped to Plymouth in a fishing boat. Next day Skippon surrendered and the King took possession of forty-two artillery pieces, 5,000 muskets and a large amount of powder and shot. But he could not support such a large number of prisoners so Essex's army was allowed to march away on condition that they took no further part in the war until they reached Southampton.

On 3 September the King and his army set off on the long march back to Oxford. On 10 September, having established that Plymouth was too strong to assault, he left Grenville to reinvest it and marched to Exeter where he received some money and clothing for his men. From there he sent detachments to contain local Parliamentary garrisons in Taunton and Lyme and moved on to Chard, where he arrived with his army on 23 September.

Soon after receiving Digby's letter of 15 August Rupert started to move south. On 26 August he arrived at Bristol from where he hoped to direct Charles Gerrard's recruiting in South Wales and at the same time retain some control of events in the north-west, which he had left in the hands of Lord Byron.

Two other events that affected Rupert happened in the middle of August. On 18 August Montrose set off from Carlisle with two attendants to join a detachment of Irish Macdonnells sent by the Earl of Antrim to the Western Highlands. Meeting them shortly afterwards, he launched the campaign which justly earned him the glory that has ever since attached itself to his name. On the same day that Montrose left Carlisle, Rupert's brother, Charles Louis, arrived in London and was lodged by Parliament in the royal palace at Whitehall.

Within a few days of Rupert's departure, Byron, together with Langdale's Northern Horse, suffered a defeat in Lancashire; they were obliged to withdraw into Cheshire. Shortly afterwards Langdale was again worsted by Meldrum and Brereton at Malpas as a result of which the remains of the Northern Horse, numbering around 2,000, moved south into Monmouthshire. In early September Montgomery Castle, which stood between the Royalist recruiting grounds of North Wales and their headquarters at Shrewsbury, was handed over to Parliament by Lord Herbert of Cherbury.

At the end of August the King wrote[9] assuring Rupert of his support and affection, and urging him to be more friendly to Digby. The messenger bearing this letter also told Rupert that the King would have to delay promoting him until the position regarding Charles Louis was clear, since he could hardly employ him as commander-in-chief if Parliament was going to set up his brother as King.

Rupert remained based at Bristol for the next two months and it was during this period, when he was trying to stop the rot in the north-west and recruit a new army in South Wales, that the strain of the past two years, and in particular of the defeat at Marston Moor, caught up with him. There can be little doubt about the depression that afflicted him at this time. Sometimes it was exacerbated by accounts of fresh disasters, or of further intrigue amongst those around the King. Occasionally it was lightened by a letter from a friend such as the Duke of Richmond, reminding him of the King's unwavering support and the extent to which the whole Royalist cause depended on him.

Rumours circulated that Rupert was no longer his usual energetic self and even that he had given way to drunkenness and debauchery. But there is little reliable evidence to support this and subsequent accounts have relied heavily on a letter allegedly written by Trevor from Bristol on 13 October[10] which is plainly a figment of someone's imagination, as it includes a description of events that took place several weeks later when neither the Prince nor Trevor were in Bristol. But even if the debauchery is discounted, he was plainly run down by the extremes to which he had pushed himself for so long. It used to be a joke in the Royalist army that Rupert could not tire, and his physical courage was, and remains, legendary. But nowadays it is accepted that there is a limit to the endurance of even the strongest and Rupert had clearly pushed himself beyond it. It is hardly surprising that he became even more suspicious than usual and, although he soon recovered his physical strength, it took him longer to regain his mental equilibrium. During this time he sometimes seemed perfectly normal but on other occasions he became excessively upset by matters of little importance.

On 30 September Rupert met up with the King at South Perrott, not far from Crewkerne. In discussion it was decided that the Royalists should concentrate their remaining resources so as to safeguard Wales, the Oxford area and the south-west. To this end the King would return with his army to Oxford, attempting to relieve the three important outlying garrisons of Basing House, Donnington Castle and Banbury on the way. Rupert, accompanied by Hopton, would return to Bristol and move the Northern Horse and Gerrard's 2,000 recruits from Monmouthshire and South Wales into Gloucestershire, which was the only route by which they could reach the main Royalist army. The King hoped that as they moved they would draw off part of the Parliamentary army which would help him to achieve his objectives. But if this did not happen, Rupert was to bring his men straight on to join up with him at Sherborne or Marlborough. One way or the other the King undertook not to be drawn into a battle until Rupert arrived.[11] Rupert was back at Bristol by 6 October.

The Parliamentary leadership, being unaware of the King's limited aims, was at this time concerned for the safety of London. Waller, now separated from Browne, had moved forward to Shaftesbury, and the remains of his army acted as a covering force behind which Parliament tried to unite Manchester's army with those of Essex's men that had got back from Cornwall.

If the King's army was weakened by casualties, sickness and desertion, Parliament's forces were devastated by dissension. Within Manchester's Eastern Association army, reduced as a result of the campaign in the north to around 6,000 men, a major dispute had arisen between Cromwell and Crawford. Cromwell, because of his opposition to the Scots attempt to impose Presbyterianism on the English, had denigrated their part in the victory of Marston Moor and had taken every opportunity to boost the part played by the Independents with particular reference to his own regiments of horse. Crawford, who was himself a Scot and a highly competent professsional, resented this and supported Scots accusations that Cromwell had been indecisive, if not downright cowardly, in the battle and that others, including Crawford himself, had been obliged to intervene in order to get Cromwell's horse back into action after their first check. Manchester himself had been disturbed by Vane's suggestion that the King should be overthrown and was alarmed by the increasing influence of the Independents. It might be an exaggeration to say that he feared them more than he feared the King, but he certainly held back from investing Newark as Cromwell recommended and refused a Parliamentary request to take his army into Lancashire to oppose Rupert's forces on their return there. He maintained that his army should concern itself with the defence of the Eastern Association and he remained in Lincoln and subsequently Huntingdon until news of Essex's defeat in Cornwall forced him into moving to Reading where, reinforced by a further 1,800 men from London, he arrived on 29 September. During all this time he was on the worst possible terms with Cromwell, whose forthright rudeness came close to insubordination.

On 15 October the King reached Salisbury and Waller fell back on Andover. Manchester, who had previously refused to join Waller in Dorset, now marched to Basingstoke, sending urgently for the London trained bands to reinforce him. Essex's horse under Balfour and his foot regiments under Skippon, which were being rearmed at Portsmouth after their long march back from Lostwithiel, also started moving towards Basingstoke.

Essex himself, who had returned to London some weeks earlier blaming everyone but himself for his disaster in the west, was trying to co-ordinate these moves. But neither Waller nor Manchester was prepared to take orders from him, so Parliament decreed that the campaign should be directed by a committee consisting of all three of the generals. Fortunately Essex became ill and subsequent operations were handled by Waller and Manchester, assisted by Balfour and Skippon.

The King's original intention was to move from Salisbury to Marlborough where he expected to meet up with Rupert, but Goring persuaded him and the war council that an opportunity existed to beat Waller before he joined up with the rest of the

Parliamentary forces. An attack on 18 October successfully drove him out of Andover causing him many casualties, but he merely fell back on Basingstoke. Two days later the Parliamentary concentration there was complete and the King, with 9,000 men, found himself opposed by about 17,000 of the enemy (i.e. Waller, 3,000; Manchester, together with his London reinforcements, about 8,000; Balfour and Skippon, 6,000).

The King, flushed with the success of his campaign in the west and his skirmish with Waller, seemed in no way daunted by the odds against him but he did realise that he could not relieve Basing House, which was behind the enemy concentration at Basingstoke. He accordingly swung north-east towards Donnington Castle, causing the enemy besieging it to withdraw. Hearing that Banbury was at its last gasp, the King detached Lord Northampton's brigade of horse to relieve it, arranging for them to be reinforced from the Oxford garrison on the way. He placed the rest of his army in a strong defensive position north of Newbury to await the arrival of Rupert and the return of Northampton. At this moment Sir John Urry, who had deserted from the Parliamentary army in June of the previous year, decided to rejoin his former friends, taking with him up-to-date information regarding the size and disposition of the King's army.

The King now found himself obliged to defend himself against a force twice the size of his own, contrary to his agreement with Rupert not to fight until he joined him. Fortunately the outcome was not as bad as it might have been, the King eventually getting his army back to Oxford having relieved all of his beleaguered garrisons with the exception of Basing House. But both Prince Rupert and the King have been blamed for allowing such a risky situation to develop; Rupert for not getting his reinforcements to the Royal army until too late and the King for allowing himself to be drawn into a battle at all. The case against the King can perhaps be dismissed on the grounds that his boldness paid off. The case against Rupert can only be decided by examining what he had to do and the time available for doing it.

In essence Rupert had to arrange for the move of 2,000 foot soldiers recruited by Gerrard in South Wales for a distance of about sixty miles to a crossing of the River Severn, picking up the Northern Horse in Monmouthshire on the way. These troops then had to get across the river in the face of such interference as the Parliamentary garrison at Gloucester could arrange: this turned out to be slight although the lines of communication of the force with South Wales were cut after it crossed the river.[12] The force next had to march south for about thirty miles towards Bath where they would join Rupert and the troops that he was bringing with him from Bristol. When the battle took place on 27 October they were still about thirty miles short of the rendezvous at Marlborough and fifty-seven miles from Newbury. Had they completed the course, the Welsh recruits would have covered approximately 137 miles partly through hostile country, a march that could be expected to take between two and three weeks. In other words had they started as soon as Rupert got back to Bristol and had they been pushed hard, they should have arrived in time.

But it is not known whether they were armed and ready to march when Rupert met the King at South Perrott, nor whether the logistic arrangements for such a move had been made. It may be that it was the preparation, which should have taken place in August, that was faulty and that Rupert did not grip the problem until after meeting the King, by which time it was too late. A third possibility is that neither the King nor Rupert envisaged any urgency when they met and that it was only when Rupert received a letter written by the King from Blandford on 11 October that the need for speed became apparent. But each one of these possibilities implies some criticism of Rupert, who was responsible for the preparation of this force both before and after his meeting with the King and who should have had his finger on the pulse of enemy moves and intentions throughout. It is difficult to escape the conclusion that he was not operating with his accustomed vigour, which fits in with the general impression that he was run down and depressed at this time.

The right of the Royalist position north of Newbury rested on the Kennet and the left on a tributary of this river called the Lambourn. The centre lay astride a heavily fortified house and its outbuildings, now called Shaw House. To the left rear of the position, about one mile from Shaw House, was Donnington Castle, now fully replenished. South of this, between the Lambourn and the Kennet, was the village of Speen. The front was held by the King's foot under Astley, the village of Speen was fortified and held by Prince Maurice's army, and the majority of the horse was held in a large field in between.

On 26 October the Parliamentary armies closed up to the Royalist position, but considered it too strong to attack frontally. The council of war therefore decided to split their force. The larger part, commanded by Waller, consisting of Essex's army under Skippon and Balfour, together with Waller's horse under Haselrigg and Cromwell's horse, would set off through the night on a thirteen-mile detour round the north of the Royalist position, giving Donnington Castle a wide berth and finally advancing between the Lambourn and the Kennet to take the Royalist position from the rear. Meanwhile Manchester would make a feint attack on the main Royalist position in the morning to pin them in their positions, and a further assault when Waller's attack came in later on.

It would have been surprising if such an ambitious and complicated plan had worked in the light of the communications available in the seventeenth century, and this one did not. Waller's march took longer than was expected and was in any case observed from Donnington Castle. Manchester's feint attack was pressed rather too hard and it proved difficult to get the men going again when Waller attacked: although Manchester did eventually mount another attack it was too late to take the heat off Waller and he was again beaten off by Astley. Waller's own attack started shortly after 3 p.m. when there was only about an hour and a half of daylight left, and although Speen was eventually captured, Balfour's horse made little progress in the small water meadows between Speen and the Kennet and Cromwell's regiments were charged as they attacked to the north of Speen, first by Cleveland and then by Goring who forced them to retire. When it got dark the King was still in possession of the battlefield, but he was in no condition to renew the contest against such heavy odds.

During the night Prince Maurice and Astley withdrew the army successfully across the Thames at Wallingford leaving the artillery in Donnington Castle. The King with the Prince of Wales, riding hard through the night, met up with Rupert at Bath the following afternoon.

Early next morning Waller and Cromwell with their regiments of horse set out in pursuit of the Royalist army, but could not follow it through the close country beside the river without the support of foot soldiers. Leaving their men at Blewbury, Waller and Cromwell returned to try and get Manchester to bring the army up, but he decided to attack Donnington Castle instead, in order to gain possession of the Royalist guns. The attack was made half-heartedly and failed, after which Manchester belatedly agreed to move forward to Blewbury.

Arriving on 4 November, Manchester discovered from outposts that had been pushed forward to Witney and Faringdon that the Royalist army was assembled at Burford. But now the King had around 15,000 men with him: not only had Prince Rupert joined him, but Northampton's brigade had returned after relieving Banbury and additional troops had reached him from Oxford. On receipt of this information Manchester held a council of war which decided that the whole army should march back to Newbury. This they did on 6 November, having had the decision endorsed by Parliament.

By this time it had become clear that Parliament had no intention of offering the crown to Charles Louis. Furthermore Lord Forth had conveniently broken his shoulder when his horse fell in the recent fighting, and his coach, containing his ancient German wife, was one of the few prizes taken by Manchester's troops after the battle. The way was therefore clear for the King to appoint Rupert to the chief command in the army, which he did at Burford on the very day that Manchester withdrew to Newbury. In an attempt to avoid jealousy, Rupert suggested that the title of General should be given to the fourteen-year-old Prince of Wales, rather than to himself, and that he should be known as the King's Lieutenant General, a proposal to which the King happily assented.

The Royalist army now advanced towards Newbury for the purpose of collecting the artillery that had been left in Donnington Castle, the enemy doing nothing to intercept them. As they drew up to the castle they met some feeble resistance which they easily brushed aside. They then withdrew towards Oxford with no more interference than a half-hearted attack on their rear which Rupert quickly dispersed. By this time the enemy were thoroughly demoralised by the indecision of their commanders, shortage of supplies and the fatigue engendered by marching to and fro to little purpose. Despite orders from Parliament to stay in the field, they could do no more and went into winter quarters, leaving the King free to resupply Basing House. The Royalist army then went into winter quarters also, the King reaching Oxford on 23 November where he justly received a hero's welcome.

10

COMMANDER OF THE KING'S FORCES

At the time that Rupert took over the chief command from Lord Forth, the King and most of his supporters at Oxford were in high spirits. Five months earlier the city had been surrounded and the King had been forced to steal out in the night, suffering the indignity of being chased into the West Midlands by two Parliamentary armies. Now he had turned the tables on his opponents, repulsing Waller at Cropredy Bridge, defeating Essex in Cornwall and fighting off Manchester at Newbury, before returning safely to Oxford, having relieved all his main garrisons in the south in the process. To add to this, news was being received that Montrose had won important victories outside Perth and at Aberdeen and was running rings round Argyll's forces in the Highlands.

All this was causing deep depression in Parliament, which had raised and equipped large numbers of fighting men only to see the fruits of their labours apparently undermined by the squabbling and ineptitude of their generals. As soon as the armies went into winter quarters, Essex, Manchester, Waller and Cromwell took their various disputes on to the floor of the two Houses of Parliament. The rows and arguments that ensued caused the House of Commons, largely under the influence of the Independents, to pass the so-called Self-Denying Ordinance under which any member of the Lords or Commons holding a military command was obliged to resign it. But the House of Lords, which was solidly Presbyterian, initially threw it out so that for the winter months the existing commanders continued to operate.

As soon as Rupert started to formulate plans for the future, he must have seen how misplaced was the euphoria of the King and his more optimistic advisers. If events had gone well in the south, the same could not be said of the country as a whole. In the north, the town of Newcastle had recently been taken by the Scots and most of Yorkshire and Lancashire was under Parliamentary control with the exception of a number of isolated Royalist garrisons, some of which were still able to exert an influence on the surrounding countryside in the same way as Massey was able to intervene in the country around Gloucester. Only in Wales and the south-west was the King's position still relatively secure.

Towards the end of 1644, a threat of a different kind was beginning to show itself in the counties bordering Wales. This developed out of the failure of efforts made by Royalist leaders in Worcestershire and Shropshire to get the King to reorganise his forces in the area, with particular reference to the way in which they were supplied and quartered. The result was that a number of poorly armed groups, usually led by the local gentry, formed up amongst local communities for the purpose of defending themselves against marauding bands of soldiers of both sides.[1] Although these groups, which came to be known as Clubmen, were supposedly neutral as between the two main antagonists, and although as they spread to other parts of the country they caused almost as much trouble to Parliamentary forces as they did to the Royalists, their initial impact was felt by the King who was already being hard put to maintain his position in this region.

The King, though obviously acquainted with the various weaknesses of his position, persisted in thinking that in the long run an ever-increasing flood of Confederate Irishmen would arrive to redress the disadvantages that were assailing him in England. He also hoped to receive assistance from France and the Netherlands. He therefore continued to give his confidence to those like Digby whose unwarrantable optimism mirrored his own, regardless of the extent to which their views ran counter to the facts. And nowhere were the facts more discouraging than in Ireland itself.

Before sending troops to the King, the Confederate leadership wanted Ormonde, the staunchly Protestant Lord Lieutenant, to join his forces to theirs and expel the Scots from Ulster. This was a ridiculous suggestion, but even treating with the Confederates at all was seen as a betrayal by most of the Protestants in the country, who were still frightened of a further massacre like that of 1641. The Royalist leader of the Protestants in Munster, Lord Inchquin, was so concerned for his people's safety that he expelled all the Roman Catholics from Cork, at the same time seizing the military stores kept there. He then declared for Parliament, which quickly sent him arms so that he could hold and defend the ports of Youghal, Kinsale and Cork itself. He next urged Ormonde in the interests of the Protestants to cease all dealings with the Confederates, which Ormonde was unable to do because of the instructions that he was receiving from the King. As a result of Inchquin's defection, Parliament and the Scots between them now had control of both the south and the north of the country. Although Ormonde continued to negotiate with the Confederates, he was obliged to do so from a position of weakness which made it unlikely that he would be able to strike the sort of bargain that would result in their reinforcing the Royalists in England, especially as the Confederates, being aware of the King's great need, were steadily raising the price of their intervention. Eventually it became clear that nothing would satisfy them short of the restoration of the Roman Catholic Church throughout Ireland and, although this was not their position at the end of 1644, every day that passed made it less likely that the King would get his Irishmen. On the other hand, negotiations with the Confederates, when known about or suspected, continued to alienate support for the King in England.

There can be no doubt that Rupert, who was in close touch with Ormonde, must have been well acquainted with these developments, in addition to which he had direct experience of Confederate reluctance. As early as the previous January he had written asking for muskets and powder which the Confederates originally agreed to send, but they then declined on the grounds that the goods were needed by the Irish destined for Scotland. They also said that they were reluctant to send men until assured that they would be well treated:[2] Parliament's abominable behaviour towards Irish prisoners of war was probably designed, in part at any rate, to dissuade the Confederates from sending men to England. Other discouraging signs included the fact that officers sent by the King from England with commissions to raise regiments amongst the Confederates were unable to do so.[3] It is unlikely therefore that Rupert shared his uncle's optimism regarding Ireland, but it is equally clear that he was prepared to get help from that quarter if it could be obtained, contrary to the recommendations of Hyde and others who felt that the value of such assistance would be outweighed by the damage it would do to support for the Royalist cause.

On his return to Oxford in November, Rupert immediately found himself immersed in the problems of his new office. Not only did he have to allocate quarters for the regiments in and around Oxford and arrange for them to be brought up to strength, reclothed and re-equipped, but he also had to deal with an alarming number of requests from commanders in the outlying areas still under Royalist control and initiate discussion in the war council regarding future operations. And while all this was going on he had to contact Essex in order to arrange for the next round of negotiations which both sides now decided to undertake.

In practice these negotiations had little chance of success because Parliament was still insisting on the two things that the King would never accept, i.e. the abolition of the Church of England in favour of a Presbyterian system and control of the armed forces by Parliament. But both sides had good reasons for letting negotiations run on. From the point of view of the Presbyterians in Parliament and their Scottish allies, they were seen as an opportunity to reduce the growing power of the Independents. From the point of view of Vane, St John and Cromwell they gave a breathing space during which they hoped to restructure the army on lines that would ensure their own superiority in the future. From the King's point of view they were necessary to keep the Royalist Parliament in Oxford satisfied that he was seeking a negotiated solution and to give time for the development of Montrose's successful operations, which were gradually strengthening his hand and undermining the position of the Scots in northern England. But above all the King hoped that the negotiations would give the Independents a chance to weaken the Presbyterians, whom he still regarded as being the main enemy.

As Rupert settled in, the familiar bickering and intrigue inseparable from life at Oxford during the Civil War must have engulfed him once more, further depressing his spirits. During his ten-month absence, much had changed in the sense that the Queen had gone and Wilmot had been disgraced; both developments strengthened his position. Furthermore, a reconciliation of a sort had taken place between him and Digby at the King's insistence. Whilst still at Bristol Rupert had written to Legge in Chester saying that he and Digby were friends, but he also said that he doubted whether they trusted each other.[4] In the same letter Rupert mentioned that factions were building up against him on the grounds that he was a principal obstacle to the achievement of a peaceable settlement. But Rupert had himself been responsible for some unpleasantness when he failed to secure the colonelcy of the King's life guard of horse. He automatically blamed Digby, but his outburst on this occasion was probably no more than a reflection of his damaged morale. For his part Digby, still jealous of Rupert, formed an unlikely alliance with Goring.

The limited operations that Rupert planned for the winter months were designed to harass Parliamentary forces in the counties bordering Wales and in the area south of the Thames. To implement them Prince Maurice was sent to Shrewsbury at the end of November to take over the command formerly held by his brother, albeit with somewhat reduced powers, and Goring, with a task force of 3,000 horse and 2,000 foot, was despatched into the southern counties in early December. During the winter Rupert also intended to consolidate the Royalist position around Oxford and in the area between Oxford and the west. A more ambitious plan, designed to take advantage of Montrose's successes in Scotland in order to recover the north of England, was being considered for the coming campaigning season.

In pursuit of these plans Rupert first installed a Royalist garrison in Chipping Campden for the purpose of isolating Gloucester from the wool trade on which it depended. At the same time Digby tried to persuade General Browne, Governor of Abingdon, whose three regiments of foot were mutinous from shortages of pay, to abandon Parliament and hand over the town.

Not surprisingly this failed and Rupert decided to take Abingdon, despite the strength of the garrison. He therefore led a force in the early hours of the morning of 11 January round to the south of the town from where he launched his attack. Although Rupert was initially successful, Browne led a counter-attack and he was beaten off. It was later alleged that Browne had received advanced warning of Rupert's attack from Lord Percy in Oxford, but this has never been proved.

Amongst the casualties at Abingdon was Henry Gage, who had become Governor of Oxford a few months earlier when Sir Arthur Aston broke his leg in a fall from his horse. Rupert replaced him with the ever-reliable Will Legge from Chester, much to the annoyance of Aston who was now recovered and who wanted his old job back. At about the same time Rupert made Gomme the quartermaster general as part of an overall attempt to fill up the senior posts in the army with reliable professionals, less likely to become involved in intrigue. But although he was successful in one way, he caused disaffection amongst those displaced and laid himself open to the charge of surrounding himself with personal supporters. None the less, by tirelessly visiting the troops in and around Oxford he maintained the devotion of the regimental officers and men, who never failed to respond to his magnetic leadership.

As always resources were inadequate to satisfy the demands of the Royalist commanders around the country, who were busily trying to restore their stocks of arms, ammunition, equipment and clothing so as to be in a position to take the field in the spring. Despite the reduction in the area controlled by the King, some money was still coming in and considerable stocks of military supplies obtained. But great difficulty was experienced in raising the money needed locally for paying and quartering troops and much of Rupert's correspondence for this period consists of disputes regarding the areas allocated for the support of the many garrisons and units. Commanders varied greatly with regard to the discipline they enforced, the less scrupulous allowing their men to make good their deficiencies by stealing from the local population.

Of these none was worse than Goring, whose men looted wherever they went even in areas which supported the King. After leaving Oxford he carried out a sweep south of the Thames through Hampshire as far as Farnham, but was soon pushed back to Salisbury where he set up his headquarters in mid-January. Failing to get the orders he wanted from Rupert, he persuaded the King, thanks to Digby, to give him his orders direct which was the same arrangement that Rupert had when he was General of Horse. But in doing so he greatly offended Rupert and laid up much trouble for the future.

At the same time Prince Maurice was finding difficulty in holding his area together and was obliged to ask for extra powers. In the middle of February he moved north to Chester to repel Brereton who soon retreated, but while he was away, Shrewsbury was attacked and captured by a small force led by the Parliamentary commander in Shropshire, thanks to the fact that the Governor was ill and the soldiers of the garrison slack about their duties. This was a major setback for the Royalist cause and disrupted the whole business of putting men recruited in Wales into units and preparing them for war, a process that had been based on Shrewsbury for the past two years.

Rupert was supposedly more upset at losing Shrewsbury than by his defeat at Marston Moor and for good reason, since at Marston Moor he merely failed to recover something that was already lost, whereas in the case of Shrewsbury, the lines of communication to one of the two areas still capable of supplying the men and money needed for the prosecution of the war, i.e. Wales, were put in jeopardy. A complete block had now been established south of the Royalist-held country around Chester and Wrexham, resulting from Parliament's control of Oswestry, Montgomery Castle and Shrewsbury. There was still a large area open to the Royalists south of this block through Ludlow and Hereford to Worcester, but south of this again Gloucester acted as an obstacle on the direct route from South Wales via Monmouth into the Cotswolds or south to Bristol. If Parliament gained control of the Ludlow to Hereford gap, the situation would be grim indeed.

The other area still providing men and money, i.e. the south-west, was not yet seriously threatened. The Parliamentary presence at Taunton was a nuisance, but provided it was well contained, movement to the north of it from Bridgwater to Minehead and Barnstaple was perfectly possible, as was movement to the south of it to Exeter. Oxford was still the King's headquarters and strong points round about it had to be maintained to provide for its safety. Garrisons in the East Midlands such as Newark, Lichfield and Ashby were still secure and would be able to provide a few regiments to reinforce the Royalist army should it wish to operate in the area: they also constituted a thorn in the side of Parliament which rightly saw that they could be used as jumping-off points for Royalist excursions into the north or into the Eastern Association. But if the war was to be kept going for long enough for help to arrive from Ireland or abroad, the lines of communication between Oxford and Wales must be kept open. For this reason Rupert decided that he would have to go to Shropshire in person, but before doing so he had to attend to two other matters.

The first of these was the concern felt by the Northern Horse, billeted in and around Banbury, that while they sat idly in their winter quarters, Parliament was reducing remaining pockets of Royalist resistance in the north unopposed. Langdale believed that if he and his men appeared in Yorkshire they would be joined by large numbers of people hostile to Parliament. Whether this was correct remained to be seen, but offensive action would at least add to the problems of the Committee of Both Kingdoms, already worried by Montrose's operations. Accordingly a plan was made for them to make a dash to relieve Pontefract Castle. If this sparked off a Royalist uprising, the King might be able to send troops to exploit it. If not, the Northern Horse could still return to the King in time to take the field with the main Royalist army in the spring. In the event Langdale, who left Banbury on 23 February, was wholly successful in relieving Pontefract Castle, defeating Lambert, who had taken over command of the northern army from Lord Fairfax, on the way. But there was no uprising and Langdale, with no foot of his own, could only withdraw to Bridgnorth in Shropshire after demolishing the enemy's siege works and restocking Pontefract against a resumption of the siege.

The second matter involved establishing the Prince of Wales, together with his own council, at Bristol as commander-in-chief of the four western counties of Somerset, Dorset, Devon and Cornwall. One good reason for separating the King and the Prince of Wales was that it would minimise the possibility of them being captured together by Parliamentary forces. The King also thought that, at fourteen, the Prince ought to be exercising some responsibility of his own. Rupert strongly opposed the idea as it meant setting up a second centre of authority which would give Royalist leaders the opportunity of playing one off against another. But the King, who was planning to send Hyde and Culpepper away to Bristol with the Prince as part of his council, was looking forward to being rid of these opponents to his hard-line policies and he decided that the plan should go ahead. Hopton would act as the Prince's military adviser. In addition the Prince's council included his governor, the Earl of Berkshire and two former military commanders, Lords Capel and Forth.

The task of the Prince's council was to co-ordinate the activities of the various Royalist commanders in the area, notably Sir Richard Grenville besieging Plymouth, Sir John Berkeley at Exeter and Sir Edmund Wyndham who, having failed to recapture Taunton, was trying to prevent the garrison commanded by Robert Blake from sending raiding parties into the surrounding countryside. Also in the Prince's area of responsibility at the time were Parliamentary garrisons at Poole, Weymouth and Lyme and Goring's task force from the King's army. It soon became clear that co-ordinating the activities of so many independently minded commanders, including Goring who took his orders from the King when he did not like what the council suggested and from the council when he did not wish to comply with the King's instructions, was well beyond its powers. The Prince himself took little part in discussion. Instead he contented himself with embarking on one of his first recorded affairs, this time with his childhood nurse, Lady Wyndham, who evidently enjoyed the opportunity of contributing to his further education.

Although Goring was difficult to handle, he was still highly effective on the field of battle. Early in February he had almost succeeded in capturing Weymouth but had been pushed out again by the defenders, reinforced from the sea. On hearing that Waller was approaching from the east with a task force of his own, including some regiments of horse from the Eastern Association commanded by Cromwell, he retired to Taunton where he tried to get Berkeley and Grenville to help him carry it by storm. But when Waller saw that Weymouth was safe, he started to withdraw, followed by Goring who left Taunton and pursued him back through Dorset, beating up Cromwell's horse in their quarters on the way. This was the situation when the Prince and his council arrived in Bristol.

Two other decisions were taken in the last few days of February. First, the King prorogued his Oxford Parliament, which was representing the war-weariness of Royalists around the country more forcibly than the King liked. Second, the peace negotiations finally broke down to the satisfaction of the King who was particularly incensed by Parliament's barbarity in executing the aged Archbishop Laud, but to the regret of many, including Rupert, who were beginning to realise that there was little likelihood of winning the war militarily, because the amount of territory controlled by the Royalists was too small to supply the resources necessary for keeping a sufficiently large army in the field. Only if the area under Royalist control was considerably enlarged could the situation be restored.

These matters being concluded, Rupert was free to set off for the Welsh borders. The general concept of operations agreed in Oxford at this time was that he would move to Ludlow with a further detachment of the Oxford army to collect the recruits which should have gone to Shrewsbury. He was then to try to raise extra forces locally and link up with Prince Maurice. After this the two Princes would be joined by the King with the remainder of the Oxford army, and the combined force would move north to defeat the Scots and re-establish Royalist control over the north of England.

It was hoped that all this could be managed while Parliament was reorganising its armies in the south. Despite its initial failure to pass the Self-Denying Ordinance, Parliament had agreed early in February to combine what was left of the armies of Essex, Manchester and Waller into what would be known as the New Model Army. Shortly afterwards it selected Sir Thomas Fairfax to be its commander. Politically this was a good choice as, being a member neither of the Lords nor of the Commons, he would not have to resign his command if the Self-Denying Ordinance became law. Furthermore he was a middle-of-the-road Puritan who could be relied on to obey Parliament's orders without becoming involved in any sort of political intrigue. From a military point of view it was an even better choice as he was an experienced professional of proven tactical ability, a good disciplinarian and a capable organiser. Although seven years older than Rupert, he was between ten and twenty years younger than the Parliamentary commanders that he was replacing.

Rupert established himself in Ludlow early in March only to discover that Prince Maurice, who had gone to take the pressure off Byron in Chester, had recently suffered a reverse at the hands of Brereton near Nantwich. There is no record of the factors considered by Rupert when making his plans at this time, but it is clear that he was obliged to react to two separate threats. The first was to Hereford, which was being harassed by Massey aided by Parliamentary supporters in Herefordshire: Rupert also suspected treachery judging by a letter that he wrote to Legge at the end of the month.[5] The second was in the north where a detachment of the Scots army was already marching to support Brereton.

Rupert first moved towards Hereford where he was involved in a minor action, capturing some of the enemy. Despite this success, he was worried about the ability of the Royalists to maintain control in Wales. He also felt that until he could gather up some more recruits he would be unable to force his way through to Maurice.

When Shrewsbury was lost, the Parliamentary commander had hanged thirteen of the prisoners taken on the grounds that they were Irish. Rupert accordingly hanged thirteen of his recently acquired prisoners as a warning to Parliament not to restart this disgraceful practice. Parliament was greatly annoyed by this and instructed Essex to write to Rupert pointing out that 'there was a very great difference between Englishmen and Irishmen'.

Despite this unpleasantness and his concern for the position in Wales, it seems that moving away from Oxford had finally restored his spirits. Letters to Legge written in March and early April are optimistic so far as operations in the immediate future were concerned, except that in the south-west he anticipated muddle and an erosion of the Royalist position resulting from the uncertain command arrangements. There is even a touch of his old sardonic humour when he begs Legge to ensure that the King does not bring too many beefeaters and scullions with him when he marches from

Oxford, because of the problems of accommodating them. The after-effects of Marston Moor were receding in the face of Rupert's robust temperament, buoyed up in all probability by his ability at the most unlikely moments to relax with his hawks or his hounds. This is well illustrated by a letter sent by Byron to Rupert in which he describes the site of a recent skirmish as being in the place where Rupert killed a buck during the retreat after Marston Moor. On an earlier occasion Rupert had been hawking so close to the enemy that Essex had captured his falconer and his hawks, which he courteously returned.

During the first three weeks of April, Rupert was at his most energetic. On 8 April he paid a flying visit to Oxford where a meeting was held to assess the situation. On this occasion he supported Hertford in saying that it was unlikely that they would ever win the war and that the remaining military strength should be used to get the best peace possible. In this they were opposed by Digby who remained as optimistic as ever, humorously denigrating the Parliamentary armies and their new commander.[6] But Digby's optimism was based on his desire to maintain his influence with the King rather than on any logical assessment of the relevant factors.

Two days later Rupert attended a meeting of the Prince of Wales's council in Bristol in an attempt to get some order into the military affairs of the Prince's command. By this time the situation had deteriorated considerably as Goring, who had been told to send his horse to watch Waller and his foot and artillery to assist in the siege of Taunton, had taken offence and left his army altogether to take the waters in Bath. In addition to advising the Prince's council, Rupert drew off some of the arms that he had captured in 1643 to equip the forces he was now raising along the Welsh borders.

Ten days earlier Rupert had ordered Maurice's major general of foot to bring some men, recently recruited in Wales, to Hereford. On his return to Hereford he set off with these reinforcements to join Maurice and together they captured Beeston Castle some eight miles south-east of Chester. Their combined force then moved rapidly south and on 22 April defeated Massey at Ledbury twelve miles east of Hereford.

Over a period of sixteen days Rupert had travelled more than 300 miles, taken part in important meetings in Oxford and Bristol, captured a castle and won a small battle. He had also on the King's orders done his best to break up the Clubmen, executing some of their leaders in the process.[7] Together with his brother he had at least inflicted a check on Parliamentary activity along the Welsh border and the opportunity now existed for the King to join them with the foot and artillery from Oxford in order to carry out the next part of the plan.

But at this point a further complication developed. After Rupert's visit to Bristol, Goring had resumed command of his horse and in an operation of great speed and violence attacked Waller and Cromwell, causing them considerable casualties. Waller again withdrew out of Dorset and, as the Self-Denying Ordinance had at last got through Parliament, he, as a member of the Commons, laid down his command, as also did the Earls of Essex and Manchester as members of the House of Lords. Cromwell should also have done so, but when he reported to the headquarters of the New Model Army at Windsor, he was given a short reprieve and told to take a brigade of horse into the country to the north and west of Oxford to round up all the draught horses in the area which were needed by the King to drag his artillery pieces.

Immediately after Ledbury, Rupert had sent Maurice to Oxford with 1,000 horse to escort the King's forces to Worcester where the junction of the two armies was to take place. But as a result of the various detachments which had been made from the Oxford army, the King was too weak to move while Cromwell's force was in the vicinity, especially as Cromwell had now received orders to impede his move and had been reinforced by some extra detachments of horse and about 550 foot from Abingdon. Making the most of his opportunity, Cromwell narrowly missed overwhelming a force commanded by Lord Northampton at Islip and followed this up by capturing a Royalist strong point at Bletchingdon. He then tried to storm Faringdon, but this proved too much for him. Meanwhile the King sent to Goring and Rupert to come to his assistance and, as these two approached, Cromwell withdrew to Newbury, losing nearly 200 of his horse in a brush with Goring in the process. Rupert entered Oxford on 4 May. Goring arrived next day and a meeting of the war council ensued.

While these events were taking place the New Model Army was making ready for war. The establishment laid down by Parliament was for eleven regiments of horse each 600 strong, one regiment of dragoons 1,000 strong, twelve regiments of foot 1,200 strong and an artillery train. In terms of units this represented a reduction from the combined forces of Essex, Waller and Manchester so that it was possible to dispense with the services of a number of surplus officers. But it did not represent a reduction in the numbers of men available as the units in those armies were very under strength. In practice Parliament was obliged to order the conscription of 8,600 men in an attempt to fill the foot regiments of the New Model. But by aiming for a relatively small army, i.e. no more than 22,000 when fully recruited, it was within the powers of Parliament to ensure that it was paid, equipped and supplied in such a way that it would not have to plunder the countryside in which it was operating to survive. At the same time it would be able to detach one or more small task forces and still be large enough to outnumber anything that the Royalists could put into the field against it.

Under the influence of the Independents, the opportunity was taken to get rid of most of the Scots professional officers and where possible to promote Independents at the expense of the Presbyterians.[8] Skippon was selected to be the major general of foot, a Dutch professional called Vermuyden was made commissary general and second-in-command of the horse, and Thomas Hammond became lieutenant general of the ordnance. The post of lieutenant general of the horse was left vacant because Fairfax wanted Cromwell to fill it, providing that Parliament could be persuaded to relax the provisions of the Self-Denying Ordinance in this case. Many of the surplus officers, including Scots such as Manchester's former major general, Lawrence Crawford, were sent to join one of the regional armies which remained in being, notably those commanded by Brereton in the north-west, Massey in Gloucester and Sydenham Poyntz who had taken over from Lambert in the north.

On 1 May the New Model Army, though not yet fully recruited, took to the field for the first time, marching west to the relief of Taunton. But Parliament had had a difficult time deciding where the army should be employed, some favouring the march to the west while others thought that it should move towards Oxford. In opting for the relief of Taunton it was felt that some provision should be made for the security of the Eastern Association in case the King should decide to turn on this rich Parliamentary heartland: clearly the King's intentions were not yet known to the Committee of Both Kingdoms. As a result, four regiments of foot were detached to Cromwell's force which was given this task, Cromwell himself getting a further extension of his command.

But by the time that Fairfax reached Salisbury on 5 May, Parliament had heard of the arrival of Rupert and Goring in Oxford. This caused so much consternation that they ordered Fairfax to split his army again, sending a large enough detachment to relieve Taunton and leading the remainder back towards Oxford. On receipt of these orders Fairfax detached a further 4,000–5,000 foot and around 2,000 horse towards Taunton under the command of Colonel Weldon and countermarched his army as instructed.

When Cromwell withdrew, Rupert and Goring concentrated their forces with those of the King between Evesham and Stow-on-the-Wold. For a brief moment the King found himself commanding an army of 11,600 men.

At the war council that followed, most of those present suggested that the King should keep his army concentrated and move into the south-west to join the Royalist forces there and fight the New Model Army. Rupert did not like this plan for several reasons. First, because he distrusted the ability of the Royalists in the south-west to combine in support of the King: Grenville and Berkeley had consistently undermined each other's operations in the past. Second, because the Northern Horse were set on the idea of a campaign in the north and would be extremely reluctant to move into the south-west: if made to do so they would be likely to lose most of their strength through desertion. Third, because even if the Royalists beat Fairfax in the south-west, they would only have succeeded in retaining what they already controlled. Rupert felt that Royalist fortunes could only be restored by defeating the Scots and re-establishing control in Yorkshire and Lancashire, thereby greatly enlarging the area from which money and recruits could be obtained. A campaign designed to achieve this would also relieve the pressure on Chester, which was by now in danger of being captured.[9]

Rupert therefore urged that the Royalists should stick to the original plan, allowing Goring to return to the south-west to harass Fairfax while the main Royalist army moved north into the Midlands from where they could recruit and pick up extra units from the garrisons at Dudley, Lichfield and Newark, at the same time threatening the Parliamentary position there and in the Eastern Association counties. The King would then be in a position to move north and attack the remains of the Scots army, now besieging Pontefract, which had recently been weakened by being obliged to send detachments to assist Brereton in Cheshire and to strengthen the Covenanters in Scotland who had lost a further battle against

Montrose at Inverlochy in early February. It was even considered possible that the Scots, who were at loggerheads with Parliament because of the activities of the Independents, might come to an agreement with the Royalists rather than fight them. The threat posed by the move of the King's army into the Midlands would inevitably cause the withdrawal of the New Model Army from the south-west, as had in fact already happened, and once the situation there was restored Goring's detachment could rejoin the main army. Goring fully supported Rupert's views, which the King endorsed.

In accordance with this decision Goring returned to Taunton with 3,000 horse. Weldon's detachment from the New Model Army had arrived a few days earlier, just in time to save Taunton from being captured by the Royalists. Goring's arrival in turn enabled the Royalists to confine Weldon's men in Taunton with the garrison. At the same time the King's army set off for the Midlands, reaching Droitwich, just to the north of Worcester, on 11 May. By this time the New Model Army had reached Romsey on its way back from Blandford.

As Rupert had foreseen, the northward move of the Royalist army caused consternation in Parliamentary circles. At the time, Parliament's Northern army was widely split up and contingents from Lancashire, Yorkshire, Derbyshire, Staffordshire and Cheshire, totalling nearly 6,000 men, were ordered to join the Scots without delay. The Committee of Both Kingdoms then got the impression that the King intended to pass through Cheshire into Lancashire and Yorkshire, gaining recruits as he went; Leven was therefore asked to send men to help Brereton hold the passes into Lancashire, Brereton himself having abandoned the siege of Chester to meet this threat. This committee was so concerned by the King's moves that it ordered Fairfax to send a further detachment from the New Model Army of 2,000 horse and 500 dragoons, under his commissary general Vermuyden, to join Leven. Meanwhile Cromwell was ordered to take his brigade from Ely to Warwick so as to be in a position either to cover a sudden move by the King towards the Eastern Association or to move north to join Leven.[10]

From Rupert's point of view the important thing was to defeat the Scots before they were reinforced and before the New Model Army could catch up with him. But the King's army had to secure the areas through which it passed before it could gather up the garrison units which it so badly needed to bring it up to strength: for example 300 men from Camden under Sir Henry Bard and 400 from Dudley Castle under Colonel Leveson. But this slowed down the move of the army so that by 26 May it had only reached Burton-on-Trent, still sixty-five miles from Pontefract. Three days earlier Fairfax reached Oxford and laid siege to it, Cromwell having been diverted there on the way to Warwick with the idea that the King, seeing his capital threatened, might turn back to save it.

Oxford was well fortified and supplied and was thus capable of resisting a siege, so Parliament's decision to invest it should have been to the King's advantage as it meant that he would not be followed too closely by the New Model Army. But many of the King's courtiers and officers had their wives and families in the town and were reluctant to move on into Yorkshire until the siege was lifted. The King and most of his senior advisers, including Rupert, were bombarded with letters from individuals in Oxford urging a return, one bewailing the fact that even the Duke of York might have to go short of food. After much acrimonious discussion it was decided that, before moving north, the army would capture Leicester in the hope that it would cause Parliament to withdraw its forces from Oxford in order to defend the Eastern Association.

As this might lead to a battle with the New Model Army before the move north, and as Fairfax was no longer a danger in the south-west, Rupert sent urgent orders to Goring to bring his regiments of horse to Market Harborough. But Goring, who had negligently lost a number of men when two of his own detachments accidentally fought each other, refused the summons. Instead he sent a letter advising the King to return to Oxford and saying that if he did so, he would join him, after which they could jointly fight Fairfax.[11] As the Prince of Wales's council had already discovered, Goring was now virtually a law unto himself, although in this instance he was supported by Culpepper.

The King's army, moving by Ashby and Loughborough, arrived outside Leicester on 29 May having been joined by Sir Richard Willys, with 1,200 horse from Newark, on the way. Willys had taken over as Governor of Newark from Robert Byron who had been captured the previous November: he was a staunch supporter of Rupert. The army now consisted of 5,520 horse and almost exactly the same number of foot with an artillery train of twelve guns and two mortars. With a total of around 11,000 men it was almost as large as it had been before Goring took his 3,000 into the south-west. Opposing it behind the defences of Leicester were 1,270 Parliamentary soldiers assisted by perhaps another 1,000 active men from the town. The lengthy fortifications could not be fully manned by so small a force and were in any case not particularly strong. In addition the Governor had been persuaded not to demolish a number of houses outside the city walls which would give cover to an approaching enemy.[12]

Rupert, annoyed at having to delay the move to the north, was determined that no time should be wasted in capturing Leicester. He decided to launch his main attack from the south and during the evening and night of 29 May he personally supervised the erection of a battery which was ready by the following morning. At midday he summoned the Mayor to surrender the town, offering favourable terms as an inducement, but the Mayor, playing for time, asked to be given the night to think it over. After some further delay Rupert gave the town fifteen minutes to surrender before starting to batter a breach in the walls with his guns, which he succeeded in doing by 6 p.m.

At midnight Rupert launched an all-out attack from four directions. One brigade, commanded by Astley's son Bernard, advanced from the north. Another, commanded by Sir Henry Bard, attacked from the east. Colonel Russell with Rupert's regiment of foot attacked an enemy gun battery on Horsefair-Leys, while the main attack on the recently made breach was commanded by Colonel Lisle. The King's life guard of foot supported Lisle.

Within an hour all these columns were successful and the gates were thrown open so that Lord Northampton's regiment of horse could get in to help round up the defenders. But still the enemy continued to resist in isolated pockets. By all the laws of war the Royalists were entitled to give no quarter and some members of the garrison, including many Scots, were killed. Inevitably too there was much pillage and rape. Eventually Rupert got control of the situation and stopped the worst excesses of the night, a fact that was recorded by the Parliamentarian Sir Samuel Luke who wrote that 'in the end, Prince Rupert coming in, his mercy put an end to their cruelties so far as it concerned the English. The Scots were all put to the sword, being 200 in number.'[13]

It is difficult to find agreement regarding the costs of storming Leicester, but there were probably about 200 Royalist casualties, in addition to which men were left to garrison the town when the Royalists moved on, which further reduced the King's army: others must have deserted with their loot as always happened after a town was taken by storm. On the other hand the Royalists captured nine artillery pieces and 1,000 muskets, together with much powder and other supplies. Over 1,000 prisoners were taken, including two colonels and a lieutenant colonel, one of whom was exchanged for Henry Tillier who had been captured at Marston Moor.

The capture of Leicester was followed by yet another meeting of the war council at which three possible courses of action were considered. The first of these, which received little support, was that the army should march back towards Worcester to meet up with Sir Charles Gerrard who was once again bringing recruits from South Wales to the number of around 3,000. The second option was to pursue the original plan and turn on the Scots. The third was to return to Oxford and relieve the siege.

Rupert naturally put all his weight behind the move to the north on the grounds that this was the only course offering a chance of long-term success. His argument was strengthened by the arrival of news that Montrose had won yet another victory in Scotland at Auldearn near Inverness on 9 May. At this time Montrose said that if the King could spare him 500 horse, he would lead an army of Scottish Royalists into England by the end of the summer. Rupert assured the council that Oxford was in no danger and Langdale reiterated the extreme reluctance of the Northern Horse to move away from the north. It is abundantly clear that Rupert insisted on the northern option and that he was backed by most of the military leaders. But the civilians, led by Digby and Ash-burnham, were equally adamant that the army should return to Oxford.[14] Quite apart from their concern for their families, they felt that with most of the civilians being in Oxford, the soldiers were gaining too much influence with the King. They were also absurdly optimistic about the outcome of a battle with the New Model Army, which they continued to ridicule. The King, who was himself under pressure from Oxford, decided to back the civilians and ordered a move to the south.

But the sack of Leicester had already brought about the relief of Oxford. Fairfax, who had since the inception of the New Model Army been marching hither and thither in accordance with detailed directions from Parliament, now received instructions to take what-ever steps were needed to destroy the King's army. His first reaction was to insist that Cromwell, who had been moved back into Cambridgeshire as the King approached Leicester, should be made his lieutenant general of horse and this was agreed. He next sent orders for Cromwell to move to Stony Stratford and for Vermuyden to return from the north. Fairfax himself left the Oxford area on 3 June.

The King's army, less 400 of the Newark horse which had to return to protect that vital stronghold, moved south from Leicester on 4 June. On 5 June it reached Market Harborough and on 8 June it arrived at Daventry where it stayed for the next three days while a large number of cattle were rounded up and sent under escort to replenish Oxford. Judging by letters written by the King to the Queen and by Digby to Nicholas in Oxford, both were full of confidence and predicting total victory within a few days. They were still expecting to be joined by Goring, whose letter refusing to leave the south-west had not yet arrived. Indeed it never did arrive because it was intercepted by Fairfax who therefore knew that the King's hopes in this direction would be disappointed.

On 11 June Fairfax reached Stony Stratford where he found Vermuyden who had already arrived nearby at Newport Pagnell. At this point Vermuyden gave up his appointment for personal reasons and returned to Holland. He was replaced by a clever and politically minded Independent called Henry Ireton.

By now Fairfax was only ten miles from the King. In order to give Goring a chance to arrive, the King decided to withdraw back to Market Harborough. In an attempt to give Fairfax the slip he set off initially in a westerly direction hoping that the enemy would think that he was heading for Worcester. He then swung north, but Fairfax was too close to be put off.

On 12 June Fairfax reached Kislingbury, a short distance from Daventry. Early in the morning of 13 June he was joined by Cromwell and together they marched to Guilsborough. In the course of the same day the King reached Market Harborough. That evening an advanced guard of the Parliamentary horse overran a detachment of the Royalist rearguard at the village of Naseby some five and a half miles south of Market Harborough. This incident brought home to the King how closely he was being pursued by Fairfax and led to yet another council of war.

Rupert had always known that battles were unpredictable. Earlier in the war he had sometimes been prepared to risk battle with stronger Parliamentary forces because of the qualitative superiority of the Royalist horse. But this had not worked at Marston Moor because the enemy had too great a numerical advantage, allied to some skilful leaders and some effective regiments, particularly those of the Eastern Association many of which were now present in the New Model Army. Although Rupert could not have

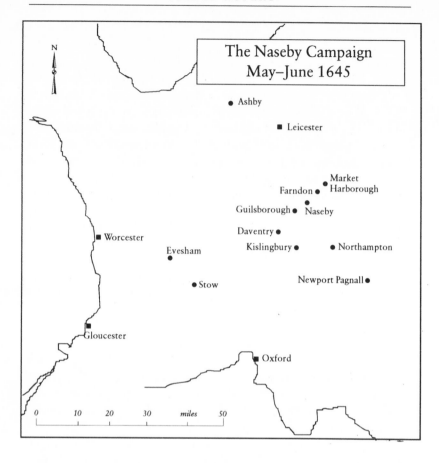

The Naseby Campaign
May–June 1645

N

● Ashby

■ Leicester

Farndon ● ● Market Harborough

Guilsborough ● ● Naseby

Daventry ●

Kislingbury ● ● Northampton

■ Worcester

Evesham ●

● Stow

Newport Pagnall ●

■ Gloucester

■ Oxford

0   10   20   30   *miles*   50

known exactly how strong Fairfax was, because of the comings
and goings of enemy detachments, he knew for certain that he was
facing a greatly superior enemy. He therefore advised a further
retreat towards Leicester where numbers could be augmented from
the garrison, with the additional possibility that either Gerrard or
Goring would arrive before the battle took place.

But as usual he was opposed by Digby and Asburnham who,
devoid of any military understanding, persuaded the King that
further retreat would affect morale and that the army should
advance boldly towards the enemy. The King's Secretary at War,
Sir Edward Walker, writing some years later, made it clear that
the decision was taken not only to fight, but also that the Royalist
army should turn and seek Fairfax out rather than be pursued by
him. Walker, who was normally critical of Rupert, went on to say

that these decisions were made contrary to Prince Rupert's opinion and that it was everyone's misfortune that the court faction led by Digby and Ashburnham was constantly opposed to the army.[15] The die was cast and Rupert had to make the best of it.

As soon as it got light the Royalist army started to deploy along a ridge about two miles south of Market Harborough between East Farndon and Little Oxenden in accordance with a plan that Rupert had been considering over the past ten days. He also sent the scoutmaster out to look for the enemy, who had spent the night at Guilsborough nine miles to the south of Market Harborough. After some time the scoutmaster returned to say that he had ridden four miles to the south of Market Harborough without seeing any sign of the enemy, whereupon Rupert himself went with a body of horse to discover where they were.

Fairfax had also got his army on the move at first light and was heading for Naseby about four miles ahead. The Royalist scoutmaster, who had probably reached the ridge just to the south of the village of Clipston, would not have been able to see the Parliamentary army which was still south of the Naseby ridge. But when Rupert arrived he did see a body of enemy horse apparently retreating from a position north of Naseby into the village itself. In fact what he had seen was Fairfax and Cromwell completing a reconnaissance of the ground north of the village. In pursuit of the decision to seek out and fight Fairfax, Rupert sent word back to the King to bring the army forward from the position it was occupying between East Farndon and Little Oxenden and occupy the ridge to the south-west of Clipston centred on Dust Hill, which was about one and a half miles north of Naseby.

The route from the ridge on which they were deployed to the new position on Dust Hill involved the foot in a march of two miles to the south through Clipston after which they had to move east to their deployment positions, which would have taken those on the right of the line another mile. In order to protect the army when it turned to march east, the Northern Horse were deployed to the south of Clipston in a position which would be on the left of the Royalist line when it finally deployed. The Northern Horse would therefore have been the first Royalist troops seen by Fairfax and they would have arrived before the leading foot regiments of the New Model Army. When Fairfax saw the easterly move of the King's army he thought that Rupert was trying to deploy up-wind of him which would have given the Royalists an advantage as it meant that the smoke of battle would be blowing into their opponents' eyes. As his own army arrived he deployed it opposite the Royalists on the forward slope of the ridge north of Naseby. When both armies were deployed they were therefore each on a slight ridge with an area of lower ground between them. In the centre the distance between the forward troops of each army was about 600 yards, slightly further on the flanks.

On the right or eastern wing of the Royalist army Rupert placed a force of about 1,710 horse in two lines supported by 200 musketeers. In the front line was his own life guard and Prince Maurice's life guard, each amounting to around 130 men, his own strong regiment of 400 horse and a second composite regiment of 300 made up of the remains of Prince Maurice's regiment and the Queen's regiment. In the second line, commanded by Sir William Vaughan, were three regiments amounting to a further 750 men.

On the left wing was the Northern Horse, also deployed in two lines, supported by a further 200 musketeers. Although Langdale had with him the remains of over twenty regiments, some consisted of no more than thirty or forty men with a high proportion of officers: there was even one regiment that consisted of nothing but officers. Altogether it is estimated that there were the same number of horse on the right wing as on the left, that is to say a little over 1,700, deployed in two lines. Of these the front line, commanded by Langdale himself, consisted of the regiments from Yorkshire, Lancashire and Derbyshire while the second line, which was probably commanded by Blakiston, consisted of regiments from Northumberland and Durham.

The centre was commanded by Lord Astley and consisted of three brigades of foot (tertias) commanded by Sir Bernard Astley, Sir Henry Bard and Colonel George Lisle as at the storming of Leicester. Altogether there were 3,200 foot under Lord Astley's command deployed in two lines, in addition to which he had a brigade of horse under Colonel Thomas Howard numbering 880 men which was positioned between the first and second lines. This brigade consisted of the remains of seven regiments of horse mainly drawn from Midlands garrisons and organised into three divisions. Also in the centre were the ten Royalist guns.

Rupert had again decided to keep a sizeable reserve consisting of the King's life guard of foot, 300 strong, and his own regiment of foot, 500 strong. In addition there was the King's life guard of horse which, with the addition of numerous courtiers and gentle-

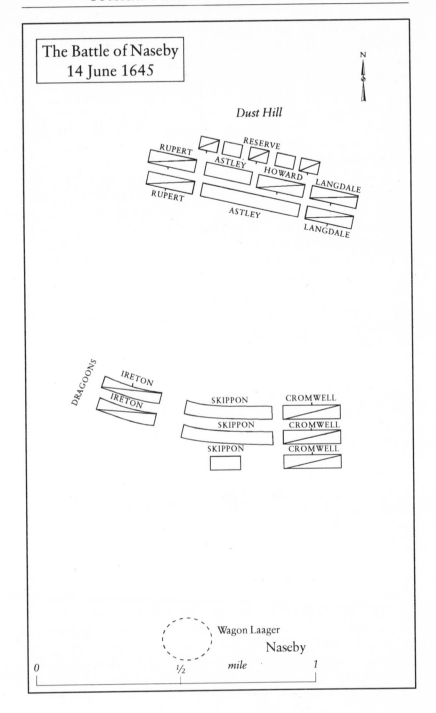

The Battle of Naseby
14 June 1645

N

Dust Hill

RUPERT

RESERVE

ASTLEY

HOWARD

LANGDALE

RUPERT

ASTLEY

LANGDALE

DRAGOONS

IRETON

IRETON

SKIPPON

CROMWELL

SKIPPON

CROMWELL

SKIPPON

CROMWELL

Wagon Laager

Naseby

0   ½   mile   1

men volunteers, numbered around 500, together with that part of the Newark horse that had not already returned to Newark amounting to a further 400–500 men. This reserve, which totalled 800 foot and nearly 1,000 horse, would, if properly handled, constitute a formidable part of the King's overall capability and was designed to deal with any Parliamentary incursion achieved by the concentration of greatly superior numbers on any part of the field. The holding of a large reserve is the only way to compensate for overall numerical inferiority.

The reserve was drawn up along the crest of the ridge just in front of the King's position. On the right was half of the Newark horse. Next to them was the King's life guard of foot. In the centre and immediately in front of the King was the King's life guard of horse. To their left was Prince Rupert's regiment of foot, which would therefore have been to the right rear of the Northern Horse, and on the left was the other half of the Newark horse.

In the event the Royalists' numerical inferiority was probably even greater than Rupert had foreseen as Fairfax had mustered 14,000 men to oppose the King's 9,000. He deployed them in a conventional manner with the horse on the two wings and the foot in between. The hedge that ran at right angles to the front, on the left of the position, was lined with the only regiment of dragoons in the New Model Army.

The Parliamentary left was commanded by the new commissary general, Henry Ireton, who had with him, in addition to the dragoons, five strong regiments of horse plus a half-regiment of horse belonging to the Eastern Association that had not been incorporated in the New Model Army. Altogether he had 3,300 horse to oppose the 1,700 of the old Oxford horse and he deployed them in two lines, the front commanded by himself and the second by Colonel Fleetwood.

The Parliamentary centre, commanded by Skippon, consisted of eight regiments of foot containing 6,400 men which was almost exactly twice as many as Lord Astley's foot. Skippon deployed them in two lines. In the front line were five regiments and in the second line were two full regiments and half of a third. The other half, amounting to 400 men, was held in a third line as a reserve. It was the only reserve held by the army as a whole. Skippon also had the New Model Army's eleven field guns; the three siege guns stayed in the wagon laager which was immediately behind the reserve and close to the village of Naseby.

The Parliamentary right was commanded by Cromwell, who had

six regiments of horse plus the other half of the Eastern Association regiment. Altogether he had 3,900 men with which to oppose Langdale's 1,700. The reason why he had more men than Ireton was that an extra regiment of horse unexpectedly arrived after the deployment was made and this was placed on the extreme right of the line. Cromwell deployed his regiments in three lines, the first commanded by Whalley and the second by himself. The rear line consisted of six reserve troops for use where required. Cromwell's original large regiment (the Ironsides) had been broken up when the New Model Army was formed. One half had been used to form Fairfax's regiment of horse and the other half had become Whalley's regiment of horse. Both these formidable regiments were in the front line of the Parliamentary right wing.

One surprising aspect of the New Model Army was that there was no brigade level of command so that Skippon, Cromwell and Ireton had to give their orders direct to each of the regiments under their command.[16]

Once the deployment of the Royalist army was complete, Rupert rode across and took personal command of the right wing. Although the King was in overall command, it would have been normal for the Lord General, which in practice was the office that Rupert held, to have been with him. At Naseby this was particularly important, because of the way in which Rupert had designed the battle. As he had kept a large reserve to restore the situation in any part of the battlefield where things were going badly, it made sense for him to be stationed where he could advise the King on the timing and nature of its use. For example, he might suggest that one part should go in one direction and another somewhere else, or alternatively that the whole reserve should be launched in one great thrust, in which case he might have to lead it in person.

Even today no one seems to know why Rupert led the right wing. Some claim that he asked to do so because he could not tolerate the thought of sitting next to the King and having his advice accepted at one moment and overruled at the next on the prompting of courtiers such as Digby. Another possibility is that he felt that the only way to overcome the heavy numerical superiority enjoyed by the enemy on both wings and in the centre, was personally to lead an attack of such ferocity in one place that Fairfax would have to abandon his design for the battle as a whole in order to repel it. If for either of these reasons Rupert wanted to command the right wing, he could argue that either Lindsey or Bellasyse, both of whom were with the King, were sufficiently experienced soldiers to advise on the use of the reserve. But possibly the King wanted his nephew to command the right wing. After his victories at Cropredy Bridge and Lostwithiel, he may have thought that he was as well capable of controlling the battle as Rupert. This possibility is borne out by the fact that, for no apparent reason, both he and Digby were still expecting an overwhelming victory. But whether the decision was made by Rupert or the King, it proved to be a mistake.

In order to seize the initiative, the Royalists attacked all across the front. The exact time is not recorded, but it was between 10 and 11 a.m. The foot started to advance slowly across the open ground with the horse on either wing keeping abreast of them, halting every now and then when they found themselves getting too far ahead. At a given moment the 200 musketeers that were positioned between the forward regiments of horse fired a volley at the enemy, whereupon the horse charged.

As Rupert's wing closed in on Ireton, Okey's dragoons fired on them from their position behind the hedge, but they in turn were engaged by the Royalist musketeers who had been with the regiments of horse before they charged.

The right of Rupert's front line, consisting of his own life guard, Prince Maurice's life guard and most of his regiment of horse, smashed through the centre and right of Ireton's first line, but the two weak Royalist regiments on the left were repulsed by Ireton himself. The two regiments in Rupert's second line then charged in order to dispose of Ireton's second line. Rupert and Maurice with the survivors of this encounter swept on up the slope until they came to the enemy's wagon laager just to the west of Naseby, driving most of Ireton's wing before them. But Ireton, with the best part of two regiments from the right of his front line, was still operational and apparently unaware of the disaster that had overtaken the rest of his command. He now turned inwards to assault the Royalist foot, but he was unhorsed, wounded and captured in the fighting that ensued: he was released later in the day.

In the centre Astley initially made ground thanks to the superior quality of his veteran regiments which for some time drove the enemy foot back in disorder, severely wounding Skippon when he moved forward to rally his men. But through shortage of numbers, the left of his front line did not extend quite far enough, so that Fairfax's own regiment of foot on the Parliamentary right was not engaged.

The King from his position on the ridge behind the battle would have measured the progress of Astley's advance from the Parliamentary colours falling one by one and he would also have seen Rupert fighting his way through the enemy horse on the right. But it would have been the events that were taking place on his left that principally occupied his attention.

Cromwell's front line under Whalley did not wait to receive the charge of the Northern Horse, but moved forward to meet it. But Whalley's regiments did not all move forward at the same speed, because of some difficult going on their right. As a result his left-hand regiment struck the right of the Northern Horse hard, dispersing three or four troops which disappeared off to the rear and reformed behind Prince Rupert's regiment of foot. By contrast in the centre his men were only able to push the main body of the Northern Horse back; they did not manage to break it. But as more and more of Whalley's troops got clear of the bad going, the Northern Horse were subjected to increasing pressure. In an attempt to restore the situation, the left-hand half of the Newark horse now joined in the mêlée, but whether they did so on the King's order, or on their own initiative in accordance with their understanding of the way in which the battle was designed to be fought, is unknown. Cromwell then sent forward one of the regiments in his second line to decide the outcome of the struggle. The Northern Horse, now heavily outnumbered, broke and fell back about a mile.

It is likely that this happened at about the time that Rupert was cantering up to the Parliamentary wagon laager, although Rupert may have taken longer to fight his way through Ireton's men than Cromwell did to disperse the Northern Horse. Precise timing is impossible to work out as the participants were not equipped with accurate ways of recording it.

On Cromwell's orders, Whalley did not follow the retreating Northern Horse, but detailed two regiments to screen them off. The remaining three regiments rejoined Cromwell who now led them, together with the three regiments not so far engaged, against the left flank of the Royalist foot, their right flank being asssailed by Ireton's men as previously described. Astley, heavily outnumbered and assailed from both flanks as well as from the front, could not be expected to last long unless reinforced.

The King still had under his hand the whole of his reserve with the exception of half of the Newark horse and, had he launched them at this point, he might have stabilised the situation in the centre and gained time for the Newark horse to reform and for Rupert to get his regiments back into the battle. It is clear that the King understood what was required as he moved forward to put himself at the head of his life guard of horse in order to launch the attack. But at this moment of crisis, the very turning point of the battle, an unimportant Scottish earl appeared from amongst those standing with the King, seized the bridle of his horse and swung it round to the right, that is to say away from the direction of the impending advance. This was taken by the nearest troops to mean that they were to retire and something like a minor panic set in until the whole body could be halted several hundred yards to the rear. By this time the opportunity to arrest the disintegration of the Royalist centre had passed.

The man who grabbed the King's bridle was the Earl of Carnwath, an eccentric, quarrelsome and ineffective supporter of the King's cause in Scotland. He had joined Montrose early in 1644, at which time his daughter, dressed as a man, commanded a troop of horse, her banner displaying a naked man hanging from a gibbet! There is no doubt that Carnwath's action was the immediate cause of the disintegration of the King's army, but there has never been any suggestion of treachery. As he said at the time, he acted to preserve the King's life, the surprising thing being that the King failed to fend him off. Had anyone treated Gustavus Adolphus in this fashion he would have received short shrift and had it been Rupert, he would have been killed on the spot.

The King was not the only person to see that the battle had reached its climax. Fairfax also realised that the destruction of the Royalist foot must be completed before their reserves could be thrown in, or their horse return to the battle. The part of the Royalist centre that was holding out most strongly was Lisle's brigade on the left. Its forward regiment had fought its way through that part of the Parliamentary line commanded by Manchester's young cousin, Edward Montague, but it was now contained. If the regiment behind could be broken, the whole of the Royalist centre would be in danger of collapse.

In order to dispose of this last bastion of resistance, Fairfax directed his regiment of foot, which had so far seen little of the fighting, to attack it from the front whilst he personally led his regiment of horse round to the rear and launched it from that direction. It was often recorded that in battle the mild-mannered Fairfax was transformed into a creature of elemental force, clear-thinking, energetic and brave, and at no time was this more apparent than at Naseby. In the face of his furious assault resistance crumbled. Shortly afterwards the other magnificent regiments of the Royalist centre started to disintegrate. They had put up a great fight against heavy odds, but when it was clear that no relief would be coming from the King's reserve, they began to surrender one by one.

Meanwhile Rupert, conscious of the need to keep in touch with the battle, had returned to the King with most of the horse that had started on the right wing. Contrary to the assertion later made, that he had led an uncontrollable chase of the enemy for miles beyond the battlefield, he had in fact only followed them for a little over 1,000 yards. But his men had been subjected to some hard fighting and their horses were blown, so that it would take time before they would be ready to put in another attack.

Meanwhile the King, having given up the idea of launching a counter-attack, was trying to rally what was left of the Northern Horse. By this time the foot regiments of the reserve seem to have been committed although it is difficult to know exactly where or on whose orders: it may be that the advancing enemy had pushed forward as far as their positions. Such evidence as does exist suggests that the King's life guard of foot had become engaged with the Parliamentary dragoons, who had by now joined in the assault on the right of the Royalist foot, and that Prince Rupert's regiment of foot was fighting fiercely in support of Lisle's brigade. Certainly this regiment sustained heavy casualties in the battle somewhere and lost five of their colours.

The enemy horse that Rupert had chased from the field now started to return in dribs and drabs. Fleetwood, who had commanded Ireton's second line at the start of the battle, formed them up opposite the Newark horse in roughly the place that Cromwell's horse had occupied at the start of the battle. As the fighting in the centre died down, Fairfax redeployed his regiments so that the Parliamentary army again presented a solid front with regiments of horse on both flanks and foot in the centre. But the foot took longer than the horse to sort themselves out and Fairfax, who was determined to avoid any part of his force being overwhelmed by an attack from the remaining Royalist horse, was not prepared to advance until the whole army was ready. He did however allow some of his horse to move forward far enough to maintain a desultory fire on the Royalists with their carbines.

Amongst the Royalists there were still a few who thought that another charge would disperse the enemy, but most could see that only a rapid withdrawal could save what little remained of the army. Accordingly the order for retreat was given and they set off at best speed, being pursued by the enemy horse for twelve miles to within two miles of Leicester. The rest of Fairfax's army moved to Market Harborough where he set up his headquarters. Altogether the fighting had lasted for no more than two hours.[17]

The battle of Naseby was a total defeat for the King. Although most of the horse got away, they had sustained heavy casualties. Astley's well-trained regiments of foot were entirely destroyed with the exception of a few isolated groups that managed to disperse. The King also lost all his guns and his baggage train, including his coach with his personal papers and letters. It is estimated that the Royalists had about 1,000 men killed and another 4,500 captured including 500 officers, many of them the experienced professionals essential for turning recruits into soldiers. By contrast Parliamentary losses were probably no more than 200–300 killed and wounded. Contrary to the usual practice Fairfax did not release the prisoners after disarming them, but sent them all to London where those that would not accept employment abroad or in Ireland were kept in prison to prevent them rejoining the King's army.

To cap it all the enemy, who had happily accepted the surrender of Royalist soldiers in the battle, deliberately killed or maimed many of the female camp followers on the grounds that they were Irish whores. In fact they were the usual collection of women who moved with the army to help with the cooking, washing and care of the wounded, many being the wives of the men in the ranks. Comparatively few of them would have been Irish, but there might have been an appreciable number of Welsh speakers judging by the composition of the army.

As the King's principal military commander, Rupert has naturally been criticised both for the way in which the campaign developed and for the conduct of the battle.

In considering the campaign, the first thing to understand is that its aim was exactly the same as Rupert's campaign of the previous year: to recover the north, which had been lost when the Scots invaded. Only control of a lot of extra territory would enable the

King to raise armies of the size required to combat Parliament. Without control of this extra territory, isolated victories in the south would do no more than cause a delay while Parliament raised new forces: the Royalists would never be able to raise a large enough army from the west and south-west both to defeat Parliament's armies and to take London. The fact that the King's victories in 1644 did not pose a threat to London, or cause a Parliamentary collapse, conclusively proves this point.

Rupert's conduct from the time that he took over from Lord Forth makes it abundantly clear that he understood this fact. Throughout the winter his efforts were directed at securing the west and south-west so that the King's main army would be free to go north. By the beginning of May conditions existed for a successful move north and Rupert persuaded the King to embark upon it.

But things went wrong once the campaign got under way. In the endless debates that followed every change of circumstance, Rupert consistently urged that the aim should be maintained, but the King followed his advice one day and ignored it the next. As a result momentum was lost and precious resources were squandered, as for example on the taking of Leicester and on the garrisoning of it. Goring's failure to answer the King's summons certainly aggravated the situation, but even without him it might have been possible, by withdrawing from Market Harborough on 14 June, to incorporate the 1,500 men garrisoning Leicester and Willys's 400 from Newark into the army before fighting, and, if the battle could have been put off for long enough, Gerrard's 3,000 might also have arrived. At the very least a more favourable defensive position might have been found.

But although Rupert is on record as having opposed most of the bad decisions made in the campaign, it is impossible not to feel that he had lost some of his forcefulness. He is reported as having become more diplomatic in his handling of the war council and it is possible that as a result he was not putting his case forward as clearly as before. Whatever the cause, there is no doubt that the only person deserving credit for the way in which the campaign was conducted was Fairfax.

Few accounts of the battle of Naseby give any clear idea of how it developed, and the impression has got round that it was a rehash of Edgehill, with Rupert smashing the enemy on his wing and then taking all the best Royalist regiments away from the battle in an uncontrollable pursuit, in marked contrast to Cromwell who managed to break the opposing horse on his wing and then, keeping his men together, turn them on to the flank of the Royalist foot.

The facts are somewhat different. At Edgehill Rupert's horse were far superior to his opponents and at the very sight of him the enemy turned and fled, taking some of the foot with them. On this occasion the fault lay with Byron, who failed to turn on the Parliamentary foot as ordered. At Naseby Rupert's right wing was faced with an enemy of almost double his own strength which included two of Cromwell's old Eastern Association regiments and two that had formerly been in Waller's army. That Rupert was able to break through these veterans and chase some of them off the field was a tribute to his unsurpassed skill in the heat of battle. And he only achieved it after heavy and prolonged fighting in which the commanding officers of both his own and his brother's regiments became casualties, together with a number of other officers. Furthermore, despite the ferocity of the struggle and the difficulties of control caused by the loss of these commanders, Rupert was able to halt the pursuit and reorganise his regiments within a comparatively short period and lead them back to the King.

By comparison Cromwell's task was easy. With an even greater superiority than Ireton, all he had to do was to despatch a suitable force under Whalley to beat off the Northern Horse, reinforcing it with an extra regiment when he saw that he had not sent enough in the first place. This still left him with three regiments to launch against the Royalist centre and, once he saw that the Northern Horse was unlikely to take any further part in the battle, he was able to take regiments away from Whalley to add to the number fighting the foot. All this he did with commendable efficiency, following it up by reordering the horse at the end of the battle and by organising the pursuit. But the picture of Cromwell leading a charge and then, after a period of heavy fighting, wheeling his men away from the enemy to attack the foot is fictitious.

There are, however, three aspects of Rupert's performance that can justifiably be questioned. The first concerns Rupert's decision to move the army forward from its initial position south of Market Harborough to the ridge to the north of Naseby. There seems to have been little advantage in doing this from a topographical point of view and, had the Royalists stayed in their original position, they might have been able to launch their attack while the Parliamentary army was deploying, thereby gaining some advantage. There is no evidence to show why Rupert asked the King to bring the army forward, but it may have been that he felt that he was acting in accordance with the decision of the council of war to follow up the enemy and attack him, rather than to wait to be attacked.

The second point concerns the way in which Rupert deployed the army, the controversial aspects of which relate to the size of the reserve and the fact that he used Howard's brigade of horse to reinforce the centre rather than to strengthen the wings. In the event it is unlikely that Howard's regiments would have made much difference to the outcome of the contest between the Northern Horse and Cromwell, especially as it was composed of second-class regiments. On the other hand they did play a useful part by helping to fend off enemy horse that were attacking Astley's flanks. Turning to the reserve as a whole, it was no fault of Rupert's that it did not get used as intended, and eventually all of it, other than the King's life guard of horse, was used to good effect. On balance Rupert's deployment seems sensible and has not been much criticised.

The third point is the vexed question of Rupert's command of the right wing, which has already been discussed. All that can be said is that if this was Rupert's decision, as opposed to the King's, he must be held to blame for it.

The final point concerns the withdrawal at the end of the battle. It has been suggested that instead of a rapid retreat, Rupert should have organised a bound-by-bound withdrawal designed to keep the enemy horse at bay. Whether this would have enabled more of the army to get away is hard to tell. It would certainly have led to further casualties amongst the horse and it would have been a difficult operation to undertake in view of the state that the surviving units were in at the time. But the way in which the retreat actually took place reflects little credit on Rupert, or indeed on anyone else.

Having retreated to Leicester, the King and Rupert, together with the survivors of the battle, continued through the night until they arrived at Ashby next morning. Fairfax did not follow them, but immediately laid siege to Leicester which surrendered on 18 June. By this time the remains of the Royalist army had passed through Lichfield, Wolverhampton and Bewdley and were fast approaching Hereford.

Even before the King and his entourage arrived at Hereford a violent row broke out between Rupert and Digby, who was predictably putting it around that the defeat at Naseby had been Rupert's fault. The final straw came when Rupert saw a letter that Digby had drafted for the King to send to the Prince of Wales. Taking it to the King, Rupert said that if the King sent it, he would resign. There is no record of the letter having been sent, nor did Rupert resign, so it can be assumed that the King did not go so far as to sign it.

By this time Gerrard had joined forces with the King, who therefore had a small number of foot soldiers in addition to the horse that had escaped from Naseby. It was now decided that Rupert should visit the Prince of Wales, who had moved to Barnstaple from Bristol to avoid the plague. The purpose of Rupert's visit was to co-ordinate the Prince's arrangements for the defence of the south-west with the King's plan to move with some of his army by boat across the Bristol Channel. Rupert left the King on 26 June and on the same day Prince Maurice left for Worcester to take charge of events along the Welsh border.

Meanwhile Digby, realising the importance of retaining the support of the Royalists in Oxford, wrote a long and subtle letter to Legge[18] in which he tells him not to believe the lies spread about Rupert (spread by Digby himself) to the effect that he had wanted to fight at Naseby when in fact he had advised against it. Digby then goes on to say that it was a pity that Legge was not present at Naseby, because he would have been able to prevent Rupert from making a number of mistakes, each of which he records in detail. In so doing, Digby manages to blame Rupert for just about everything that went wrong. Throughout, he laces his letter with profuse professions of love and admiration for Rupert who he maintains persists in distrusting his efforts to help him. Legge's forthright reply[19] refutes every criticism of Rupert raised in Digby's letter, in addition to which he directly accuses Digby of saying and doing things contrary to Rupert's interest, 'not in an open and direct way but obscurely and obliquely'. He concludes by blaming Digby for the harm he has done to Rupert and tells him that, although no one is more ready to say so than himself, many others speak of it.

By the time that Rupert met the Prince of Wales at Barnstaple, it had become clear that Fairfax intended to give the Royalists little time to prepare their defence. As soon as Leicester was captured the Committee of Both Kingdoms decided that the Scots should move south to follow the King and prevent such forces as he had from doing further damage in the Midlands, while Fairfax moved immediately to destroy Goring's army, the only significant Royalist force left in the field. By 28 June, when Rupert was at Barnstaple, Fairfax reached Marlborough: on the same day Carlisle surrendered, thereby removing a threat to the Scottish lines of communication that had been partially inhibiting their operations in England for the past year. By 2 July Fairfax was at Blandford and Goring, abandoning the siege of Taunton, moved forward to hold the line of the Rivers Yeo and Parrett, to the south-east of Langport.

From Blandford Fairfax moved west to Beaminster and then swung north through Crewkerne until he made contact with Goring's men guarding crossings over the Yeo at Ilchester and Load on 7 July. By this time Fairfax had taken under command a force led by Massey from Gloucester, 4,000 strong, which was operating to the south of Taunton and also the brigade under Weldon that had been besieged in Taunton itself. With these additions and with the eight regiments of horse and twelve of foot that he had brought with him from Leicester, Fairfax must have had at least 17,000 men. Goring's immediate aim with his 7,000 men was to hold off Fairfax as best he could in order to cover the withdrawal of his guns and baggage train into Bridgwater. If this went well, he hoped to get most of his men away to join the King.

The King meanwhile had moved to Raglan Castle where he was enjoying the stately hospitality of the aged Marquess of Worcester. There the King was building castles in the air based on the prospect of thousands of Irishmen pouring through Chester and Bristol to join a new army which would soon be large enough to turn the tables on Fairfax and avenge the defeat at Naseby. In pursuit of this design he sent Worcester's son, the Roman Catholic Earl of Glamorgan, to the Irish Confederates as his special envoy, thus undermining the negotiations being carried out by the ever-faithful Ormonde.

The speed of Fairfax's advance, and the number of troops that he had concentrated in the area, caused the King to postpone the plan for taking his army across the Bristol Channel.[20] By this time Rupert, who was thoroughly aware of the impending danger, had left Barnstaple for Bristol where he went to make sure that the city was well prepared to withstand a siege. He intended to see Goring on the way but it is not certain that he managed to do so. He also sent word to Prince Maurice at Worcester to move to Bristol with three regiments of horse: his own regiment, Prince Maurice's regiment and Vaughan's regiment. Maurice sent the regiments but was unable to come himself because the Scots were close at hand and he felt in honour bound to stay and defend Worcester.

On the same day that Fairfax reached Goring's outposts along the River Yeo, Massey caught and destroyed a body of horse that Goring had sent towards Ilminster as a diversion. Meanwhile Fairfax pushed his army across the river and, turning west, closed up on the evening of 9 July to Goring's main defensive position which was in marshy gound east of Langport behind a tributary of the river. On 10 July Fairfax fought the battle that he afterwards regarded as his greatest feat of arms. Goring's army was dislodged from its position and driven from the field, although Goring himself and many of his men escaped to Bridgwater, retreating next day to Dunster from where he wrote to inform the King of his situation. Digby forwarded the letter to Rupert at Bristol.

The disaster at Langport coincided with another setback for the King's cause when Parliament published a collection of his private letters captured at Naseby in a document entitled 'King's Cabinet Opened'. These letters confirmed what Parliament had frequently maintained, that is to say that the King was trying to get reinforcements from abroad and that he was negotiating with the rebels in Ireland to send large numbers of Roman Catholics to help him subdue his own Protestant subjects. At one point the King goes so far as to describe the loyal Parliament that he had assembled in Oxford as a mongrel Parliament, for no better reason than that it wanted him to conclude a treaty with the Parliament at Westminster. Nothing could have been better calculated to sow seeds of dissension amongst the King's war-weary followers than the publication of these papers.

Following the battle of Langport Fairfax advanced to Bridgwater, a well-fortified place which not only commanded the lines of communication between the Royalists in Devon and Cornwall and the major port of Bristol, but which also contained considerable quantities of arms, ammunition and supplies. At the same time the King renewed his efforts to get men across the Bristol Channel, moving to Cardiff where he assembled twelve boats with which to attempt the crossing. But the Parliamentary naval commander who was supporting operations against the Royalists in South Wales sailed into Cardiff and captured the Welsh boats, thereby finally putting an end to this plan.

On 16 July, despite misgivings from his senior officers expressed at a council of war, Fairfax decided to take Bridgwater by storm rather than endure the delay of a siege. After several days' preparation, during which four regiments of foot made as though to attack from the north, the assault was launched with a further eight regiments from the south on 21 July. The garrison fought back stubbornly and it was not until the morning of 23 July, with the whole town in flames and most of the defenders dead, that the Governor surrendered.

While Fairfax was engaged at Bridgwater, Rupert was also active. On the day of Fairfax's war council Rupert led a small body of horse for twenty miles across the Quantocks and beat up the quarters of some of Cromwell's horse at Wells. On 18 July he held a meeting with one group of Clubmen outside Bristol to persuade them to help him defend the city. Three days later he held a meeting with another group on Lansdowne Hill and then made a quick visit to the garrison of Bath which he found to be in low spirits. That same night he crossed the Severn for a meeting with the King near Chepstow during which it was agreed that the King would make Bristol his headquarters and bring with him enough troops to ensure its security. An interesting aspect of this visit to the King was that Ashburnham, who was usually to be counted amongst Rupert's critics, warned him confidentially that Digby, following his exchange of letters with Legge, was determined to ruin him. Rupert was back in Bristol by the evening of 22 July.

On 24 July the King wrote a muddled and evasive letter to Rupert saying he had changed his mind about coming to Bristol. This made sense, as the fall of Bridgwater meant that Bristol was isolated from the Royalists in the south-west. The King went on to say that he had not made up his mind what to do instead. In Bristol the rumour was that he intended to go to Scotland to join Montrose. Rupert now decided to make his opinion of the general situation plain and wrote to Richmond asking him to pass it on to the King. His letter is of such importance that part of it must be quoted direct.

It is now in every mouth that the King is going for Scotland. I must confess it to be a strange resolution considering not only in what condition he will leave all behind him, but what probability there is of him to get thither. If I were desired to deliver my opinion what other ways the King should take, this should be my opinion which your Lordship may declare to the King. His Majesty hath now no way left to preserve his posterity, kingdom and nobility, but by a treaty. I believe it a more prudent way to retain something than to lose all.

Rupert goes on to say that the King's expectations from Ireland are misplaced, as the Confederates have no more than 5,000 men that they could send, and that the negotiations are only designed to cheat the King. He concludes by referring to the large number of Royalists who are deserting and says that if the King is not concerned for those that remain, he is, as they have nothing to look forward to but ruin and slavery.[21]

Coming from the King's Lord General, who was also his loving but exasperated nephew, this constitutes plain speaking indeed. The King's reply, written from Cardiff on 3 August, contains a wonderfully expressed statement of his most fundamental feelings both as sovereign and as a man.

> Now as for your opinion of my business and your counsel thereupon, if I had any other quarrel but the defence of my religion, crown and friends, you had full reason for your advice. For I confess that speaking as a mere soldier or statesman, I must say there is no probability but of my ruin; yet as a Christian I must tell you that God will not suffer rebels and traitors to prosper, nor this course to be overthrown: and whatever personal punishment it shall please him to inflict on me, must not make me repine let alone give over this quarrel . . .

He goes on to say that he would no longer be offered any terms short of submission, which he cannot contemplate because it would involve abandoning God's cause and damaging the interests of his successor and his friends. Thus whilst realising that his prospects are bad, he has no alternative but to fight on so as to end his days with honour and a good conscience. The King then acknowledges that those remaining with him can expect nothing better than to die or end their days in misery, and urges Rupert to have no further truck with the idea of a treaty, but in consideration of the love between them, to stick it out for as long as possible. The King concludes by assuring Rupert that he will not allow himself to be cheated by the Irish. On the following day the King wrote again about some current business and finished by saying that as it might be a long time before they saw each other again, Rupert was to have implicit faith in his friendship and affection, adding that he was as concerned to protect him as to protect one of his own children.

There now occurred one of the most remarkable episodes of the whole war as the King tried to reach Montrose, taking with him

2,200 horse and 400 foot. On 5 August, when the King left Cardiff, Leven with an army of around 7,000 was besieging Hereford, having bypassed Worcester. But this was not the only hazard facing the King, as a number of the strongholds which he could have expected to visit on his way north had by now given up all hope of relief and surrendered. These included several small places in Shropshire and Cheshire and the important garrisons at Pontefract Castle and Scarborough. The King therefore had to chose his route with more than usual care.

The King first marched to Lichfield, bypassing Hereford as he went. Leven, hearing of this move, despatched David Leslie with 4,000 horse to follow the King. But the King had a good lead and by 18 August had reached Doncaster. He was now in danger of being caught between Leslie's horse approaching from the south-west and Sydenham Poyntz who was closing in from the north. The King therefore retired in haste due south into the Eastern Association territory, coming to rest in Huntingdon on 24 August. He now realised that he was not being followed by Leslie, who had been diverted to Scotland following yet another victory won by Montrose at Kilsyth near Glasgow on 15 August. The King was thus able to make for Oxford where he arrived on 28 August, leaving again after two days for Worcester. Leven, who was still outside Hereford, could not without his horse face the King: he therefore retired to Gloucester. The King relieved Hereford and moved on to Raglan Castle.

Even before the King set off, Royalist forces in Pembrokeshire had been defeated at the battle of Colby Moor by the local Parliamentary commander, reinforced from the sea. As a result, one of the few useful recruiting grounds still available to the King was lost.

After capturing Bridgwater, Fairfax decided to remove the threat to his lines of communication, before tackling Bristol. Okey was sent with the dragoons to capture Bath, which he did without difficulty. At the same time Sherborne Castle was invested: it surrendered on 14 August.

While these activities were taking place Rupert spared no efforts to ensure that Bristol was well prepared to resist a siege. Amongst other things he brought 2,000 bushels of corn into the city from Wales, also driving in a large number of cattle from the surrounding area. He arranged for lead to be cast into musket balls to supplement the existing supply and ordered additional match to be manufactured for the muskets.

The garrison consisted of about 800 horse and 700 foot. The horse were probably the three regiments sent by Maurice from Worcester, together with Rupert's life guard. A few of the foot may have been survivors of Naseby, but mostly they were recently recruited levies from Wales. For so small a force there seems to have been a large number of senior officers. Amongst these were Lord Hawley, a veteran of Hopton's early campaign in Devon, Bernard Astley, Henry Tillier who had been exchanged just before Naseby, Will Murray who commanded the artillery train at Naseby, John Russell who commanded Rupert's regiment of foot, Colonels Robert and Walter Slingsby, Mathew Appleyard, recently Governor of Leicester, Somerset Fox and Lieutenant Colonel Henry Osbourne. As usual Bernard de Gomme was also with Rupert.

On 22 August enemy appeared to the south of Bristol and Rupert sent out a body of horse commanded by Sir Richard Crane to harass them. In the action that followed Crane was mortally wounded. Having so recently lost Dallison, the commander of his regiment of horse, Rupert must have felt this as a great personal blow, especially as Crane, who had been captured with him at Vlotho, had been at his side throughout the war. Nowadays people are scarcely expected to survive the sight of a fatal accident without the assistance of professional counsellors, and one-tenth of the stresses and strains that Rupert had experienced over the preceding three years would be regarded as ample excuse for a nervous breakdown. But at the time all that an observer would have seen of Rupert's grief would have been an even more furious expenditure of energy.

During the afternoon Rupert set fire to an outlying village on hearing that Fairfax intended to quarter men in it. Next day he set to work to build a traverse or mound of earth outside the Temple Gate in the south which had been the target of Prince Maurice's unsuccessful attack two years earlier. Rupert also set up a battery of guns in the marsh to fire across the open ground in front of this traverse. At the same time the enemy set up another traverse and a battery to guard against a sortie. In this fashion the work proceeded on both sides as Bristol was slowly but surely invested. During one of the many sorties Rupert lost another senior officer when Bernard Astley was killed.

Fairfax's plan was that Massey with his 4,000 men should guard against a relief force sent from Devon. To the north-west of the city on Durdham Down he posted four regiments of horse to pre-

vent Rupert breaking out should he try to do so, an option that
Rupert did in fact consider. These regiments would also be well
placed to prevent the King bringing a column to the relief of the
city from the north, assuming it got past the Scots at Gloucester.
A squadron of Parliamentary ships took up their station at the
mouth of the Avon to cut off supplies reaching the city by sea.
Excluding Massey's men, Fairfax now had at least 12,000 surrounding Bristol, more than twice the number that Rupert had
when he stormed it in 1643; the defenders had about the same
number on each occasion.

From 24 August Rupert was completely cut off from the outside
world. Although Goring talked about leading an army to relieve
Bristol, Grenville refused to provide men for the purpose, knowing
perfectly well that a sufficiently large force could not be raised
from their combined resources. The King wrote to Rupert to say
that he would come to his rescue, but the letter never got through.
In any case Rupert knew that the King was incapable of relieving
Bristol with the men at his disposal. But the plague-ridden civil
population numbered no more than 12,500 and, with the supplies
that he had got in, Rupert reckoned that he could withstand a
siege for four months providing that Fairfax did not mount a full-
scale assault. An assault would be a different matter altogether
because, like Fiennes before him, he was not strong enough to man
the lengthy outer perimeter properly and if he abandoned it to
concentrate on the city walls, Fairfax's guns would be in a position
to set fire to the city.

Despite his large numerical superiority, Fairfax was reluctant to
launch an attack which would inevitably result in heavy casualties.
His first line of approach was to smuggle numerous letters into the
town, signed by himself and Cromwell, calling on the citizens to
refuse their help to the garrison and to do all in their power to
assist the Parliamentary forces. But Rupert intercepted some of
them and, by imprisoning many enemy supporters, frustrated this
manoeuvre.

Fairfax next approached Rupert direct with a letter, dated 4
September, which started as a summons to surrender the city but
which continued as an eloquent personal appeal. Reminding him
of all the support that Parliament had given to his family over the
years, and acknowledging his many soldierly qualities, Fairfax
went on to say that if the Prince found himself able to spare the
city from the inevitable result of an assault, it would endear him
to the hearts of the English people. In his letter Fairfax reiterated

the usual declaration that he only fought to restore the King to his Parliament, the true guarantor of his crown and honour.

It does not appear that Rupert was unduly impressed, as all he did on receiving the letter was to call for a glass of sherry and swear vigorously for a few moments. But seeing an opportunity for spinning out time, he wrote to Fairfax on the following day asking to be allowed to enquire whether the King would agree to the city being surrendered, which Fairfax naturally refused.

Rupert now held a council of war at which three courses of action were considered. First, that Rupert should try to break through the lines of the besiegers with the horse, after which the outer line of defence would be abandoned and the foot would hold the castle for as long as possible. This was turned down because it was felt that the horse would not get away and that it was dishonourable to leave the whole burden of defence on the foot. The second course was to abandon the outer line and concentrate the whole force inside the castle, but this was also turned down because the whole force could not get inside, and those left outside, together with Royalist supporters amongst the civilian population, would be at the mercy of the enemy. The third course, which was adopted, was to conduct the best general defence possible in the hope that the initial assault, at least, would be repulsed with such heavy loss that Fairfax would revert to a siege. This in turn might be called off after a few weeks with the approach of winter.

In order to delay matters further Rupert again wrote to Fairfax suggesting that if no relief force appeared by a certain time he might surrender under certain very favourable conditions which he knew that Fairfax could not accept without reference to Parliament. But Fairfax was not to be so easily put off and, after exchanging a few more letters with Rupert, he launched an all-out attack at 2 a.m. on 10 September.

Fairfax's plan was to direct Weldon's brigade of four regiments on to the Temple Gate area. At the same time three regiments of Rainsborough's brigade would attack from the north-east on to the outer defences between Prior's Hill Fort and the River Frome, while his fourth regiment attacked the fort itself. Behind Rainsborough were three regiments of horse ready to pass through any breach that might be made. This left Fairfax with a reserve of four more regiments of foot together with the four regiments of horse on Durdham Down.

Weldon's assault on the Somerset side of the town was no more successful than Prince Maurice's assault had been in 1643, but

Rainsborough's men broke through the outer defences in several places after about an hour's heavy fighting. Once through, they soon opened up a way for their supporting regiments of horse which by sheer weight of numbers beat off a counter-attack launched by the Royalist horse. At the same time two of the regiments that had broken through the perimeter turned inwards on Prior's Hill Fort, taking it from the rear at the same time as it was being assailed from the front. It took three hours to overwhelm the Royalist garrison which was then put to the sword.

When it got light Rupert could see that the position was very grave. Some of the perimeter forts still held out but the majority of the defenders were by now behind the main city walls, which were being assailed from all sides. The fort at Lawford's Gate at the extreme east point of the perimeter had been overrun and the men in it killed, a fate that was likely to overtake the occupants of the remaining perimeter forts one by one, as they could no longer be supported by the Royalists from within the beleaguered city. Soon the enemy were getting into the city itself and the defenders were falling back on the castle.

At this point Rupert called another council of war which was not attended by Hawley, Appleyard or Slingsby, who were still in the outlying forts. It might still be possible to hold the old castle for a week or two, but this would be at the expense of seeing the city destroyed and the defenders outside the castle killed. There was also some question as to how long the water supply in the castle would last once the city as a whole was lost. Finally, there was nothing to gain by continued resistance as there was no prospect of relief or even of gaining time for other Royalist forces to carry out some important operation elsewhere while the New Model Army was tied down in front of Bristol. The council therefore asked Rupert to get what terms he could.

Rupert now had a difficult decision to make. From the point of view of his personal honour he was bound to fight on for as long as possible, regardless of the effect that this would have on his men or on the population of Bristol. But as a practical and professional soldier Rupert would not have felt justified in sacrificing men who might still have a useful part to play in the future, not to mention the second greatest city in the kingdom, for the sake of satisfying his private honour. If it came to justifying his actions he would be able to point out that he had with 1,500 men fought with an army ten times his own strength for six hours, which was twice as long as the duration of the battle of Naseby, and in this time had inflicted more casualties on them than they had sustained in that battle. He therefore sent to Fairfax with a conditional offer to surrender the city.

Although Fairfax would have been within his rights to refuse any terms other than that the survivors should throw themselves on the mercy of Parliament, he agreed to negotiate. Rupert sent Tillier, Vavasour and Mennes to meet him and they found him as generous in victory as he had been resolute in battle. It was eventually agreed that the defenders should march out the following morning with their swords, pikes, colours and drums, the Prince's life guard carrying loaded carbines. Furthermore the Royalists would be escorted to within a few miles of Oxford by a Parliamentary regiment of horse in case of trouble with Clubmen along the way.

When he heard of it, the King regarded the surrender of Bristol as a mortal blow and a betrayal of the trust that he had in his nephew. His bitter sorrow and indignation were seized on by Digby as the opportunity he was looking for to ruin Rupert. He hinted at treachery and fanned the flames of the King's wrath for all he was worth. Without even waiting to hear what Rupert had to say, the King wrote to Rupert stripping him of all his commands and ordering him to leave the country at once. The dramatic steps that Rupert took to restore his reputation and to be reconciled with his uncle are highly relevant to an understanding of him as a person, but irrelevant to an assessment of him as a soldier. With the exception of a brief period as a brigade commander in the French army, his military career ended with the surrender of Bristol.

11

AFTERMATH AND ASSESSMENT

O<small>N</small> <small>THE</small> <small>MORNING</small> of 11 September the Royalist garrison of
Bristol marched out of the city with Prince Rupert at their head,
carefully turned out in scarlet laced with silver and riding a spectacular black Arabian. He was met by Fairfax and Cromwell who
escorted him for two miles across the downs, showing him
the greatest respect and treating him with courtesy. After they
left him Rupert is said to have told one of the Parliamentary
officers that he had never before received such satisfaction in
unhappiness.

The regiment detailed off to escort the Royalists to Oxford had,
before the formation of the New Model Army, been Waller's regiment of horse and its colonel was John Butler. At Naseby it had
been on the left of the Parliamentary line and had taken the full
force of Rupert's charge, both Butler and his major being wounded.
Butler had long regarded Rupert as little better than the devil incar-
nate. But during the journey he changed his mind to such an extent
that he wrote to Waller in London saying that he was honoured
to have been with Rupert and that he was sure that they were all
much mistaken about him. He asked Waller to use his influence to
ensure that no Parliamentary pamphlet was published to Rupert's
discredit for the surrender of Bristol, as he could not have held it
without more men.

In some extraordinary way Rupert had won the respect of Fairfax, Cromwell and Butler in the same way as he had impressed his
captors in Austria. Although his youthful good looks had been
replaced by a lean hardness that could be frightening, his gallantry
and integrity continued to strike a response from brave men regardless of their political allegiance.

*   *   *

With the loss of Bristol the King moved north, intending once more to join Montrose. But unknown to the King, Leslie had overtaken Montrose and totally defeated him at the battle of Philiphaugh, on 13 September, scattering his forces and removing all threat to Argyll's government. The King himself, in trying to improve the situation around Chester, lost most of his remaining horse and was obliged to move rapidly through the Midlands and seek refuge in Newark.

Meanwhile Rupert was fuming with resentment at the King's refusal even to see him, let alone hear his reasons for surrendering Bristol. The King, thinking back to Rupert's letter recommending a treaty with Parliament, was suspicious that Rupert had surrendered Bristol to force his hand. Digby went further, obliquely hinting at the possibility that Rupert was aiming for the crown, in support of which he showed the King reports from Oxford to the effect that Rupert was being treated with exaggerated respect by some of the courtiers there. Rupert, who was doubtless conscious that rumours of this sort would circulate, arranged for a pamphlet to be published in which he described the state of Bristol when he arrived, and the subsequent action taken to defend it, all supported by the proceedings of the various councils held and of the treaty reached with Fairfax. This showed that his decisons were based on sensible military responses to developing circumstances and were reached after proper discussion with his senior officers. What remains unexplained is why more had not been done to improve the defences of Bristol in the two years since the Royalists captured it, with particular reference to strengthening the perimeter wall in certain places and improving the water supply in the castle itself.

Eventually Rupert's patience gave out and he decided to force his way to Newark to confront the King, despite the fact that he had been told to stay in Oxford and that he no longer had so much as his life guard to escort him. But he had many supporters in Oxford, eighty of whom volunteered to accompany him on his ride. Leaving on 8 October, he was joined by Prince Maurice at Banbury and together they arrived at Newark on 16 October after a series of skirmishes with Parliamentary forces detailed off to stop him. In one of these Rupert came near to losing his life when a Parliamentary soldier, who was a deserter from Rupert's regiment of horse, rode up to him and fired at point blank range. Fortunately the pistol misfired and Rupert put a bullet through his head even as he cried for quarter.

The King, on hearing of his approach, sent orders forbidding him to enter Newark, but Rupert ignored them and the Governor,

Sir Richard Willis, accompanied by Charles Gerrard, rode out to meet him with a guard of honour of 100 horse. By this time Digby, hearing of Rupert's approach, asked the King to appoint him lieutenant general of the forces north of the Trent and hastily departed. Travelling with the remains of the Northern Horse commanded by Langdale, he got almost to Dumfries before being attacked and having his force scattered by the enemy. Digby and Langdale escaped to the Isle of Man.

Rupert meanwhile had forced his way into the King's presence and demanded a court martial. The court that subsequently assembled consisted of Lords Lindsey, Cork, Astley, Belasyse and Gerrard together with Richard Willis and John Ashburnham; a fair mixture of Rupert's friends and enemies. It swiftly found in favour of Rupert, and the King made a statement absolving him from any disloyalty or treason in surrendering Bristol. Rupert's honour was vindicated and, now that they were freed from the influence of Digby, a complete reconciliation between uncle and nephew was expected.

But the King, annoyed by the way in which Willis had befriended Rupert, removed him from his position of Governor of Newark under the guise of promoting him to the command of his life guard: he had previously removed Legge from the governorship of Oxford for the same reason. Willis and Rupert were furious, and with Maurice and Gerrard marched into the King's presence to protest. The King ordered them out and they withdrew to the Governor's house, from where they demanded a fair trial for Willis, failing which they asked that they and any of the horse in the garrison who so wished should have passes to leave the King's service. The King refused Willis a trial, but said that anyone wanting to go overseas could come and collect their passes next morning. When presenting themselves to take leave of the King, Gerrard apologised to some extent for his rudeness on the previous day but Rupert remained defiant. It seems that about 200 men accompanied him when he left Newark for Belvoir Castle.

Although the King had given Rupert and his entourage leave to go abroad, they also needed passes from Parliament to get there. Parliament would not give them passes unless they agreed never to fight for the King again, an undertaking that they refused to give. The party therefore set off once more to fight their way through enemy territory, arriving soon afterwards at Woodstock near Oxford. The King was no longer strong enough to stay at Newark so he moved to Oxford itself.

There now followed a period in which the Duke and Duchess of Richmond and Will Legge worked on the King for a reconciliation. On this occasion it was the King who had suffered wrong from Rupert's inexcusable rudeness, amounting almost to mutiny. After some time the King agreed to forgive Rupert if he would give him due satisfaction for his behaviour. Legge wrote urging him to submit himself fully to his uncle and Mary Richmond also sent a personal appeal, pointing out his uncle's desperate plight and saying that there were many in Oxford who longed for his return. She concluded by saying that she wrote as one who valued him more than all the world, and she was confident that he realised that she would do nothing against his interest. Rupert capitulated, writing to ask the King what form the apology should take. The King sent back a letter for him to sign. Rupert, who was now determined to do nothing by halves, sent back a blank sheet of paper with his signature on the bottom asking his uncle to write anything above it that he liked. The King received this with tears in his eyes and on 9 December Rupert arrived in Oxford to be embraced by the King, who is said to have greatly repented of all the ill usage that his nephew had received in the past. But Rupert was not restored to any of his commands, for the simple reason that there was nothing left to command. By this time the war was irrevocably lost.

After the fall of Bristol, Fairfax had again turned back to clear up strong points in his rear before moving into Devon. During the ensuing month his forces captured Devizes, Berkeley Castle, Winchester and Basing House, all Royalist strongholds that had for long been thorns in Parliament's side. By the third week in October the New Model Army set off to mop up Royalist resistance in Devon, capturing Tiverton Castle before briefly going into winter quarters around Exeter. In November Goring, who was by now a total alcoholic, gave up and retired to France. By the end of the year the Prince of Wales was at Tavistock.

During this period other Parliamentary forces and the Scots continued to reduce Royalist strongholds further north, capturing such places as Bolton Castle, Welbeck in Nottinghamshire, Beeston Castle in Cheshire and, by the end of the year, Skipton Castle in Yorkshire and Hereford. These disasters were followed by the loss of Belvoir Castle in January and Chester itself in February.

As the winter progressed the catalogue of disaster continued.

When Fairfax resumed his advance in January he detached Fleetwood with three regiments of horse and some dragoons to watch
Oxford from Islip. He then pushed on through Devon and Cornwall. On 20 March the last remaining Royalist forces in the south-
west, commanded now by Hopton, surrendered, the Prince of
Wales having departed for the Scilly Isles some weeks earlier. The
following day Lord Astley with 3,000 recruits that he had somehow collected from Wales was defeated at Stow-on-the-Wold by
Parliamentary forces that had formerly been besieging Chester.
Sitting on a drum at the end of the battle Astley addressed his
captors with the prophetic words, 'You have done your work and
may go play, unless you fall out amongst yourselves.'

During the winter the King lived quietly in Oxford following a
regular routine, walking around the defences, giving audiences,
attending church and playing frequent games of tennis, usually
with Rupert. Freed from the cares of military planning and civil
government, the King had plenty of time to enjoy the opportunities
available for learned discussion and the appreciation of the arts
which he so greatly enjoyed. Rupert's activities at this time are not
recorded, but he doubtless found ways of filling his time in this
his longest period of inactivity since his imprisonment at Linz. He
would have enjoyed the company of his brother and his other
friends in Oxford such as Legge and the Duke and Duchess of
Richmond, and it is likely that his relations with the Duchess stayed
on the same level as they had been during the past three years. But
there were other women in Oxford with whom he could associ-
ate in a more physical way, one of whom, Goring's sister Lady
Catherine Scott, is supposed to have borne him a son. But as
this lady was free with her favours and had several illegitimate
children, there is no proof that any of them were fathered by
Rupert.

During this time, when the King could do nothing to arrest the
dissolution of his forces, he considered many ideas for restoring
his fortunes. One of these was that he should escape to the Continent and another was that he should join the defeated Montrose
in the hope of restarting a guerilla war in Scotland. He even thought
of allowing Fairfax 'to restore him to his faithful Parliament'. In
the end he decided to hand himself over to the Scottish army which
was by now outside Newark, in the hope that he could exploit the
differences that existed between the Scots and Parliament thereby
regaining some political influence for himself.

Rupert was strongly opposed to this idea, as he realised that the

King would never accept the conditions that the Scots would impose on him as the price of their support for any bargaining that he tried to carry on with Parliament. Rupert went so far as to ask that his opposition to the plan should be recorded in writing. But when the King made it clear that his decision was final, Rupert offered to accompany him. The King, who was intending to travel in disguise, declined the offer on the grounds that Rupert's great height would give the party away should they meet up with any Parliamentary troops. It is not unlikely that the King also felt that Rupert would be an embarrassment in the Scottish camp, not only because of his dislike of the Scots, but also because he might disapprove of the political duplicity that the King would have to use in order to promote his cause under such difficult circumstances. On 27 April a little party consisting of John Ashburnham and the King's chaplain, Michael Hudson, passed over Magdalen Bridge. They were accompanied by the King disguised as a groom. The last time that Rupert set eyes on his uncle was when he bade him farewell as he left Oxford.

Rupert stayed to give what help he could to Sir Charles Glemham, formerly Governor of York and then Carlisle, who had been made Governor of Oxford when Legge was deposed in the aftermath of Bristol. Rupert, Maurice and Gerrard all took part in the sorties made to harass the enemy and in one of these Rupert was slightly wounded when a bullet struck his shoulder. As his pistol dropped from his hand, it went off and shot his opponent's horse!

On 20 June Oxford surrendered on favourable terms. Rupert and Maurice were permitted to stay in England with their servants for up to six months, provided that they did not go within twenty miles of London. But at this time the Thirty Years War was drawing to a close and Charles Louis suggested that the three brothers should meet briefly to discuss family matters regarding the recovery of the Palatinate. Although Rupert and Maurice detested the part that Charles Louis had played in the Civil War, they agreed to meet him outside Guildford, which was very near the twenty-mile limit. No record exists of the discussion that the brothers had together, but Parliament maintained that, in spite of Fairfax's having agreed to the location of the meeting, the Princes had infringed the terms of the treaty and would now have to leave the country within ten days. Rupert therefore left England for Calais on 5 July and Maurice left for the Hague three days later.

*　　*　　*

Rupert made his way directly to St Germain, outside Paris, where Queen Henrietta Maria had her court. She had recently been joined by the Prince of Wales, who had spent some months in Jersey after leaving the Scillies. Prince Charles had throughout the war been a fervent admirer of Rupert and received him with great warmth, as did Anne of Austria, the Queen Mother and Regent of France. But her sister-in-law, Henrietta Maria, was less forthcoming until she received a letter from King Charles, now with the Scots, telling her to treat Rupert well.

At this moment Rupert's greatest need was employment since he was, as usual, short of money and it was the Regent of France rather than the exiled Queen of England who was capable of providing it. Louis XIII had died in 1643, a few months after his great minister, Richelieu, leaving his forty-two-year-old wife, who was in fact daughter of a Spanish as opposed to an Austrian monarch, to govern during their son's minority. She employed as her principal minister Cardinal Mazarin, a Sicilian of her own age, with whom she developed close emotional ties. Soon Mazarin arranged that Rupert should raise a force of Englishmen to serve with the French army against the Spaniards in the Spanish Netherlands. Rupert was of course debarred from fighting the Imperialists by the terms of his release from prison in 1641.

At this time France had two armies in the field, one commanded by Turenne on the Rhine facing the Imperial army and the other commanded by the Prince de Conde along the Netherlands border. Conde, who was a year younger than Rupert, was on the crest of the wave having defeated the Spaniards at Rocroi in 1643 and the Bavarians at Freiburg in 1644. In May 1645 Turenne had been badly defeated by the Imperialists as a result of which Conde had moved rapidly to the Rhine where he avenged Turenne's defeat with a terrific victory at Nordlingen in which the enemy commander was killed and Conde himself severely wounded. By comparison the operations conducted in 1646 had been on a reduced scale although, soon after Rupert arrived in France, Conde succeeded in capturing the important port of Dunkirk.

There were by this time plenty of English Royalists in France and during the winter Rupert collected what amounted to a brigade of around 2,000 men for use with the French in the coming campaigning season. One of those whom he declined to employ was Goring, who promptly joined the Spanish army instead, dying destitute in Spain in 1657. No details are available regarding Rupert's military activities during the winter, but it is not difficult to work out that he must have spent some of his time collecting together men and equipment and some time training them. It is also known that he was much in the company of the Prince of Wales who was reluctantly courting one of his French cousins. Although Prince Charles desperately needed the vast fortune that this lady possessed, he was not attracted to her person. To spin out the negotiations for as long as possible he pretended that he knew no French: Rupert's task was to interpret for him. The result of this strange courtship pleased Prince Charles better than it did those of his advisers who were looking forward to the financial windfall.

It might seem strange that Rupert did not manage to fit in a visit to his mother during the winter, but ever since the autumn of 1642 her sympathies had been with Charles Louis and on one occasion in 1642 she even published the fact that she disapproved of the part that Rupert was playing against the English Parliament. A further problem was that Rupert had failed to join in the condemnation of his younger brother Edward who had converted to Rome after marrying a beautiful and well-connected French Roman Catholic. But by far the biggest uproar in the Palatine family was caused by Rupert's youngest brother Philip, by this time eighteen years old, who murdered one of his mother's admirers because he claimed to have been intimate not only with Elizabeth herself but also with Louise. Philip, in a rage, had not even waited to fight a duel, but had plunged his hunting knife into the man's throat, as a result of which he was obliged to fly the country. Elizabeth was furious, but Rupert supported Philip, as indeed did all of his brothers and sisters including Charles Louis. With so many causes of contention between them it is hardly surprising that Rupert did not hasten to join her.

At the start of the 1647 campaigning season Conde was sent to lead a revolt in Catalonia, mainly because Mazarin was worried by the power and influence that he was building up in France. Soon afterwards Rupert was sent with his brigade to the Netherlands border to join a force of 7,000 Frenchmen marching to the relief of Armentières, which was being besieged by 20,000 Spaniards. The force which he was sent to join was commanded on alternate days by a young and irresponsible Frenchman called the Comte de Gassion and the aged Danish Marshal Rantzau. This arrangement was not unusual in the seventeenth century, but in this case it was complicated by the fact that Rantzau thought, with good reason, that Gassion was totally unfit to command.

The day after Rupert's arrival, Gassion took him on a reconnaissance of an enemy position which was on the far side of a river. At

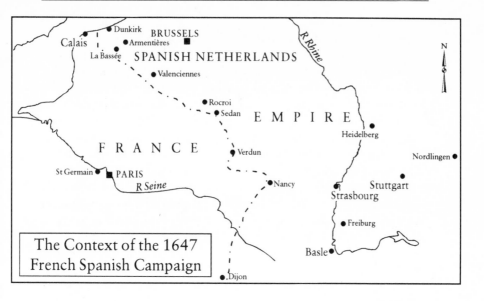

The Context of the 1647
French Spanish Campaign

one place on the river bank, Gassion told Rupert to wait for him and then went on by himself to a small house from where he could get a good view of the enemy lines. While he was looking across, an enemy patrol arrived by boat and closed up on him without his noticing until he was suddenly confronted by a man aiming a musket at him. With great presence of mind he made out that he was a Spanish officer and then when the man lowered his weapon he made a dash for it, Rupert coming forward at great peril to himself to help him escape. Rupert was appalled at Gassion's unprofessional behaviour, especially as Gassion said that he was dogged by bad luck of that sort.

Next day Gassion took his whole force across the river prior to attacking the Spaniards who outnumbered him by more than two to one. But the ground was such that the horse could not be used at all, which ruled out what remote chance of success there might otherwise have been. Gassion now called a council of war at which Rupert gave it as his opinion that an attack was inadvisable under the circumstances, a view with which Rantzau agreed. As a result the force withdrew and Armentières fell to the Spaniards.

Having taken Armentières, the Spaniards moved south towards their base at La Bassée with the French force, of which Rupert's brigade were part, some way abreast of them. Gassion once more decided to watch the enemy from close quarters and asked Rupert to accompany him. Rupert took with him his page, Robert Holmes, and the master of his horse, Mortaigne. As they got close to the enemy, Gassion and Rupert left their attendants a short way off and went forward by themselves to take a closer look. At this point they were ambushed by a troop of horse. Rupert and Gassion managed to escape by getting over some boggy ground whereupon Mortaigne and Holmes came up to support them. But in trying to hold up the leading enemy, they were both wounded, Mortaigne in the hand and Holmes, who was unhorsed, in the leg. Rupert was not prepared to leave Holmes, who had been an officer in Prince Maurice's regiment for the past three years, but neither Gassion nor any of his attendants were prepared to help. Rupert and the wounded Mortaigne were therefore obliged to ride forward alone in the face of the Spanish troopers. Eventually Rupert managed to get Holmes on to the back of his horse and carried him to safety.

The Spaniards now turned south-east and marched fifty miles to Landrecies on the Sambre with a view to capturing it, crossing the River Scheldt on the way. The French then tried to relieve this garrison but were unable to do so. Rupert, with three extra regiments of German horse, was given the task of covering the retreat and managed to beat off an attack mounted by 6,000 Spaniards. At this point Gassion's artillery became bogged and Gassion considered the possibility of abandoning it. But Rupert said that if he could be given some extra troops, he would get the guns out, which he succeeded in doing.

A day or two later the distrust that Rupert felt for Gassion broke into open hostility when Gassion left Rupert with a small number of men to hold a position covering the retreat. After beating off several attacks, Rupert realised that it was time to withdraw, but Gassion told him to stand fast. But it was not even Gassion's day for commanding the force and Rupert withdrew. At about this time it seems that Gassion's erratic behaviour was becoming the subject of comment outside the confines of his own little army because shortly afterwards he received a reprimand from the court saying that if he wanted to be a general he should stop behaving like a Croat, a term then used to denote an ill-disciplined light horse auxiliary.

Having failed to relieve Landrecies, the French were told that while the Spaniards were busy besieging it, they should double back and capture La Bassée. Rupert was sent on ahead with a body of horse, arriving just in time to confront 350 Englishmen serving in the Spanish army who had been sent to reinforce the garrison. Rupert quickly captured these people, most of whom were only too pleased to change sides and serve under him. Some of Rupert's foot now arrived and within three weeks he captured La Bassée without French help, which apparently made Gassion jealous.

Shortly afterwards Gassion and Rupert were riding together with a small escort on business connected with gathering forage. In some way information of their whereabouts was passed to a Spanish detachment from Armentières which set off to intercept them. As the French party was riding along, Rupert, noticing a dog looking intently into a nearby covert, suspected an ambush and moved towards Gassion to warn him. At that moment the enemy opened fire and it was apparent that they were surrounded. The French immediately broke through the ambush position, a few of their number being taken prisoner in the process. As soon as they were clear, Gassion said to Rupert that they should turn and attack the Spaniards and made to dismount as though to fight on foot. Rupert and one or two of his officers accordingly dismounted, whereupon Gassion and his men rode off with all the horses, leaving Rupert to the enemy. Rupert's party just managed to escape on foot, but not before Rupert received a bullet wound in his head. The wound was serious and Rupert had to be evacuated by stages to St Germain where he arrived in September. Rupert was saved the trouble of avenging himself on Gassion, who was killed a few weeks after Rupert was wounded.[1]

That was the end of Rupert's service with the French army. During the campaign of 1647 he had played a small part with his customary skill under difficult circumstances. Everything that he did displayed his mastery of the military art and his swift capture of La Bassée confirmed his skill in siege operations. But the campaign is hardly significant in an assessment of Rupert as a soldier. It was however to be his last. His future wars would all be fought at sea.

To assess Rupert as a soldier it is necessary to analyse his performance as an operational commander and, separately, as one concerned with the overall direction of the war, but before doing so it is worth looking carefully at his qualifications.

Without doubt the first qualification that a military commander must possess is a knowledge of his job. This quality involves accumulating and retaining basic facts and being in a position to exploit them by clear thinking and accurate expression. In all of this Rupert excelled when it came to matters directly related to the handling of operations. Even before he became General of the Horse in 1642 he had been avidly collecting knowledge both from the experience of his early campaigns and from study, particularly during his prolonged imprisonment. He had thought deeply about minor tactics and had developed the headlong charge for which he is still famous. In addition he understood the elements of moving and maintaining a force in the field as well as of laying siege to a town and taking it by storm. He had also thought deeply about the way in which the great leaders of the time had organised and used their armies. It was the complete mastery of his profession more than anything else that endeared him to the officers and men of his armies, although the very speed and accuracy with which he summed up a military situation on purely military lines and the curt brevity with which he customarily expressed himself could antagonise those who were looking at matters from a different point of view.

But the collection of knowledge, combined with an ability to think and express himself clearly, is not the only quality needed by a commander. He also needs to be possessed of vast energy, so that he can push himself and his followers to the very limits of their endurance when there is anything to be gained from it. He needs mental energy as well as physical energy so as to be able to keep turning things over in his brain whenever he is awake. Throughout the first part of the Civil War Rupert was renowned for his energy, to such an extent that he was even credited with superhuman powers on occasions. No one knew when or where he was going to turn up next, so great was his ability to ride night and day to confuse the enemy and galvanise his own followers into activity. His mental energy was scarcely less impressive, especially as he often managed to plan his next operation while physically immersed in manoeuvring and fighting the current one. With regard to expenditure of energy, Rupert's performance up to July 1644 had much in common with Napoleon in the Italian campaign of 1796. Only in the autumn of 1644 did Rupert seem to slow down a little, recovering his old form by the spring of 1645.

Another important quality is courage, which a commander needs so as to put himself in the best place to see what is going on in a battle and to control events. He also needs it so as to encourage his troops by his example. Throughout his life Rupert was a byword for courage. No braver man has ever lived and it is a miracle that he survived so many battles and skirmishes with so little hurt. It is perhaps ironic that he received the first wound of his life when carrying out a sortie from Oxford after he had been relieved of all his commands and that he sustained his only serious wound in an absurd and unnecessary skirmish in a minor operation in France. Perhaps with a little less courage Rupert would have avoided these wounds and still been able to carry out all his operational tasks, but in this case he would have denied himself the legendary reputation that is revered to this day.

As a brave and energetic man with a detailed knowledge of his job, Rupert was justifiably possessed of self-confidence to a high degree and this in turn led to his men having complete confidence in him. But those who were not themselves soldiers were not always capable of recognising his great military qualities for what they were, sometimes mistaking his knowledge and confidence for arrogance. No doubt his quick and furious temper counted against him and the fact that he was a man of absolute integrity made it hard for him to dissemble his feelings, although he evidently became more diplomatic in his dealings with people in the latter stages of the war.

On balance it must be conceded that Rupert had the qualities needed by an operational commander to a high degree and it is now necessary to see how he used them.

In a general sense it could be said that the business of operational command consists first of making a plan which relates the resources available, or capable of being made available, to the achievement of a particular operational aim, and second, of implementing that plan.

In order to make an operational plan the first thing is to collect as much information as possible about the enemy, the terrain, and the condition and location of one's own troops. The next thing to do is to see what additional resources can be made available and how. It is then necessary to work out two or three different ways of combining these resources together for the achievement of the aim, considering such things as the best way to take advantage of ground, the grouping of units or brigades including the proportion to be held in reserve, the timing of moves, etc. In all of this the business of being able to provide food, powder and shot at the time and place required is most important and often determines the rest. When this is done, all that remains is to choose one of the alternatives, which can then be elaborated into a plan.

From the earliest days of the Civil War Rupert took great trouble to gain information about the enemy, thereby giving rise to some of the myths about him as mentioned in this book. Naturally over a period of three years he was not always successful. In particular he does not seem to have kept his finger fully on the pulse in the days leading up to the second battle of Newbury and he has also been blamed for not knowing enough about Fairfax's movements in the two days preceding the battle of Naseby. But on the whole he was very successful at collecting information about the enemy. Furthermore, as a result of the way in which he constantly moved around amongst his own units, he had a better knowledge of their condition than most commanders of the time who tended to rely on written reports.

One of the most important differences between being an operational commander in the seventeenth century and being one today is that in the seventeenth century commanders had to raise, train and equip their own armies as well as use them. Thus for example, when planning to relieve York, he had to include in his plans arrangements for raising a sufficiently large force, which he did by combining troops from Ireland with the few that he had brought with him from Oxford and then adding to them levies that he raised himself in Wales and along the Welsh borders and later from Lancashire, Cumberland and Derbyshire. And when it came to raising forces he was second to none, continuing to do so right up to the time of his dismissal when most other Royalist commanders were finding it impossible.

In combining the various parts of his force he was both clever and flexible. Where necessary he was prepared to use his horse as foot, as at the siege of Lichfield, and equally he would mount musketeers to move them quickly, as he did on the approach to Newark. His plans for combining his varied resources to fight a battle were usually conventional, although at both Marston Moor and Naseby he made his centre more flexible by adding a brigade of horse to it. He was also more prepared than most commanders to keep a worthwhile reserve, as he did in these two battles, but this may have been forced upon him by his numerical inferiority.

One of the most impressive aspects of his planning was the arrangements that he made for the movement of his army before a battle. It was this factor above all else that gave the Royalists their opportunities at Edgehill and the first battle of Newbury and that also enabled him to relieve Newark. By the speed of his movement he even came within striking distance of beating the vastly superior allied forces outside York at Marston Moor.

Part of his success at moving his forces so quickly undoubtedly arose from the way he drove them on, but most of all it resulted from careful planning. One aspect of this planning was his system for starting with a small force and building it up as he went along, thereby avoiding the necessity of providing administrative support for the whole body throughout the move. Another was the logistic planning itself, which relied on his knowledge of what could be obtained from the many Royalist garrisons throughout the country. Using this knowledge he was able to map out in his mind various alternative ways in which he could move, possibly preparing several routes to allow himself tactical flexibility. Little of this planning has been recorded so it is difficult to quote chapter and verse, but it is clear that he was seldom held up by having to let his men forage each evening for their subsistence, which indicates that it must have been ready for them at different places along the route. Occasional reference is made to the way in which he prepared a route in advance, as for example the route that he took back to Lancashire after his defeat at Marston Moor. Another aspect of his movement planning was the way in which he arranged to demolish hedgerows and build bridges to enable his force to move away from established roads.

There is no doubt that Rupert planned swiftly and effectively, as is evident from the fact that his subordinates were always clear what they had to do. In this connection it is interesting to notice that Legge, when refuting Digby's letter regarding Rupert's arrangements for Naseby, said amongst other things, 'I am so well acquainted with the Prince's ways that I am confident all his general officers and commanders knew beforehand how or in what manner he intended to fight.'[2] In the seventeenth century, when there were few staff officers and when armies were small, planning was very much the personal business of the commander. There can be no doubt that in this field Rupert was highly proficient and can stand comparison with any of the other generals in the Civil War.

Once a plan has been made, an operational commander has to ensure that all those involved are properly prepared to play their part before he can attempt to implement it. Activities under this heading include making sure that orders are sent, received and understood by subordinate commanders right down the chain of command, and that these people and as many of the troops as possible have a chance to see and get an impression of their commander. In addition they should be given a chance to train with the other units in the force and they should understand the operating procedures that their particular commander employs, for example Rupert's method of charging the enemy.

Throughout his career, Rupert took great trouble in preparing his forces. As General of the Horse he quickly decided on the extent to which tactical doctrine, as expressed in the various publications of the day, should be amended in order to take account of his own experience and of the weapons and equipment available to the Royalists. He then spent long hours going round his units making sure that eveyone understood exactly what he wanted, in the process of which he became well known to many of the junior officers and men. When he took command of a task force, he did the same for those units that had not been under his command before, so far as time allowed. Thus when he went to Shrewsbury in February 1644 he spent some weeks preparing the diverse regiments that went to make up his new army before setting off to relieve York, a period in which he undertook a number of small local operations and pulled off the famous relief of Newark. Even on his way to York he made use of delays caused by his need to wait for powder after capturing Bolton, and by his need to collect information about the enemy when he was at Skipton, to give short periods of training to units recently incorporated into his force. Throughout the war it is clear that he continued with this policy, even on occasions annoying some of his senior subordinates such as Wilmot and Goring who resented being told to alter procedures with which they had long been familiar.

Although a commander always has a lot to do in the way of making his plan and ensuring that his troops are prepared to put it into effect, the real test lies in implementing it. In this respect a commander has to hold a balance. On the one hand he must try to force his plan through in the face of the manifold difficulties that are bound to arise: in this connection, if he starts with adequate strength, a good plan and proper reserves, he should be able to ward off the adverse effects of enemy action without changing it. On the other hand it may happen that new developments indicate that a major change of plan is needed, and a commander often comes under pressure to make such a change when things are going wrong. He then has to decide whether to stick to his guns and force the enemy to fall in with his original ideas, or to change his plan in order to achieve his aim in a different way. The dilemma can only be dealt with by a commander who has great strength of will and sound judgement, because he not only has to overcome the enemy but also carry his own side with him.

Once Rupert had decided on his plan, he was tenacious in sticking to it, although he was prepared to change it if action by the enemy obliged him to do so. His main problems arose when the pressure came from his own side, as for example when Newcastle tried to dissuade him from fighting outside York. The usual procedure in those days was for commanders to hold a council of war before the start of each new phase of an operation at which they listened to the views of all of their senior commanders before deciding what to do. It seems that in the early part of the war Rupert sometimes failed to summon his council, probably because he was too busy and in too much of a hurry to deal with it. Certainly a complaint to this effect was made to the King regarding his conduct of the retreat through Lancashire after Marston Moor. Possibly as a result of this he was more careful later on and there are records of the frequent councils held during his defence of Bristol.

In all other respects he implemented his plans with great skill, energy and daring. His ability to turn up at the right place at the critical moment was uncanny and in a battle he was quick to see a tactical opportunity and act on it.

Rupert has been criticised for getting himself too closely involved in his battles and therefore being unavailable to influence them at the right moment. Naturally such criticism focuses on the occasions when the battles were lost and care has been taken in this book to analyse his reasons for placing himself as he did at Marston Moor and Naseby. But no one criticises his even more daring behaviour in the battle outside Newark where he very nearly lost his life, nor at his capture of Bristol, nor when he turned the flank of the Parliamentary line at Chalgrove Field with no more than his life guard, because in each case the battle was won. It must also be remembered that at that time it was customary for commanders to expose themselves in precisely the same way that Rupert did and that his actions were not just those of a reckless hothead. Gustavus Adolphus and Conde, for example, were always in the thickest of the fighting and the same can be said of Fairfax, who was the only other English operational commander in the Civil War of a stature comparable to Rupert. (Cromwell's day came later, but even he got himself wounded at Marston Moor.)

In assessing Rupert as an operational commander it is fair to say that he possessed the required qualifications and characteristics to a high degree. It is also fair to say that his operational planning was first class and that he prepared the men under his command for their tasks as well as possible, given the circumstances under which he was operating. He certainly gained and retained the respect and even devotion of the officers and men who served under him, with the exception of a few of the senior officers whose opposition arose more from rivalry or jealousy than from an objection to his performance as an operational commander. Rupert was undoubtedly chiefly responsible for the superiority which the Royalists established over their opponents in the early days of the war and which they retained for at least the first year.

The way in which Rupert implemented his plans with the armies that he built up and prepared is a different matter. In this respect his fortunes were mixed, although his participation in lost battles, apart from Marston Moor, occurred when he was acting as a subordinate commander to the King, for example, at the first battle of Newbury and Naseby. Against this he had a string of remarkable victories to his credit, often under extremely difficult circumstances, such as Powick Bridge, the storming of Lichfield, Chalgrove Field, the capture of Bristol, the relief of Newark and the battles in Lancashire on the way to York. In addition the way in which he handled the retreat from Brentford and the interception of Essex before the first battle of Newbury should not be forgotten, nor his part in the victory at Edgehill. On balance it is probably fair to say that his failures prevent him from being regarded as one of the very best operational commanders, but that his many successes entitle him to be regarded very highly in this field.

When it comes to assessing Rupert's contribution to the higher direction of the Civil War it would be natural to look separately at the periods when he was General of the Horse and Lord General, on the assumption that his influence would be greater in the latter post. In fact the reverse is true, Rupert's influence being less towards the end of the war, when the King was under the influence of the irresponsible Digby, than at the beginning when he was advised by a larger group of infinitely more sensible people. But throughout, Rupert played a part in assisting the King to formulate his overall policy for defeating the rebels and in helping him determine the long-term military policy which the operational commanders would have to put into effect.

In a general sense a military man operating above the level of operational command needs a slightly different set of qualities to those required by an operational commander. For example he still needs to know his job, but in this case his knowledge has to embrace a wider understanding of the overall situation, including details of the civil government, law, foreign affairs and the political background to the struggle. He certainly needs energy, but mainly of the mental variety so as to keep absorbing facts that enable him to argue convincingly with the civilians. He needs courage, but primarily moral courage, so as to be able to give unwelcome advice and to stand up for the operational commanders should they be subjected to damaging intrigue. He also needs determination in order to ensure that overall military plans, once made, are adhered to unless a major change of circumstance calls for a reappraisal. In short, the principal military adviser to a King or government needs the ability to influence great events rather than to direct lesser ones. He needs breadth of vision and the ability to persuade as well as to compel; patience as well as stamina.

Any comparison of these attributes with those possessed by the twenty-two-year-old Rupert in 1642 shows up certain shortcomings. Quite apart from the fact that he was neither patient nor diplomatic at that stage of his life, he was also unfamiliar with the civil background to the conflict, taking a relatively simplistic view of the best way to deal with rebels. Furthermore the warfare that Rupert had so avidly studied was mainly of the straightforward variety, waged between opposing rulers, although he probably had some views on insurgency based on his knowledge of William the Silent's uprising against Spain.

But being highly intelligent he easily picked up the underlying difference between these two sorts of war, realising that the ultimate aim was to gain the allegiance of the enemy rather than to destroy him lock, stock and barrel. In this connection it is interesting to see how the King, whilst theoretically understanding this and explaining it beautifully to Rupert by letter,[3] was quite incapable of offering the hand of friendship to rebels such as the three earls who tried to change sides in August 1643, whereas Rupert, who may not have worked out the theory so clearly, was the first to welcome them and took greater trouble with his prisoners than did the King.

It must also be realised that insurgency in the seventeenth century had little in common with modern insurgencies because allegiance was governed by power as opposed to persuasion. In practice what mattered was to be in a position to dominate a given area militarily. That alone enabled one side or the other to raise men and money on the one hand and to punish opposition or reward support on the other. And military domination of an area was governed by conventional military operations. In this respect Rupert was quick to isolate the strategic essentials, realising the importance of grabbing London before the enemy could build up its defences and, when the opportunity was finally lost at the first battle of Newbury, being a consistent advocate of holding key areas such as the north, the Welsh borders and the south-west. Throughout the war his strategic sense remained sound.

In the early stages of the war Rupert's problem lay in dealing with people rather than concepts. Whereas he quickly won the trust of his soldiers he was less good with the civilians who surrounded the King, although many, either because they understood the impatience of youth or because they recognised his great value to the Royalist cause, managed to work with him. Some, such as Nicholas, Richmond and possibly Jermyn, liked and admired him and therefore tried to ease his path: others such as Falkland, Hyde and Culpepper gritted their teeth and did their duty. In the case of the regional commanders a similar situation arose: Derby and Loughborough got on well with him while Hertford and Newcastle objected to the way he rode roughshod over their sensibilities.

By the time Rupert became Lord General he had become more tactful at handling such people, but the rigours of the first two years, the intrigues as much as the operations, had slowed him down and deprived him of some of his spark.

Throughout the war Rupert's main problem was with the King, not because he did not get the King's support for most of the time, but because the King was incapable of following a consistent line even after it had been discussed and agreed. In fact the King was surprisingly constant in his underlying principles, i.e. his determination to uphold the episcopal Church and retain control of the armed forces, but he vascillated wildly in the means by which he pursued these basic aims.

Furthermore as the war progressed the King took every opportunity to distance himself from those of his supporters who were looking to a negotiated constitutional solution, giving his trust to those who sought a purely military victory. And as the prospect of outright victory receded, more and more of his immediate circle found themselves pushed to one side, despatched on missions or sent to advise the Prince of Wales. It was this that enabled Digby, who said whatever he thought would please the King, to become so influential and ultimately to discredit Rupert himself. Rupert, who never became involved in intrigue, was quite incapable of dealing with this sort of behaviour even though he worked himself into a fury as he saw what was going on. Although this was to his credit as a man, it represented a weakness in one concerned with the higher direction of the war. It is an unfortunate fact that senior commanders, working between the operational commanders and the sovereign or government, need to understand the principles of political self-defence even if they wish to remain aloof from politics itself. That Rupert was slow to learn this lesson must count against him in an assessment of his contribution to the higher direction of the war.

But perhaps one word in his defence may be said at this point, based on the fact that Digby was not just another politician. Ronald Hutton, in his magisterial book on Charles II, describes Digby as one of the most destructive individuals of his age. He goes on to say, 'If it is the skill of the impressionist painter to reduce solid objects to particles of light and form, so it was the art of Digby to take the components of complex and delicate political situations and create from them scenarios of compelling (and fallacious) simplicity and plausibility. Had he only written a history of his times with the skill with which he misled its rulers, he would be regarded as a wronged hero. Having persuaded Charles I to lose his field army in the suicidal attack at Naseby and then to dismiss his best general, he led the remaining Royalist cavalry to destruction . . .' What chance had the young Rupert of defending himself against such a person?[4]

In looking at Rupert's contribution to the higher direction of the war it must also be remembered that for most of the time he was making it at the same time as he was acting as the King's foremost operational commander in the field. Against this background it can be said that, with little initial understanding of the overall situation, he quickly grasped the essentials and gave sound military advice regarding the conduct of the war. He assessed every change in the military balance as it occurred and was not afraid to point out the increasing weakness of the King's position, even to the extent of telling him when all was lost. He certainly did his best to ensure that the King pursued the agreed aim during the duration of each campaign, although in this respect he was seldom successful. In short he put up a creditable performance, but his temperament and political experience were such as to limit his effectiveness in this field.

In comparing Rupert with the famous soldiers of history, it is clear that he does not rank with men such as Marlborough, or Napoleon, or Gustavus Adolphus for example. These people were in a different league because they were not only great operational commanders in their own right, but also designers of the political events for which the military forces that they wielded were being used. Rupert was a first-class operational commander and a conscientious and useful top-level military adviser who ultimately lacked the political skill needed to make his views prevail.

But in addition to this he managed in some indefinable way to capture the imagination, not only of his contemporaries, but also of many people down the years. For example, in describing the key players of the Civil War, Richard Ollard, having discussed Fairfax, Cromwell, Warwick, Charles I and Hyde, goes on to say, 'But for what actors call star quality, the ability to attract every eye in the house from his first entrance, Rupert is supreme. He not only personifies the concept of the Cavalier, he transcends it. The fearless cavalry leader, the grand seigneur, splendid in dress and style of life (though austere in avoiding self-indulgence), . . . the image of Rupert is part of everyone's apprehension of the Civil War . . . Rupert's flawless courage on the battlefield was matched by a brilliance and boldness in strategy and tactics that no commander on either side surpassed . . .'[5] Lord Ballantrae, who as a brigadier led one of Wingate's columns in Burma, concludes a passage describing Rupert by saying, 'As a professional soldier whose hobbies are sailing and travel, I find I love him very much.'[6]

Rupert's career as a soldier lasted fourteen years and when it came to an end following his wound in France, he was still only twenty-six years old. Ahead of him was a much longer career as an operational commander at sea and as a director of England's naval affairs, which brought to his life a lasting achievement. On land his achievements did not last, because they were swallowed up in the wreck of the Royalist cause. The forces which he raised and trained, and which fought with such lustre under his command, were eventually broken up and dispersed, leaving the regular soldiers of the future to trace their descent from the New Model Army. But none can deny that he was a magnificent soldier. In the English Civil War he won undying fame, a commodity incidentally that would have been regarded as singularly useless by the ever practical Rupert.

BIBLIOGRAPHY

ASHLEY, Maurice, *Rupert of the Rhine*, Hart Davis, MacGibbon, 1976.

ATKYNS, Richard and GWYN, John, *The English Civil War*, ed. P. Young and N. Tucker (reprints Atkyns' *Vindication* and Gwyn's *Military Memoirs*), Longman, 1967.

BENNETT, Martyn, *Battlefields of the English Civil War*, Webb and Bower, 1990.

BUCHAN, John, *Montrose*, Thomas Nelson, 1931.

CHURCHILL, Sir Winston, *A History of the English-Speaking Peoples*, vol. 2, Cassell, 1956.

CLARENDON, Edward Hyde, Earl of, *History of the Great Rebellion*, ed. R. Lockyer, Oxford University Press for Folio Society, 1967.

CLEUGH, James *Prince Rupert*, Geoffrey Bles, 1934.

CRUSO, John, *Military Instructions for the Cavallrie*, 1632, reprinted with notes and commentary by P. Young, The Roundwood Press, 1972.

EDINGER, George, *Rupert of the Rhine: the Pirate Prince*, Hutchinson, 1936.

ESSON, D. M. R., *The Curse of Cromwell*, Leo Cooper, 1971.

FERGUSSON, Sir Bernard, *Rupert of the Rhine*, Collins, 1952.

HALEY, K. H. D., *The British and the Dutch*, George Philip, 1988.

HART, B. H. Liddell, *Great Captains Unveiled*, Blackwood and Sons, 1927.

HAVRAN, Martin, *Caroline Courtier: the life of Lord Cottington*, Macmillan, 1973.

HILL, C. P., *Who's Who in Stuart Britain*, Shepheard and Walwyn, 1988.

HUTTON, Ronald, *Charles II*, Clarendon Press, 1989.

KENYON, John, *The Civil Wars of England*, Weidenfeld and Nicolson, 1988.

KROLL, Maria, *Sophie, Electress of Hanover*, Gollancz, 1973.

LINKLATER, Eric, *The Survival of Scotland*, Heinemann, 1968.

MacMUNN, Sir George, *Gustavus Adolphus, the Northern Hurricane*, Hodder and Stoughton, undated.

MALCOLM, Joyce Lee, *Caesar's Due: Loyalty and King Charles 1642–1646*, Royal Historical Society, 1983.

MORRAH, Patrick, *Prince Rupert of the Rhine*, Constable, 1976.

OLLARD, Richard, *Clarendon and his Friends*, Hamish Hamilton, 1987.

OLLARD, Richard, *This War Without an Enemy*, Hodder and Stoughton, 1976.

OMAN, Carola, *Elizabeth of Bohemia*, revised ed., Hodder and Stoughton, 1964.

ROGERS, H. C. B., *Battles and Generals of the Civil War*, Seely Service, 1968.

ROSS, W. G., *Oliver Cromwell and his Ironsides*, W. J. Mackay and Co., 1889.

ROYALTON-KISCH, Martin, *Adriaen van de Venne's Album*, British Museum Publications, 1988.

RUBINSTEIN, H., *Captain Luckless: James First Duke of Hamilton*, Scottish Academic Press, 1975.

RYDER, Ian, *An English Army for Ireland*, Partizan Press, 1987.

SCOTT, Eva, *Rupert Prince Palatine*, Constable, 1904.

SMITH, Geoffrey Ridsill, *Without Touch of Dishonour*, Roundwood Press, 1968.

STEWART, A. T. Q., *The Narrow Ground*, Faber and Faber, 1989.

STUCLEY, John, *Sir Bevil Grenville and his Times*, Philimore and Co., 1983.

THOMSON, George, *Warrior Prince*, Secker and Warburg, 1976.

TOYNBEE, M., and YOUNG, P., *Cropredy Bridge*, Roundwood Press, 1970.

TREVOR-ROPER, Hugh, *Catholics, Anglicans and Puritans*, Fontana, 1989.

WARBURTON, Eliot, *Memoirs of Prince Rupert and the Cavaliers*, Richard Bentley, 1849.

WARWICK, Sir Philip, *Memoirs of the Reign of King Charles the First*, James Ballantyne and Co., 1813.

WEDGWOOD, C. V., *The King's Peace*, Collins, 1955.

WEDGWOOD, C. V., *The King's War*, Collins, 1958.

WEDGWOOD, C. V., *Montrose*, Collins, 1952.

WILCOCK, John, *The Life of Sir Henry Vane the Younger*, St Catherine Press, 1913.

WILKINSON, Clennell, *Prince Rupert the Cavalier*, George Harrap, 1934.

WILSON, John, *Fairfax*, John Murray, 1985.

YATES, Frances, *The Rosicrucian Enlightenment*, Routledge and Kegan Paul, 1972.

YOUNG, Peter, *Edgehill 1642*, Roundwood Press, 1967.

YOUNG, Peter, *Marston Moor 1644*, Roundwood Press, 1970.

YOUNG, Peter, *Naseby 1645*, Century Publishing, 1985.

NOTES

PREFACE

1. Eliot Warburton, *Memoirs of Prince Rupert and the Cavaliers*, Richard Bentley, 1849.
2. Eva Scott, *Rupert Prince Palatine*, Constable, 1904.
3. George Edinger, *Rupert of the Rhine, The Pirate Prince*, Hutchinson, 1936.
4. Patrick Morrah, *Prince Rupert of the Rhine*, Constable, 1976.

CHAPTER 1

1. Warburton, vol. 1, p. 441, fn. 1.
2. K. H. D. Haley, *The British and the Dutch*, George Philip, 1988, p. 37.
3. Ibid., p. 47.
4. Frances A. Yates, *The Rosicrucian Enlightenment*, Routledge and Kegan Paul, 1972, p. 12.
5. Martin Royalton-Kisch, *Adriaen van de Venne's Album*, British Museum Publications, 1988, p. 22.
6. Carola Oman, *Elizabeth of Bohemia*, Hodder and Stoughton, revised edition 1964, p. 222.
7. Ibid., p. 231.
8. Warburton, vol. 1, p. 39.

CHAPTER 2

1. Haley, p. 125.
2. Royalton-Kisch, p. 23.
3. George Thomson, *Warrior Prince*, Secker and Warburg, 1976, p. 10.
4. Oman, p. 259.
5. Ibid., p. 57.
6. Morrah, p. 23.
7. Maria Kroll, *Sophie, Electress of Hanover*, Gollancz, 1973, p. 29.
8. Royalton-Kisch includes a number of pictures showing Frederick and Elizabeth engaged in social activities with the Stadholder.
9. Scott, p. 12.
10. Edinger, p. 35.
11. Clennell Wilkinson, *Prince Rupert the Cavalier*, George Harrap, 1934, p. 21.
12. C. V. Wedgwood, *The King's War*, Collins, 1958, p. 136.
13. Scott, p. 17, quoting a letter from the Queen of Bohemia to Sir Thomas Roe of June 1636 and his reply, July 1636.
14. Warburton, vol. 1, p. 49, fn.
15. Ibid., p. 449.
16. Scott, p. 19.
17. Edinger, p. 32.
18. B. H. Liddell Hart, *Great Captains Unveiled*, William Blackwood and Sons, 1927, pp. 182–3.
19. Sir George MacMunn, *Gustavus Adolphus, the Northern Hurricane*, Hodder and Stoughton (undated, probably 1920s), p. 38.
20. Ibid., p. 127.
21. Ibid., pp. 244–5.

22. Liddell Hart, p. 110.
23. Ibid., p. 111.

24. MacMunn, pp. 233–6.
25. Scott, p. 15, quoting Spruner's *Pfalz-graf Ruprecht*, p. 17.

CHAPTER 3

1. Morrah, p. 31, quoting Lansdown MSS in British Museum.
2. Warburton, vol. 1, p. 57.
3. Edinger, p. 37.
4. Morrah, p. 32, quoting Lansdown MSS.
5. Ibid., p. 31.
6. Scott, p. 25.
7. Ibid., p. 30.
8. James Cleugh, *Prince Rupert*, Geoffrey Bles, 1934. p. 44.

9. Scott, p. 34, quoting Lansdown MSS.
10. Scott, p. 37.
11. Maurice Ashley, *Rupert of the Rhine*, Hart Davis, MacGibbon, 1976. p. 14.
12. Edinger, p. 51.
13. Bernard Fergusson, *Rupert of the Rhine*, Collins, 1952, p. 20.
14. Ibid., p. 20.
15. Warburton, vol. 1, p. 453.

CHAPTER 4

1. Ashley, p. 21.
2. Clarendon, *History of the Great Rebellion*, ed. Roger Lockyer, OUP for Folio Society, 1967, p. 188.
3. Wilkinson, p. 17.
4. Warburton, vol. 1, p. 457.
5. Cleugh, p. 56.
6. Scott, p. 45.
7. Eric Linklater, *The Survival of Scotland*, Heinemann, 1968, p. 251.
8. Hugh Trevor-Roper, *Catholics, Anglicans and Puritans*, Fontana, 1989, pp. 41–3.

9. C. P. Hill, *Who's Who in Stuart Britain*, Shepheard and Walwyn, 1988, p. 77.
10. Trevor-Roper, p. 144.
11. A. T. Q. Stewart, *The Narrow Ground*, Faber and Faber, 1989, p. 36.
12. D. M. R. Esson, *The Curse of Cromwell*, Leo Cooper, 1971, p. 22.
13. Ibid., p. 34.
14. C. V. Wedgwood, *The King's Peace*, Collins, 1955, p. 149.

CHAPTER 5

1. Oman, p. 358.
2. John Kenyon, *The Civil Wars of England*, Weidenfeld and Nicolson, 1988, p. 30.
3. Richard Ollard, *This War Without an Enemy*, Hodder and Stoughton, 1976, p. 61.
4. Ibid., pp. 59–60.
5. Morrah, pp. 66–7.
6. Clarendon, p. 64.
7. Peter Young, *Edgehill 1642*, Roundwood Press, 1967, p. 9.
8. Morrah, p. 81, quoting *Natural History of Staffordshire* p. 336.
9. H. C. B. Rogers, *Battles and Generals of the Civil War*, Seely Service, 1968, p. 24.
10. Ibid., p. 25.

11. Warburton, vol. 1, p. 409, quoting *Rupert's Disguises*, London, 1643.
12. Warburton, vol. 1, pp. 400–1.
13. The material in these paragraphs is drawn mainly from the books by P. Young and H. C. B. Rogers quoted above.
14. The layout given is based on de Gomme's plan of the battle held in the Royal Library at Windsor Castle and reproduced in P. Young's *Edgehill 1642*, p. 64, together with Young's own assessment. Not all authorities agree, for example Rogers, p. 48, who places Sir John Byron's regiment behind Wilmot rather than Rupert.
15. See, for example, the letter of Lord

Bernard Stuart commanding the King's life guard (horse) and the account of Sir Philip Warwick, both quoted in full P. Young, *Edgehill*, pp. 282–3.

16. Clarendon, p. 59.
17. Wedgwood, *The King's War*, p. 132.
18. Sir Philip Warwick, *Memoirs of the Reign of King Charles the First*, 1702, James Ballantyne and Co., 1813.
19. Wedgwood, *The King's War*, p. 140.

CHAPTER 6

1. Richard Ollard, *Clarendon and His Friends*, Hamish Hamilton, 1987, p. 80.
2. Ibid., p. 81.
3. Joyce Lee Malcolm, *Caesar's Due, Loyalty and King Charles 1642–1646*, Royal Historical Society, London, 1983, pp. 87–8.
4. Wedgwood, *The King's War*, p. 158.
5. Cleugh, p. 88 and Wedgwood, *The King's War*, p. 159, referring to Thomason Tracts E83.28.
6. Scott, p. 101 and Morrah, p. 107.
7. John Cruso, *Militarie Instructions for the Cavallrie*, 1632, reprinted with

notes and commentary by P. Young, The Roundwood Press, 1972.
8. John Stucley, *Sir Bevil Grenville and his Times*, Philimore and Co., 1983.
9. Kenyon, p. 45.
10. Ashley, p. 48.
11. Warburton, vol. 2, p. 167.
12. Richard Atkyns and John Gwyn, *The English Civil War*, ed. P. Young and N. Tucker (reprints Atkyns' *Vindication* and Gwyn's *Military Memoirs*), Longman, 1967, p. 12. See also Rogers, p. 73.
13. Atkyns and Gwyn, p. 28.
14. Warburton, vol. 2, p. 250.
15. Ibid., p. 255.

CHAPTER 7

1. Warwick, pp. 268–9, including fn. p. 268.
2. Ollard, *Clarendon*, p. 93.
3. Wedgwood, *The King's War*, p. 243.
4. H. Rubinstein, *Captain Luckless, James First Duke of Hamilton*, Scottish Academic Press, 1975, p. 150. See also C. V. Wedgwood, *Montrose*, Collins, 1952, p. 56, and John Buchan, *Montrose*, Thomas Nelson, 1931, p. 160.
5. Wedgwood, *The King's War*, p. 249.
6. For details of how such a march would be organised by day and by night see Cruso, pp. 56–64.
7. Cleugh, pp. 103–4.

8. For example, Clarendon, p. 166.
9. Rogers, p. 107.
10. John Wilcock, *The Life of Sir Henry Vane the Younger*, St Catherine Press, 1913, p. 122, quoting Baillie, *Letters*, vol. 11, p. 88.
11. Ollard, *Clarendon*, p. 88.
12. Esson, p. 68.
13. Ian Ryder, *An English Army For Ireland*, Partizan Press, 1987, p. 31.
14. Lee Malcolm, p. 115.
15. Kenyon, p. 90.
16. Martin Havran, *Caroline Courtier*, Macmillan, 1973, p. 158.
17. Ibid., p. x.
18. Ashley, p. 64.

CHAPTER 8

1. See for example Kenyon, p. 101 and Young, *Marston Moor 1644*, Roundwood Press, 1970, p. 44.
2. Lee Malcolm, p. 119.
3. The account of the relief of Newark given here is taken from Martin Bennett, *Battlefields of the English Civil*

War, Webb and Bower, 1990 pp. 90–1 and Morrah, pp. 138–40.
4. Clarendon, p. 188.
5. Ollard, *War Without an Enemy*, p. 114.
6. Warburton, vol. 2, p. 387.
7. Clarendon, pp. 200–1.

8. Morrah, p. 147.
9. Margaret Toynbee and Peter Young, *Cropredy Bridge*, Roundwood Press, 1970, p. 39.
10. Warburton, vol. 2, pp. 415–18.
11. Ibid., p. 438.
12. Young, *Marston Moor*, pp. 53–6.
13. W. G. Ross, *Oliver Cromwell and his Ironsides*, W. J. Mackay, 1889, p. 24. Ross considers that Cromwell's regiment were cuirassiers at the time of Marston Moor, but that they later lost some of their heavy armour.
14. Young, *Marston Moor*, p. 205, quoting cspd p. 253.
15. Ibid., p. 208, quoting cspd pp. 265–6.
16. The layout of the allied army in this and subsequent paragraphs is as given in Young, *Marston Moor*, pp. 102–5.
17. Wedgwood, *The King's War*, p. 340.
18. The layout of the Royalist army given in this and subsequent paragraphs is as described by Young, *Marston Moor*, pp. 94–9.
19. For example Young, *Marston Moor*, p. 95, Kenyon, p. 95, Bennett, p. 113.
20. Young, *Marston Moor*, p. 116.
21. John Wilson, *Fairfax*, John Murray, 1985, pp. 51–2.
22. Young, *Marston Moor*, pp. 125–6.
23. Ibid., p. 129.
24. Ibid., p. 130.
25. Wilson, p. 52 and Young, *Marston Moor*, p. 134. See also Geoffrey Ridsill Smith, *Without Touch of Dishonour*, Roundwood Press, 1968, p. 79, who records that a leather cup was made out of the boots worn by Fairfax on that fateful occasion.
26. Clarendon, p. 217.
27. Wedgwood, *The King's War*, p. 349. See also Wilcock, p. 139.
28. Wilcock, p. 144, quoting Sanford, *Studies and Illustrations of the Great Rebellion*, p. 591.

CHAPTER 9

1. Winston Churchill, *A History of the English-Speaking Peoples*, Cassell, 1956, vol. 2, p. 203.
2. Warburton, vol. 2, p. 468.
3. Young, *Marston Moor*, p. 154.
4. Ibid., p. 476.
5. Bennett, p. 122.
6. Scott, pp. 156–7.
7. Warburton, vol. 3, p. 8.
8. Ibid., pp. 11–13.
9. Ibid., p. 23.
10. Morrah, p. 171, quoting letter from Trevor to Ormonde.
11. Ibid., p. 169, quoting Rupert's diary.
12. Rogers, p. 188.

CHAPTER 10

1. Lee Malcolm, pp. 212–13.
2. Ryder, p. 34.
3. Ibid., p. 34.
4. Warburton, vol. 3, p. 28.
5. Ibid., p. 73.
6. Wedgwood, *The King's War*, p. 436.
7. Lee Malcolm, p. 218.
8. Young, *Naseby 1645*, Century Publishing, 1985, p. 116.
9. Wedgwood, *The King's War*, pp. 442–3, based on the account given by the King's Secretary at War.
10. Young, *Naseby*, pp. 217–18.
11. Wedgwood, *The King's War*, p. 446.
12. Ibid., pp. 229–30.
13. Morrah, p. 178.
14. Warburton, vol. 3, p. 99; also Young, *Naseby*, p. 256.
15. Morrah, p. 179.
16. The layout of the two armies as given here is taken from Young, *Naseby*, Chapters 13 and 14.
17. The account of the battle given here is drawn mainly from Young, *Naseby*, Chapter 15, and Rogers, Chapter 20.
18. Warburton, vol. 3, pp. 125–8.
19. Ibid., pp. 128–31.
20. Ibid., p. 131.
21. Ibid., p. 149.

CHAPTER 11

1. The account of Rupert's campaign in France is taken from Morrah, pp. 215–18.
2. Warburton, vol. 3, p. 129.
3. Warburton, vol. 2, p. 167, note 1.
4. Ronald Hutton, *Charles II*, Clarendon Press, 1989, p. 17.
5. Ollard, *This War Without an Enemy*, pp. 68–9.
6. Fergusson, p. 5.

INDEX

Numbers in *italics* refer to figures